The 1917 White Sox

The 1917 White Sox

Their World Championship Season

WARREN N. WILBERT *and*
WILLIAM C. HAGEMAN

McFarland & Company, Inc., Publishers
Jefferson, North Carolina, and London

LIBRARY OF CONGRESS CATALOGUING-IN-PUBLICATION DATA

Wilbert, Warren N.
    The 1917 White Sox : their world championship season /
Warren N. Wilbert and William C. Hageman.
        p.   cm.
    Includes bibliographical references and index.

    ISBN 0-7864-1622-X (softcover : 50# alkaline paper)

    1. Chicago White Sox (Baseball team).   2. World Series
(Baseball) (1917).   I. Hageman, William.   II. Title.
    GV875.C58W55   2004
    796.357'64'0977311—dc22   2003017501

British Library cataloguing data are available

©2004 Warren N. Wilbert and William C. Hageman.
All rights reserved

Front cover photograph: Eddie Cicotte *(Brace)*

Manufactured in the United States of America

*McFarland & Company, Inc., Publishers
   Box 611, Jefferson, North Carolina 28640
      www.mcfarlandpub.com*

To the White Sox' many
patient and long-suffering fans.
We feel your pain.

Acknowledgments

It was Seneca, who might just as well have been a hard-hitting first baseman or outfielder during the era of "The Old Roman," who said: "He who receives a benefit with gratitude repays the first installment of his debt." We'd like to indicate with these few words that we have indeed received not only a single benefit, but benefits by the dozens from our good friends in SABR and elsewhere who have contributed both to our understanding of the national pastime and its colorful past, and to the story of the 1917 White Sox as it unfolds in this book. To take Seneca's passage one step further, this is another installment against the debt we owe these helpful and knowledgeable people. They are listed in alphabetical order: Bill Deane, Steve Gietschier, the Indiana-Purdue University Library Staff (Fort Wayne), Bill James, Jim Meyer, the Michigan State Library Periodicals Staff (Lansing), Dave Nemec, Pete Palmer, Mike Pearson, Dave Smith, Marshall Wright.

Contents

Introduction

The Chicago White Sox have already passed the fiftieth and seventy-fifth anniversary years of their last world's championship in 1917, and Sox fans may well be "celebrating" a centennial of their last World Series conquest, at the rate they have been going, before another championship flag hangs from the Comiskey mast. Those who follow the Chicago ball club located hard by its famous stockyards would rather not wait that long. Their patience is about as thin as that of the hardy Red Sox faithful whose frustration extends back to 1918 (just a year less), when the Bosox last captured a World Series—which, incidentally, opened in Comiskey Park, used by the Cubs as their home diamond in the Fall Classic of that year.

With the passing of lo these many years, the players, the events of that extraordinary season of 1917 and the victory over John McGraw's Giants in the World Series have slipped further and further into the dim reaches of time. That era in baseball's celebrated history featured the Deadball Era, the Reserve Clause, $4,000 salaries per annum, the trials and tragedies of the first World War, spitball pitchers and place-hitters, and the first few indications that the game was changing from its accustomed one run, slash-hitting format to a more robust offensive affair.

And it is not only an eon, as baseball marks time, that sepa-rates the gloss and glitter of that 1917 achievement from the pre-sent. More significantly, what *is* remembered about that era in White Sox history pivots on the more lurid and pulsating events of the infamous 1919 World Series, an earth-shaking cataclysm that relegated the Comiskey franchise's glorious 1917 championship to the backwaters of baseball's notoriously short memory.

We're going to set the record straight with stories of the big games and crucial series; of Red Faber, Hap Felsch, Eddie Cicotte and Joe Jackson; of Eddie Collins' dash to the pot at the end of the World Series rainbow, bringing the Sox back to the glory of their first championship forays of 1901 and 1906, restoring their status as one of the major league's elite franchises. How that was accom-plished, beginning with Charley Comiskey's 1914–16 buildup on through the 1917 campaign against American League ball clubs, and finally on to the wartime setting of the 1917 World Series, is the story here.

When Eddie Collins, who had beaten Heinie Zimmerman to home plate to score what proved to be the World Series winner, picked up pinchhitter Lew McCarty's grounder and threw him out to end the game at New York's Polo Grounds, Chicago fandom (and in those days they enjoyed a vast, if not national following) turned the City of Big Shoulders into a massive bacchanal. The 1919 season seemed an eternity away. At that moment in baseball time the Old Roman, Charley Comiskey, and his legions ruled supreme. War or no war, in Chicago they were ready to let the good times roll. There was a world's championship to celebrate!

CHAPTER 1

A Resolve to Win It All

The 1917 world's champion Chicago White Sox were a team whose roots burrowed into the soil of abject frustration over eleventh hour pennant losses as far back as 1907 and 1908. Charles Albert Comiskey, one of the founding fathers of the American League, a man who dealt poorly with losing or mediocrity, had fussed and fumed for nearly a decade until he had finally put together the kind of ball club that was capable of regaining the lofty status of a world's champion that his 1906 team had achieved. Once having scaled that mountain there was, for Comiskey, no turning back. To be the game's reigning potentate was for The Old Roman the only game in town. But getting up there and staying up there were two quite different things as so many before and after him found out. The flame of desire for baseball's ultimate laurel wreath burned with as much intensity in other cities around the league as it did in Chicago. And between 1906 and 1917 that was especially true in Detroit, Philadelphia and Boston, where championships had come in bundles.

Comiskey's frustration began with his club's failure to repeat as the Junior Circuit's pennant winner in 1907. The White Sox and Connie Mack's Athletics, who had hounded Detroit's Tigers all the way to the very last hours of that pennant race, finally succumbed to the Motor City's Bengals, leaving Ty Cobb and Company to tussle with Chicago's north side contingent in baseball's fourth World Series. The Cubs, bitter Pale Hose rivals, were themselves bent on vengeance after a galling 1906 defeat at the hands of Fielder Jones and his upstart South Siders, and the Bruins' World Series victory in 1907, of course, did little to brighten dispositions on the South Side.

During the early days of the 1907 campaign on a balmy day in May, the White Sox had staged a flag-raising ceremony to celebrate their stunning 1906 world's championship, the ceremony proceeding with all due pomp and circumstance—until the flagpole snapped. Might that perhaps have been an omen of what lay ahead

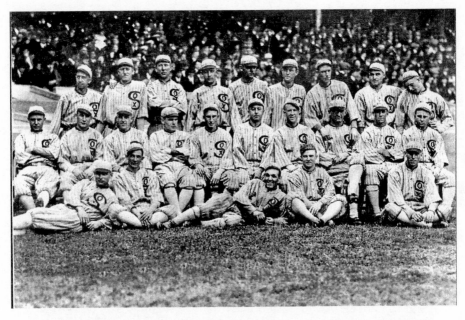

The 1917 world champion Chicago White Sox. *Standing, L to R:* Eddie Collins, Red Faber, Joey Benz, Ted Jourdan, Chick Gandil, Dave Danforth, Swede Risberg, Joe Jenkins, Lefty Williams. *Seated, center row, L to R:* Ray Schalk, Happy Felsch, Eddie Cicotte, Eddie Murphy, Fred McMullin, manager Clarence "Pants" Rowland, Coach Bill "Kid" Gleason, Joe Jackson, John "Shano" Collins, Nemo Leibold. *Front row, L to R:* Reb Russell, Byrd Lynn, Buck Weaver, Mellie Wolfgang, Robert "Ziggy" Hasbrook. (*The Sporting News*).

during a campaign that Fielder Jones, the canny Sox field general, and his charges felt they should have won? Whatever else might have been the reasons—and there were several—the final outcome spread enough dejection to cover all the bases and watering holes on the south side of town, involving everybody from the bucket-boy to Commy, the Sox' doughty major domo.

Marking off 1907 as one of those it-couldn't-possibly-happen-again seasons, the White Sox were primed for revenge as they took on the 1908 Tigers only to find themselves embroiled in another dog-eat-dog struggle that led, once again, in events painfully reminiscent of 1907, to the very last days of the season, when, but a half-game out of first place, they faced the Tigers needing only to win their last home game to salt away the pennant. But it didn't happen. The Tigers pounced on starter Guy "Doc" White and kept at it, brushing aside 40-game winner Ed Walsh and Frank "Piano Mover" Smith who were rushed into the fray. When the dust had settled the Tigers had rubbed the White Sox in the dirt of South Side Park, administering a 7-0 humiliation, thus winning their second straight American League pennant.

It was enough to make grown men shed tears of frustration, and one of them, Comiskey's manager, Fielder Jones, vowed that he'd had enough, resigning, perhaps before Charlie Comiskey could fire him. But among them all, it was Comiskey himself who bore the greatest frustration. In his mind, the only way to restore his White Sox to the ranks of baseball's elite franchises was to win the world's championship, and during those gray, cheerless days of late 1908, he vowed that he would put together another championship ball club. It would take longer than he suspected, and would cost far more than he might ever have thought possible. But whatever that would take he vowed on the spot to do. It was a challenge he faced obsessively in the years to come, even overriding his miserly habits to throw very serious money at the project that drove him much like an Ahab after his own Moby Dick.

Comiskey suffered through another five seasons as his ball club sank lower and lower in the standings while watching the Philadelphia and Boston clubs ride herd on the American League. At last, however, circumstances both within and outside of Organized Baseball meshed to a point where it became possible for an opportunistic dealer to put together the makings of a solid, if not championship ball club.

By 1914 times were increasingly tumultuous. The guns of August, booming ominously long before the 1914 season ended, threatened to spread across the European landscape—and beyond. And baseball itself was in a turmoil over the emergence of another player on the major league scene, the Federal League.

Comiskey might have been more reluctant than most when it came to dipping into the franchise largess, but that didn't mean it was out of the question. And he was far from naive in matters baseball. Himself a fine judge of baseball talent, he also had a competent group of scouts on the lookout and a purse deep enough to pull off a blockbuster deal if he might feel so inclined. By the time 1914 was drawing to a close, the hard-bitten old warrior recognized that there was angling room, especially in the City of Brotherly Love. Dame Fortune was apparently looking his way, and the crafty White Sox generalissimo was not about to snub the Good Lady. And so The Old Roman quite literally fell into the right spot at the right time with the right ingredients for a deal to set his feet firmly on the road to his ultimate goal, a world's championship.

In Philadelphia there might have been pennant winners, but the margin between mounting debt and solvency was great enough to cause Ben Shibe and his "Tall Tactician," Connie Mack, enough angst to consider, quite seriously, breaking up their championship ball club, those championships not withstanding. Commy took one look eastward and resolved to dig deeply enough into the White Sox coffers to tempt the A's to part with the brains of their ball club, at least on the field of play, none other than the Columbia alum, Capt. Eddie Collins. The American League's 1914 MVP would not come with "a song and a sawbuck." Comiskey knew that, and he dealt with the Philadelphians from the strength of powerful and persuasive monetary support. There was no sparing of the horses this time, and when the deal was consummated on December 8, 1914, the Cocky One became the Sox' new second baseman and captain for the princely purchase price of $50,000 plus a guaranteed annual salary of $15,000 for the next five seasons, and beyond that a $15,000 signing bonus. The transaction would be the cornerstone for what would soon become, when the dealing and maneuvering and angling had all been wrapped up, a world's championship ball club. To say the very least, Comiskey's deal for and with Eddie Collins rocked the baseball world. It was especially stunning precisely because it was The Old Roman, Silas Marner himself, who had raided his Drover's Bank account for an aggregate of close to 150,000 greenbacks. And he was just beginning.

The progression of the White Sox from a sixth place team in 1914 under Jimmy Callahan, longtime Chicago and Comiskey favorite, to a first place, World Series winner in 1917, looking for the world like a dynasty that was already well under way, evolved as follows:

1914, *Callahan,* *Mgr.*	*1915,* *Rowland,* *Mgr.*	*1916,* *Rowland,* *Mgr.*	*1917,* *Rowland,* *Mgr.*
Fournier, 1b	Fournier, 1b	Fournier, 1b	Gandil, 1b
Blackburne, 2bE.	Collins, 2b	Ness, 1b	E. Collins, 2b
Weaver, ss	Weaver, ss	E. Collins, 2b	Risberg, ss
Breton, 3b	Blackburne,	3bTerry, ss	Weaver, 3b/ss
Berger, UT	Roth, UT	Weaver, 3b	McMullin, 3b
Demmitt, of	J. Collins, of	McMullin, UT	E. Murphy, PH
Bodie, of	Felsch, of	Jackson, of	Jackson, of
J. Collins, of	E. Murphy, of	Felsch, of	Felsch, of
Roth, of	Jackson, of	J. Collins, of	Leibold, of
Schalk, c	Schalk, c	Leibold, of	J. Collins, of
Benz, p	Faber, p	Schalk, c	Schalk, c
Cicotte, p	Scott, p	Russell, p	Russell, p
Scott, p	Benz, p	Williams, p	Williams, p
Faber, p	Russell, p	Faber, p	Faber, p
Russell, p	Cicotte, p	Cicotte, p	Cicotte, p
Walsh, p	Walsh, p	Scott, p	Scott, p
Wolfgang, p	Wolfgang, p	Benz, p	Benz, p
		Danforth, p	Danforth, p
Won 70, Lost 84	Won 93, Lost 61	Won 89, Lost 65	Won 100, Lost 54
Tied, 6th place	3rd place	2nd place	1st place

A closer look at the White Sox during their ascendancy reveals superb pitching, always a Comiskey strong suit, to go along with a lineup of position players that came together, stayed together, knew each others' strengths and skills, and played the kind of heads-up ball that eventually paid off in the game's ultimate spoils. There were only two infield positions that remained in flux through the 1916 season and prior to the 1917 campaign, and Commy saw to it that Swede Risberg, brought in to play shortstop, and Chick Gandil, Cleveland's first baseman, were acquired to round out a stellar inner defense. With Gandil at first, Collins at second and Risberg moving in at short, enabling Buck Weaver to move over to third, the infield took on a new and polished look right from the start of spring training. It could only get better as the season moved along.

Happy Felsch, Joe Jackson and John "Shano" Collins had patrolled the vast outer acreage of Comiskey Park together from 1915 on, along with little Nemo Leibold, a smart, feisty leadoff hitter who was brought to Chicago from Cleveland during the season in 1915, giving the club strong outfield arms, superb fielding and that famous glove of Jackson's where, he insisted, "triples went to die." It was the youngster Felsch, however, who was the star outfielder of the lot. Deceptively quick, and possessed of a lethal throwing arm, he carried on the superstar outfielding Fielder Jones made commonplace during the club's earlier years.

Fred McMullin stepped into the 1917 lineup at third to fill in for Buck Weaver, whose injured hand sidelined him for six weeks. McMullin played so well that when Weaver came back to play the last three weeks of the season, manager Clarence "Pants" Rowland benched Risberg, put Weaver at short and opened the World Series that same way. A jack of all infield trades, he came to Chicago in 1915, as did another utility player, Eddie Murphy, equally valuable off the bench, especially as a pinchhitter.

By 1915, when Rowland took charge of the club, the pitching corps was already in place with but two exceptions. Red Faber, Eddie Cicotte, Joey Benz, Texan Reb Russell and "Death Valley Jim" Scott combined to give the Sox stellar pitching. Claude "Lefty" Williams and reliever Dave Danforth (1916) came on to round out a steady, formidable staff. And to handle all that talent on the mound was a Hall of Famer in the making, catcher Ray Schalk, a brainy little scrapper who reinvented the catcher's position, featuring clever signal-calling and backup infielding that made the White Sox' inner defenses solid, if not spectacular at times.

The chronological sequence of all these shifts, changes and adaptations that were designed to bring on a winner began with the replacement of the 1914 skipper, Jim "Nixey" Callahan. The appointment of his successor was another of Charlie Comiskey's more startling moves. Already on December 8, 1914, he had acquired Eddie Collins, and then a scant fortnight later he pulled Clarence Rowland, a young ex-catcher, just 33, out of the ranks of the minor leagues to manage his ball club. That maneuver caused

Clarence Rowland's 1915 White Sox, his first major league team, won 23 more games than Manager Callahan's 1914 team, finishing third with 93 wins. Team members, L to R, include: Standing, Ray Schalk,★ Eddie Cicotte,★ Larry Chappell, Ed Klepfer, Bill Lathrop, Manager Clarence Rowland,★ Mellie Wolfgang,★ Red Faber, ★ Joey Benz,★ Eddie Collins,★ Thomas Quinlan. Seated: Tom Daly, Hi Jasper, Jim Scott,★ John Collins,★ Howard Baker, John Breton, Jaques Fournier,† Happy Felsch,★ Bunny Brief. Front Row: Reb Russell,★ Baldwin, Braggo Roth, Mr. Buckner, Equipment Mgr. (kneeling), Buck Weaver,★ Wally Mayer, Ray Demmitt, and Lena Blackburne. Joe Jackson and Nemo Leibold were acquired during the 1915 season but do not appear on this photograph. (Brace Photo)

★*Member of the 1917 team.*
 †*Released during the 1917 season.*

still more reverberations around the baseball world. Who in all the world was this fellow with the unlikely sobriquet "Pants"?

Clarence Rowland, born and raised in Platteville, Wisconsin, spent a lifetime in baseball, most of it as a background figure, whether as a player, manager, scout or executive. Spotlight moments were few and far between in a professional career that extended from the early 1900s to his death in 1969 at 90. His tour of duty included minor league catching, managing in the minors (where he also was a part owner and executive with front office responsibilities), scouting, serving as the president of the Pacific Coast League from 1941 to 1954, working in the Chicago Cubs' front office as a vice president from 1955 to 1969, and, for one brief moment, managing the White Sox from 1915 through the 1918 season.

It was with the Sox—a ball club he not only assembled and groomed for victory but guided to baseball's highest honor, a world's championship—that he was enabled to stand, at least for one fleeting moment in a six-decade career, at center stage to reap the hard-earned rewards that accompany a World Series conquest. That was something no one could take away from him.

The fellow they called Pants was manager of the class B Three-I League Peoria Distillers that, in 1914, wound upin second place, three games behind league champion Davenport. That was a long, long way from The Bigs. But that didn't seem to bother Charlie Comiskey, who saw in this bright young fellow capabilities that he felt merited a long look. Some time before the 1914 season had ended Comiskey had no doubt determined that the time had come to put aside his longtime friend, the personable and much-traveled Callahan, in favor of a fresh start for the 1915 season. But the Old Roman procrastinated. He was in fact harboring the faint but not impossible hope that somehow John McGraw might be available. As the weeks progressed following the White Sox' victory over the Cubs in the 1914 City Series (the triumph was at least some balm for the woes of a lackluster season), it began to look as though there might still be a crack in the door, giving Comiskey a shot at landing the Big One, McGraw himself. But it became evident early in December that McGraw was staying put, working on a lucrative deal that would capitalize not only on his name and record, but on the volatile circumstances surrounding the national pastime.

Consquently, the White Sox' major domo put playing personnel front and center, giving him the time to rethink the managerial situation. Enter the Philadelphia deal for Eddie Collins. Having reminded the baseball world that Comiskey and his Sox were not yet dead, he promptly left town in the midst of 1914's pre–Christmas rush and concentrated on the young man he had promoted a time or two in years past, had kept an eye on, and who, more and more, was stealing into his thoughts. Though he said nary a word to anyone about his intentions, his mind was made up by the time he returned to Chicago.

The December 18, 1914, pages of the *Chicago Tribune* carried the bombshell: Clarence Rowland, the busher no one knew, had been named the new manager of the White Sox. Irving E. Sanborn's article broke the news this way:

By appointing Clarence H. Rowland of Dubuque, Ia., manager of the White Sox to succeed James J. Callahan, President Comiskey gave the baseball world its second sensation within a fortnight, the other one being the purchase of Eddie Collins of the Athletics to play second base....

Despairing of developing a winning team with recruits from minor leagues under major league management, Comiskey apparently has reversed his method by going after seasoned major league players and recruiting a manager from the minors...

Although Rowland has shown ability to handle ball players during his brief career on the diamond, his proclivity for picking out promising recruits had as much as anything else to do with Comiskey's choice of him as Sox pilot.

The Old Roman's strategy began to unfold. The ball club needed top drawer talent both on the field of play and in the dugout. Comiskey apparently felt that Rowland was top drawer talent; not only that, but he knew from past experience, as well as from the magnitude of the opportunity extended his new manager, that Rowland would work ceaselessly to bring his benefactor a championship as well as being true to the Comiskey cause. That Rowland would be a loyal operative in the House of Comiskey was made abundantly clear in his first interview with the *Tribune* correspondent, which also appeared in the December 18 issue.

Throughout my career in baseball Charles A. Comiskey has been my staunchest friend and supporter. He has been my ideal. It was on his recommendations and through him that I secured the positions of handling clubs that I did. He is now placing me in a position where I can repay him for helping me in the past. *I intend to give him all that I have in me.*

Thus, at one fell swoop Comiskey had ushered in a new age with a new look. In the process he had relegated old friends Nixey Callahan and Bill Gleason to other pursuits. Gleason, an old acquaintance and sidekick who had coached for Commy and was himself on the short list of more than one ball club not only in the American and National Leagues, but in the Federal League, as well, had been around a long time, and though he spent the 1915 season on the sidelines, his love for the game prompted him to return to

Charles A. Comiskey, White Sox owner and major force in American League baseball during the Deadball Era. (Brace Photo)

Chicago as a coach for the club under Rowland. More would be heard about this flinty little battler in due course.

Charlie Comiskey had made a splashy start toward his much-desired championship, and, having jumped feet first into the water, he kept at it until the White Sox lineup of 1915, if not totally revamped, would indeed remind him of those resourceful, heady ball clubs that were synonymous with Chicago baseball when his franchise was among the elite in major league baseball. How far Pants Rowland could take the team remained to be seen, but the die had been cast and the Old Roman liked the looks of it.

Compared to previous years, the 1915 season was an unqualified success. A 20-game turnaround under the busher from the boonies upped the Sox' victory total to 93, good for a third place finish, their best since 1908. And Comiskey's retooling continued apace. In 1915 he arranged for the purchase of Oscar "Happy" Felsch from the Milwaukee club of the American Association. Felsch responded favorably to his new surroundings, putting in 121 ball games and taking over the center field position. But the big noise came later in the season when The Shoeless One, Joe Jackson, was pried loose from Cleveland in a player-cash deal with Cleveland that separated $31,500 from the White Sox treasury. With the addition of Jackson the new Sox manager had quite suddenly become the proud possessor of a batting order that featured Collins, Jackson and Felsch in the 3-4-5 spots. And just as suddenly Chicago's south siders woke up to the new look and the new realities that were about to dawn in the American League. Wait till next year, so often a loser's mantra, was more than wishful thinking this time around.

Comiskey made one other late August move that, although raising few eyebrows, nonetheless would have significant consequences
for the seasons ahead. That was the acquisition of Claude "Lefty"
Williams from Salt Lake City where he was burning up the Pacific
Coast League with 33 wins and 294 K's, both league-leading figures.
Williams, a taciturn, precision hurler, would move into Rowland's
1916 rotation, and would become Joe Jackson's roommate during the
next years. Together they would become two of the more tragic
figures involved in the 1919 Armageddon known as The Big Fix.

To look at the final American League standings of 1915 it would
be easy, but not exactly accurate, to conclude that the pennant race
was a two-team affair between Boston, a two and one-half game
winner and World Series victor over Wilbert Robinson's Superbas,
later known as the Brooklyn Dodgers, and the Cobb-led Tigers. In
fact, Pants Rowland's Pale Hose, paced by Capt. Eddie Collins,
who turned the Sox into a smart contender almost overnight,
opened the season with three solid months of winning baseball that
found them astride both Boston and Detroit with a 35 and 21 record
going into July. But while Boston forged a 22 and 10 record during the midseason month of July, with Detroit close behind at 18
and 10, the Comiskeymen faded to 13 and 14, and by the time
August arrived the race actually did come down to the Red Sox and
the Tigers. Just the same, the White Sox turnabout under Rowland,
his field captain Collins, and the little colonel behind the plate, Ray
"Cracker" Schalk, was worthy of more than a second glance around
the league. Knowing heads realized that the Old Roman's outfit
would have to be reckoned with in 1916.

Continuing their mastery over their crosstown rivals, the Cubs,
in the 1915 City Series, the White Sox put their most successful season in many a year into the record books with a third place finish,
having tied the 1906 Pale Hose record for most wins in a single season at 93, having drawn more than a half million through the turnstiles of Comiskey's new baseball palace, and having whipped up
Chicago appetites for a 1916 pennant flag. That anticipation carried loyal South Siders through the long winter.

After finishing off the 1915 season with a blistering 11 game
winning streak and polishing off the North Enders four out of five
in the City Series (it is well to remember that during those early
years the City Series was a huge event staged with all the hoopla
and trappings of a World Series) one would have thought that the

quiet man behind the scenes who had guided the Comiskeymen to more success that season than Chicagoans dared to hope for, would have been up for kudos from the bossman himself. Not quite so. While pleased overall with the progress his club had made in 1915, Comiskey chaffed under his team's July let-down and let it be known that nothing less than the top slot would slake his thirst for the prestige and respect that a world's champion brought. And third place was not where the champions finished.

Comiskey also let it be known that he missed the hard-driving temperament that stoked winning habits. That kind of fiercely competitive spirit, synonymous with McGraw's fighting ball clubs, and of his own 1906 champions, could only be accomplished by dint of unbending will, strong discipline and a tough-minded leader. That put Pants Rowland on the hot seat, a rather strange development considering the way Commy put up with the free-wheeling Callahan and other lesser lights during some of the dismal years between 1908 and 1914. It also had the town's wags wondering if it wouldn't be long before Bill Gleason, the Kid himself, would be calling the shots for Sox. He was, after all, as feisty and gritty as ball players could be, knew the game inside and out and had years upon years of experience in playing with and handling ball players. It was Kid Gleason's presence that cast Rowland in the role of an underdog, a lesser light standing in the shadows. That he had brought the Sox along brilliantly through his first year at the helm didn't seem to cut much ice, and right or wrong, the underdog's role was his ever after.

As it turned out, Bill Gleason was indeed brought back into the game for the 1916 season, but as a coach for the Sox, not as their new manager. Charlie Comiskey's mind was made up. He rehired Rowland for the 1916 season anyway, and, as usual, let the press conjecture and say what they were inclined to say.

That the resurgence of the Sox was no fluke was evident early in the 1916 season. By the time May was over the Rowland forces were in the thick of the hunt, challenging the defending champs, Boston, the early season success of the Yankees, and Detroit, back once again to try to restore the glory of their 1907-09 championship days. By the end of May the Tigers and White Sox had battled through a dozen encounters with no advantage, each team winning six times. But during the remaining ten games the Sox posted a seven and three record to win the season series by a 13 and 9 count, good enough to relegate the pesky Detroiters to a third place finish.

It was Boston, in the end, that prevailed, defending their 1915 championship with a September surge that took the measure first of the Sox (two out of three at Comiskey Park), and then of the Tigers, with three straight that put the pennant out of reach for both Detroit and Chicago. Boston's success in Chicago, September 16–18, raised its season mark against the Sox to 14 and 8, enough to bring home the bunting and to relegate the Pale Hose to a second place finish. And that irked hizoner Mr. Comiskey. Not even a 4-0 routing of the Cubs in the City Series appeased him. Nor did another notch upward from third to second place. The major business had not been brought off, and for the Old Roman it would be a long winter—once again.

If there was backroom conjecture about Pants Rowland's fate during the November-December portion of the Hot Stove League season in 1915, it was open season on Commy's field general in 1916. As early as November 6 the *Chicago Tribune*'s James Crusinberry had addressed the managerial situation in Chicago (the Cubs, also in the market for a new skipper, were in the midst of their own talent hunt and would soon sign Fred Mitchell to guide their ball club) with these comments about the situation on the South Side:

> Like the Cub stockholders, Comiskey is up against the same problem (ed: making decisions about his personnel, coaching *and managing*) of how to find a lieutenant of whom better things can be expected with any degree of certainty. Within the ranks of the Sox themselves he has two brainy players in Eddie Collins and Ray Schalk, but it is doubtful if the keystone star would undertake the responsibility of handling the reins, and the all-American backstop's youth is against him. Besides, Schalk will have a wife to manage this season in addition to his duties as marksman.
>
> Comiskey has the same chance to get Jack Hendricks or Fred Clarke that the Cubs have, and no better. The only other tried veteran who has shown class as a major league manager and could be had without stealing him is Billy Murray, former leader of the Phillies, and later interested in the Federal League club in Newark.
>
> Has anybody a real, certified pennant winning manager up his sleeve?

Crusinberry's last comment said it all, implying that Rowland was not a "real, certified pennant winning manager." And the top brass did nothing to naysay the rumormill. In fact, Comiskey wasn't talking. Further, he didn't do anything about contracting his 1917 manager. That stood in contrast to his usual practice of getting his manager signed for the coming year, and that *ex post haste,* shortly after the conclusion of the season. All of which left Rowland, who had improved the ball club four notches to within striking distance of the winner's circle, out there on the far end of a thin limb.

Whatever misgivings The Old Roman might have had about reappointing Pants Rowland, if any, would never be known because, per custom, he kept that end of the business to himself. So things drifted along until mid-December when the move was made and, sure enough, it was Pants Roland's signature that appeared on the White Sox contract. That, once again, put the subject to rest. But not ever after...

The issue is reviewed here because the baseball fraternity, Chicago's fandom and the media never really "took" to The Busher. They seemed to feel that Comiskey could do far better. He had only to look into the Sox dugout where The Kid, Bill Gleason, also rehired for the 1917 campaign, was, in their opinion, pulling the strings and running the club. The consequence of that kind of ambivalence, along with Rowland's release as the White Sox pilot after a dismal 1918 season, tends to undercut his role and the skills he brought to a ball club that rocketed like a meteor through the latter days of the deadball era, and might very well have established the White Sox as one of the premier franchises in the game for years to come.

The passing of many years has not dimmed the "common wisdom" of the days of yore. Dick Lindberg, the astute White Sox team historian, penned these observations in his review of the Rowland-Gleason era in his *Stealing First in a Two-Team Town* (Sagamore Publishing, Champaign, Illinois, 1994, p. 98).

> Few of the veteran players listened or took him (ed: Rowland) seriously. His youth and inexperience kept getting in the way. Instructions to players took the form of a well-meaning suggestion, or sage piece of advice. Sometimes they listened, but most of the time the athletes paid no mind. He was, after all, just a "busher." Behind the scenes leadership was provided by Comiskey, of course, and a sturdy little man summoned out

of retirement when it became evident that Rowland needed help bringing the thoroughbreds across the finish line.

The leader on and off the field was "Kid" Gleason, the fifty-something coach, who developed a great rapport with the youngsters like Lefty Williams and Swede Risberg. When Rowland and Comiskey parted ways after the shortened wartime season of 1918, Gleason stepped in.

What's wrong with that picture? With all due respect to Mr. Lindberg, it should be pointed out that Kid Gleason was *not* a part of the 1915 White Sox resurgence. The team that won 93 games that summer, in contrast to the 1914 club that could muster but 70 wins, was under the sole leadership of Pants Rowland. The Busher had to be doing *something* right, or was the turnaround accomplished by the players despite their manager? That doesn't seem reasonable.

The fellow they called "The Busher," Clarence "Pants" Rowland, signed by The Old Roman, Charles Comiskey, to manage the White Sox for the 1915 season. His contract was renewed each season through 1918, and in 1917 he had the last laugh on them all, including John McGraw. (Brace Photo)

And then there is the *Chicago Tribune*'s coverage of the players' reaction to Rowland's rehiring in December of 1916. James Crusinberry reported in the Tribune's December 27 sports pages, as follows:

> That Clarence Rowland, recently reappointed manager of the Chicago White Sox, will have the staunch support of the stars of the south side team in his efforts to land a pennant for Charles A. Comiskey next season was made quite evident yesterday when Rowland received letters from three of the leading lights of the Thrityfifth Street aggregation vowing their support for the coming year.

The letters were from Eddie Collins, king of second basemen, Joe Jackson, chief slugger and Buck Weaver, former captain and always intellectual infiedler. E. Collins expressed
considerable pleasure in the fact that Rowland had been given
another chance to lead the south siders and stated that he
believed next year would be the big year for the team.

The article went on to report that Joe Jackson was determined
to get an early start, beginning his spring training in New Orleans
on his own already in January, and that Buck Weaver stated his
approval of the move, adding that the team hadn't done for Rowland what it could have. Rowland was predictably overjoyed, and
probably more than relieved.

As the new year rolled in and the serious business of getting
his charges on the dotted line commenced, the White Sox commisar
turned to getting the signatures of all the key members of his ball
club on the dotted line. In a matter of weeks the team would head
south to its Mineral Wells, Texas, digs with the usual compliment
of wannabes, yannigans, grizzled veterans and stars to ready for the
campaign ahead. This much was for certain: regardless of what
others might think, say or put into print about Rowland, Gleason
or anyone else, Comiskey's field leader would be Pants Rowland,
his first lieutenant would be Kid Gleason, and the ball players would
fall in line behind them.

Two key signators signed on directly ahead of the Comiskey
Special's embarkation for Texas. One was a gifted young athlete
from California by the name of Charles Risberg, known to his teammates as Swede, and the other, after making certain that the terms
were to his liking, came to the Sox from Cleveland, where he had
performed during the 1916 season as the Indians' first sacker, the
slick-fielding Arnold "Chick" Gandil. The latter acquisition was
cause for no little joy in Chicago where the *Tribune* bubbled over
with a March 2 headline that shouted GET YOUR SEAT FOR THE
'17 SERIES! WHITE SOX PURCHASE GANDIL. The accompanying article by sports writer John Alcock further revealed that
Gandil's purchase was at the behest of Commy's manager, yet
another evidence of Rowland's perseverance and alertness in the
player market. The signing of Gandil filled what Comiskey and his
braintrust felt was a gaping hole at first base. The advance contingent, to be joined by still others who headed south included:

Name/Position	Nickname	Yrs w/Sox	Age	Wgt/Hgt	B/T
Jenkins, Joseph, c	Joe	0	25	178/5:10	R/R
Lynn, Byrd, c	Birdie	1	22	175/6:00	R/R
Mayer, Walter, c	Mose	0	25	178/5:11	R/R
Schalk, Ray, c	Cracker	5	25	156/5:07	R/R
Gandil, Arnold, 1b	Chick	1	28	198/6:01	R/R
Hasbrook, R.L., 1b	Bob	0	23	170/6:00	R/R
Jourdan, Ted, 1b	Ted	0	21	170/6:01	L/L
Collins, E. T., 2b	Eddie	2	28	160/5:09	L/R
Hartford, B., ss	Bruce	0	24	180/6:01	R/R
Risberg, C. A., ss	Swede	0	22	180/6:00	R/R
Terry, Zeb, ss	Zeb	1	23	155/5:08	R/R
McMullin, Fred, inf	Mac	1	28	170/5:09	R/R
Weaver, Geo., inf	Buck	5	25	170/5:09	B/R
Collins, John, of	Shano	7	30	180/6:00	R/R
Eldred, L. C., of	Brick	0	23	163/5:07	R/R
Felsch, Oscar, of	Hap	2	23	178/5:11	R/R
Fournier, J., of/1b	Jack	5	25	190/6:00	L/R
Jackson, Joe, of	General	2	28	178/6:00	L/R
Leibold, H., of	Nemo	2	25	155/5:06	L/R
Murphy, Ed, of	Mique	2	26	160/5:09	L/R
Benz, Joey, p	Blitzen	3	30	195/6:00	R/R
Cicotte, E. V., p	Succotash	4	33	160/5:07	B/R
Danforth, Dave, p	Dave	1	25	177/6:01	L/L
Faber, Urban, p	Red	3	25	180/6:02	R/R
Russell, Ewell, p	Reb	4	25	185/6:00	L/L
Schellenbach, F., p	String	0	18	190/6:02	R/R
Scott, James, p	Senator	8	31	185/6:01	R/R
Williams, Claude, p	Lefty	1	23	165/5:09	L/L
Wolfgang, Mel, p	Mellie	3	26	160/5:08	R/R

The most interesting thing about that roster was the column listing the players' ages. Shano Collins was the only position player who checked in at age 30. Among the pitchers Eddie Cicotte was the elder statesman as well as the grandaddy of the ball club, but a young 33 nonetheless. The opening day lineup would average 25, as follows:

Gandil 1b, 28	Weaver, 3b, 25	Jackson, lf, 28
E. Collins, 2b, 28	Leibold, rf, 25	Schalk, c, 25
Risberg, ss, 22	Felsch, cf, 23	Williams, p, 23

It was a lineup that, barring catastrophic events, might well have played together for the next ten seasons. Alas, two such catastrophic events seared both the game and particularly the House of Comiskey. One was temporary, however devastating it might have been, soon passing into the history books as the Great War. The other simply would not pass away, leaving its mark on the Comiskey franchise ever after, and that was, of course, The Great Scandal of 1919-20 which involved the entire 1917 opening day lineup. Six of the eight men out, as they ultimately came to be known, leaving only Fred McMullin and Eddie Cicotte, both of whom were key cogs in the team's drive to the championship, started for Rowland in the season opener.

The point, however, is that the Old Roman had assembled a young, highly talented ball club that would soon show its wares and a killer instinct, forging to the head of the American League parade. It remained for Rowland and Gleason to whip that kind of talent into a frontrunner during the weeks ahead in Texas.

In addressing the upcoming season during their weeks together in the spa town of Mineral Wells, Texas, some forty miles removed from Fort Worth, the Comiskey braintrust had a number of concerns. The defending world's champions, Boston's Red Sox, were returning their entire lineup intact, and that meant that their pitching staff, which included the likes of Carl Mays, Dutch Leonard, Ernie Shore and the young southpaw who had become the best lefty in the business, Babe Ruth, would be back to bedevil White Sox hitters. Over in Detroit, 1916's third place team, the Tigers, would return their lineup intact, as well. That meant that Ty Cobb would be back to torment not only the Sox, but everybody else in the league. In order to win a world's championship a ball club is called upon to win its own league first and those two teams were just as pennant-minded as the Comiskeymen. So that was the foremost concern.

Interestingly, there was no concern over the condition of the players, all of whom reported in great shape, ready to answer the bell. That ran against the grain of the usual training camp during baseball's earlier years, which emphasized, right up there among its top priorities, boiling away the poundage that accumulated over the winter months. In case you might have wondered why on earth The Old Roman would book an out-of-the-way little spot on the map in the Hill Country of Texas for the team's training camp, the "Fat Farm" concept was the main reason behind selecting a town with medicinal waters, a spa town. Further, it had fewer distractions than Dallas or Los Angeles or New Orleans might have to offer. Consequently, the ball club could and did settle down to getting plays, signals, arms and batting eyes ready right from the opening call to action.

There was one exception to the grade A shape of the players and that was Reb Russell's mealticket, his southpaw throwing arm. Russell was the top lefty on the club, counted on for a another season of heavy duty. But in mid-March he came down with what would be described today as tendonitis in his elbow which prevented him from fully extending or twisting that arm. Russell had been a workhorse, beginning his career in Chicago with a 20-game, 300-plus inning season. Pants Rowland had penciled both Russell and "The Senator," Frank Scott, into his rotation as part of the top four of his staff. But it was evident by the end of March that the two veterans would have to be spotted in just the right places during the course of the season to keep them fresh for each start. Ol' Tex, one of jolliest and most likeable fellows on the team, would make a strong contribution to the 1917 club, but his 20-win seasons were definitely behind him. He would, in fact, have been out of baseball altogether in just a couple more seasons had it not been for his lusty hitting. Like Smokey Joe Wood, he turned to outfielding, putting in a .368 season as a reserve outfielder for the Pirates in 1922. Noteworthy, also, is his .279 average in 1917, which included a number of pinchhitting assignments.

The concern over Russell during March and on into April, further, caused both Rowland and Kid Gleason to turn a close eye on the little lefty from the Pacific Coast League, Claude Williams. Gleason, a former pitcher before turning to infielding, took the youngster under his arm. The other lefthander on the pitching staff was Dave Danforth, another southpaw, who became the premier reliever in baseball the summer of 1917. The three of them gave the Sox solid pitching and versatility from the port side.

Aside from experimenting with batting orders and dealing with the minor muscle pulls and strains, there was one other concern. Some 100 plus miles southeast, near Waco, McGraw's Giants were going through their own spring training grind. This was a club to keep an eye on. After a whirlwind finish to their 1916 season, spiced with the longest winning streak in the game's history, a 26-game wonder, they were the team to beat despite Robinson's lineup in Brooklyn. By mid-season in 1916 McGraw had finally come up with a lineup he liked. Trades, additions, a player or two from the

defunct Federal League, and a pitching staff that had finally
adjusted to the departure of the Mathewsons and Marquards of
former years had combined under McGraw's leadership to get the
Giants back into the pennant hunt. Pitchers like lefthander Ferdie
Schupp, back for another year after registering the lowest ERA in
baseball history, 0.90, Rube Benton, another southpaw who tacked
the 26th win on to that monstrous winning streak, and the third of
McGraw's lefthanded triumverate, the elongated Slim Sallee, would
combine with righthanders William "Pol" Perritt, 18-11 in 1916 and
Freddie Anderson, a spot starter and reliever, plus an old hand like
Jeff Tesreau, to give the pitching corps maturity and a variety of
deliveries and styles that would probably keep National League hitters at bay long enough for McGraw's patented slash and steal
attack to get his club out in front so that his pitching staff could
shut down the enemy in the late innings and bring his club home
a winner. Indeed, this was a ball club to keep under surveillance.

Finally, there was no keeping the war overseas far from everybody's thoughts. The way it made itself felt, a very present concern and something to be dealt with, was the conscription of men
from the ranks of professional baseball, and beyond that, talk about
curtailing the major league season, calling off the season for a number of minor leagues, and enlistments. And to bring the situation
home with emphasis, military drills were to become a part of every
team's spring training regimen. There had been talk about military
training before 1917, and by January 28 of 1917 the *Tribune* reported:

> Military drill for the White Sox at their training camp in Min-
> eral Wells, Tex., is assured, provided other American League
> clubs go through with the project (Ed: they did). President
> Comiskey of the Sox has practically been offered the services
> of Sergt. Walter S. Smiley of the United States army as drill-
> master, but is holding off until assured all the other clubs will
> adopt the military work...
>   Capt. Huston, GM of the New York Yankees, sponsor
> for the army training idea, started south with his club without
> an army man to direct military maneuvers. Capt. Huston him-
> self is competent to supervise the drill, but it is hardly likely
> he will attempt such a position with men who will be his
> employees all season...Harry Frazee of the Red Sox has
> promised to have his players tutored in the manual of arms, so
> it looks a safe bet that Comiskey will have a regular soldier
> drilling the Sox at their Texas camp.

Such drilling was a part of the entire training program that spring, and it was carried right on into the regular season with military drills that occasionally became part of an afternoon's "entertainment" at the ball park. To readers far removed from those World War I years that may come as a surprise and seem quite incongruous, but there was no underestimating the effect the war had on the administration and conduct of the national pastime. It was another part of the gigantic context and wartime culture in which baseball waged its own lesser, but still absorbing battles.

As April began to wind down to opening day festivities major league teams began the long trek homeward, playing games as they went. The White Sox worked their way northward against minor league competition with teams like the Oklahoma City Boosters and the Class A Wichita Witches under Frank Isbell, a member of the 1906 world's championship team, serving Commy as his number one minor league operative.

The Cubs, who trained in Pasadena, California, and the Pale Hose were the only major league teams to eschew "Big Time" opposition during their training. Comiskey had deliberately devised an all-minors schedule to bring along youngsters like Swede Risberg, "Brick" Eldred, R. L. "Ziggy" Hasbrook and Ted Jourdan without the anxiety over being shamed or humiliated by the Ty Cobbs and Walter Johnsons. Consequently, right on down to the last days before pulling into St. Louis for their season lidlifter on April 11, the Sox were to be found first in Minnesota's Twin Cities for games against the Minneapolis Millers and then the St. Paul Saints. Then it was on to Des Moines where the varsity crew worked over the host Boosters, a team that would go on to championship laurels in the Class A Western League that summer. Diminutive Eddie Cicotte, working his breaking and off-speed pitches to perfection, led the Sox to an 8-1 victory. The team had the look of a winner.

Pants Rowland's opening day lineup was set by this time, and he, along with the veterans who, incidentally, had tasted defeat during the Spring warmups but once, looked foward to the warm climes of St. Louis where League Park would be readied in bunting, all gussied up for the start of another major league campaign in the Mound City. There, Fielder Jones, erstwhile field boss of those early 1900s White Sox teams, and his present charges, the Browns, would welcome Rowland and Company, sending his 25-year old lefthander, Earl Hamilton, against Lefty Williams, who had opened his major league career the year before with a 13 and 7 mark.

Meanwhile out east, Boston, under the new front office leadership of New York theatrical producer Harry Frazee, with new playing manager Jack Barry, in charge of the defending champion Red Sox on the field of play, readied to meet hosting New York, sending out The Babe to meet Bob Shawkey in front of the usual first-day dignitaries plus General Leonard Wood, who would be on hand to observe the Yanks go through their military routines as well as attempting to win their engagement with the Bosox. Up north in Beantown John McGraw's Giants prepared to meet George Stallings and his Boston Braves. The Little Napoleon would open his season with 1916 acquisitions Buck Herzog, who would give the team the kind of spice and dash his champions always had, and Heinie Zimmerman, a run-producing third baseman who knew all about winning big ball games. The outfield would be composed of tiny ex-Federal Leaguer Benny Kauff, a muscular, swift center fielder, flanked by leadoff hitter George Burns and lefthanded slugger Dave Robertson whose rifle-like arm made running on the Giants a hazardous risk. Slated for opening day hurling honors was a surprise choice, Freddy Anderson, another ex-Fed whose out-pitch was a spitter.

The pennant favorites as well as the teams already relegated to also-ran status by the scribes and smart money were all lined up at the starting gate in their various stages of readiness. As usual, the 154 game schedule, consisting of 22 engagements with each team evenly divided at home and abroad, provided for two longer home stands and two lengthy road trips during the course of the season. The remainder of the games, divided among shorter stretches at home or on the road, with open dates here and there, presented the teams with far different challenges than those which confront teams playing in an age of supersonic travel.

The 1917 White Sox, for example, were slated to finish out the season with games against the American League's eastern clubs. Their final road trip started with three games in Detroit and, after a single game back in Chicago with the Browns to conclude their home game schedule, they moved on to Boston, Washington and finally to New York, a span of several weeks that necessitated their living out of suitcases from September 14 to October 1. If, after the 17 games scheduled during that stretch, they were still on top of the American League standings, it would be a major accomplishment, if not a minor miracle. The other clubs, of course, faced similar scheduling difficulties. Nonetheless, to win a pennant while finishing up a season with a lengthy road trip was a daunting challenge.

The coverage of the White Sox pennant drive in this review of their 1917 championship season follows the team through each of its home stands and road trips. Accordingly, the season's first set of games, which included a short road trip first to St. Louis and then on up to Detroit, sets the pattern for coverage throughout the season.

And so, after all the preening, posturing and predicting had been done through the course of an eventful early Spring it was time to get down to the business of playing for keeps. The 1917 season was about to begin.

CHAPTER 2

April

The quest for pennant laurels began with a road trip that booked the Pale Hose into St. Louis and Detroit, calling for four games against each team. By the time the opening set had run its course the weather had scratched two, leaving the Sox with a six game record of 5–1 atop the American League just a nose ahead of the Red Sox who were 4 and 1. Thus, the two primary antagonists of the 1916 race picked up where they had left off the year before. Only this time, the white hosed Sox were on top and the team with the red sox was in second. And that turned out to be the way the 1917 season would wind up: Chicago 1 and Boston 2. But first, the long and and difficult journey en route to the championship.

The first five wins included a crisp, 7–2 opening day conquest at the expense of George Sisler and his St. Louis Brownie colleagues, and two pitchings gems, one by Eddie Cicotte in St. Louis and the other by Red Faber in Detroit, avenging his St. Louis loss at the hands of St. Louis' Mr. Everything, George Sisler, who had homered to beat the Sox 4–3 in the second game of the season.

The season lid-lifter was actually a pitching duel between big Jim Scott and the steady hurling of portsider Earl Hamilton, who had shut down the Sox' heavy sticks through seven innings of score-

less ball that was backed by superb fielding and a few timely K's.
But Hamilton didn't survive the eighth inning. He was taken out
after yielding a pair of doubles by Buck Weaver, a three-bagger by
Shano Collins, three safeties off the bat of Chick Gandil and an
inside-the-parker by Ray Schalk, the first of but 18 four-baggers the
Sox hit all season. Scott, who followed Lefty Williams' wobbly start
with six innings of stout relief work, picked up the win and Dave
Danforth, who came on in the eighth, mopped up.

And where, you might ask, was the vaunted middle of the order
during this White Sox bombardment? It seems that Eddie Collins,
0 for 3, Jackson, 1 for 4, and Felsch, 0 for 4, left the big hits to fellows like the other Collins, outfielder John, Cracker Schalk and
Chick Gandil, who celebrated his first game back in Pale Hose livery with a double and two singles. Defensively, strikes from the
outer gardens by Shoeless Joe and Nemo Leibold cut down would-
be Browns scorers in the very first inning. That doused cold water
on a budding run-fest at Lefty Williams' expense that might easily
have run up a tough lead to overcome. And the rookie, Swede Risberg, contributed to an errorless Chicago defense, throwing out a
pair of runners on difficult plays. But he was also picked off second, indicating that the youngster had a few things still to learn in
the faster company of The Big Show.

In their first outing, thus, Pants Rowland's outfit demonstrated
sufficient weaponry from its arsenal to indicate an eventful summer ahead. Timely hitting, strong pitching when it counted, outstanding defense and speed on the bases were all in evidence. That
bode well for the grind ahead. As for the Collins-Jackson-Felsch
combination in the heart of the batting order, that would make itself
felt in due time.

On April 14 the baseball world, which was totally unprepared
at that early date in the season for what was in store that day, found
itself gasping over one of those rare baseball phenomena, a no-hitter. Just three games deep into the season the White Sox sent their
slick little skuffed-ball meister, Eddie Cicotte, to the mound to right
the previous day's wrongs. That he did, all right, setting down the
homestanding St. Louis club without a single base hit, while his Pale
Hose playmates were running amok with 11 bingos that netted 11
tallies of their own. A seven run second inning, highlighted by a
double steal engineered by Jackson and Buck Weaver, enabled The
Shoeless One to score one of those seven markers. That outburst

chased Hamilton, who had also been shot down in the season opener.

Cicotte's sensational beginning was also an indication of things to come. While it could not be expected that his season would be as extraordinary as his no-no, it nonethess augered great things for Rowland's staff ace. And it would indeed come to pass that 1917 would mark a turning point in the hurler's career, elevating him to the ranks of the greats in the game. The box score of 1917's first no-hitter follows.

At League Park, St. Louis, April 14, 1917

Chicago	AB	R	H	PO	A	*St. Louis*	AB	R	H	PO	A
Leibold, rf	4	2	1	0	0	Shotton, lf	2	0	0	1	0
Risberg, ss	5	2	2	3	2	Miller, rf	3	0	0	3	2
E. Collins, 2b	3	3	2	1	3	Sisler, 1b	4	0	0	1	11
Jackson, lf	4	1	2	5	0	Pratt, 2b	4	0	0	2	1
Felsch, cf	3	0	2	4	0	Marsans, cf	3	0	0	4	0
Gandil, 1b	4	0	0	6	0	Austin, 3b	3	0	0	3	1
Weaver, 3b	4	1	0	2	1	Lavan, ss	2	0	0	0	2
Schalk, c	4	1	1	6	0	Hale, c	2	0	0	3	2
Cicotte, (WP)	3	1	1	0	0	Hartley, c	0	0	0	0	1
						Hamilton, (LP)	0	0	0	0	0
						Park, p	0	0	0	0	0
						Rogers, p	2	0	0	0	2
						Paulette, ph	1	0	0	0	0
						Jacobson, ph	1	0	0	0	0
						Pennington, p	0	0	0	0	0
Totals	34	11	11	27	6	Totals	27	0	0	27	12

Chicago	170–102–000	11–11–1	
St. Louis	000–000–000	0–0–3	

2B: Risberg, Schalk, Jackson; SB: Shotton, Felsch; SH: Felsch, Cicotte; Sacrifice Flies: Felsch, Gandil; DP: E. Collins, Risberg, Gandil; LOB: Chicago 6, St. Louis 4; BB: Cicotte 3, Hamilton 1, Rogers 4; K: Cicotte 5, Rogers 1; Wild Pitch, Rogers; Umpires: O'Loughlin and Hildebrand; Time of Game: 2:02.

One other masterpiece graced the White Sox' opening road trip. That was fashioned in Detroit by the rangy spitballer Red Faber, who throttled the Bengals on two hits in a 4–0 win on April 16 just two a days after Eddie Cicotte's no-hitter. That victory,

One of the great Deadball Era pitchers, Eddie Cicotte. (Dennis Colgin)

combined with Reb Russell's 4–2 conquest in Detroit the next day in relief of Danforth, sent the Pale Hose home winners of five games in six tries, having given up but ten runs, for a miserly defensive average of 1.7 runs per game. At that point they stood at opposite ends in the standings with the Tigers, in the cellar with but one win in six tries.

In the Faber whitewashing job there was still another indication of the overall potency of this 1917 aggregation. Sanborn, covering the game for the *Chicago Tribune* stated it this way under a headline that announced: FABER DAZZLES TIGERS, 4 to 0, IN 2-HIT GAME:

"U. "Red" Faber let the Tigers down without a tally and with only two incompatible hits today (April 16), enabling the White Sox, by splendid work on the bases, to compile a victory in the second game of the series.

"*Compositaly considered*, it was the most joyous game of the year. The Rowland bunch looked and acted like a perfectly tuned machine. Not only did Faber demonstrate that he is ready, thereby assuring the Sox of three hurlers in tip top form, *but the whole works, offensively and defensively, looked good.* (Emphasis added)

Fielding gems, a hit and run executed neatly by Buck Weaver and Ray Schalk, who hit sharply to the right side, followed by Faber's squeeze bunt scoring Weaver, and Joe Jackson's run-scoring double, bolstered the team's offensive punch, supporting Big Red's strong outing. The second White Sox shutout of the year got them off to a great start toward their league-leading total of 22 by the season's end. The complete list follows:

Pitcher	Score	Details
Cicotte	11–0	no-hitter at St. Louis, April 14
Faber	4–0	2-hitter at Detroit, April 16
Faber	2–0	vs. St. Louis at Chicago, April 21
Scott	1–0	vs. Cleveland at Chicago, April 24
Cicotte	1–0	2-hitter vs. New York at Chicago, May 13
Benz	11–0	4-hitter vs. Philadelphia at Chicago, May 15
Cicotte	7–0	vs. Philadelphia at Chicago
Russell	1–0	12 inning game vs. Washington at Chicago, May 24
Cicotte	4–0	3-hitter at Philadelphia, June 2
Williams	8–0	4-hitter at Boston (Shore), June 15
Danforth	1–0	complete game 3-hitter vs. Cleveland at Chicago, June 24
Cicotte	5–0	1-hitter vs. Washington at Chicago, July 17
Benz	4–0	3-hitter vs. Washington at Chicago, July 18
Russell	2–0	vs. Boston (Mays) at Chicago, July 22
Scott	4–0	at Philadelphia, August 3
Faber	7–0	vs. Boston (Foster) at Chicago, August 20
Russell	2–0	beat Boston (Babe Ruth) at Chicago, August 21
Cicotte	6–0	vs. Washington at Chicago, August 23
Cicotte/ Faber	3–0	Combined 5-hitter vs. New York at Chicago, 8–27
Russell	6–0	vs. St. Louis at Chicago, August 29
Cicotte	2–0	4-hitter vs. Cleveland at Chicago, September 8
	9–0	forfeit game vs. Cleveland, at Chicago, September 9

The Sox returned home to fans who were already pumped up over their victorious swing through St. Louis and Detroit. Eagerly awaiting a home opener that, in the Comiskey tradition, was bound to be an extravaganza at the newly refurbished south side ball park, nattily attired in red, white and blue, numbers in excess of 27,000 made their way through the turnstiles in anticipation of another Sox victory. There was good news on that overcast, dank day. The first appearance of their heroes was made for the benefit of special guests Major General Barry of the Army and American League President Ban Johnson, and the first order of business was military drill, performed by "the Comiskey Regiment," the Sox themselves. When it dawned on the crowd that it was actually Eddie Collins, Joe Jackson, Eddie Cicotte and others of the first-place Sox who were parading in uniformed precision, a roar went up drowning out the snappy marches that accompanied the drill. That joy was tempered, however, by the stark awareness of the cause of the uniforms, the rifles and the drills. The Great War was, after all, a very sobering, grim reality.

So there was also bad news. Beyond the war, forbidding skies finally yielded to a downpour that made the April 19 home opener a field of mud, holding up the game that at one point would not have been renewed had it not been for the insistence of the opening day throng.

Moreover, there was Eddie Plank. Remember Gettysburg Eddie? Right, he was one of the Connie Mack aces who saw the Athletics through their championship run before heading off to the Federal League. His 1917 contract, a renewal of the 1916 pact that brought him to Fielder Jones' Browns, would turn out to be an end-of-the-line season, but not before the cagey old veteran would add the last five of his 326 career victories to his Hall of Fame record. Unfortunately for the Sox, his 6–2 triumph that day was one of them. His primary help that day came from William Chester Jacobson, a big, husky Illinoisan who was nicknamed Baby Doll during his minor league days in Mobile by a sports scribe who used the name following a game in which Jacobson homered, causing the grandstand band to strike up a popular hit of the day, "Oh, You Baby Doll."

Three of the Baby Doll's hits and eight chances afield, some of them challenging the spacious outer reaches of the ball park's outfield, gave Plank all the support he needed to subdue a trio of Pale Hose hurlers. Between them, Plank and Jacobson, the Brownies' ox-strong centerfielder, sent Sox fans home dejected and Jim Scott back to the dugout a loser.

The opening day loss was followed, however, by a four-game winning streak that added wins to the numbers of Eddie Cicotte, Red Faber, who subjected the Browns to a 2–0, six-hit shutout, running his streak of scoreless innings through two games, Lefty Williams and Jim Scott, who opened the Cleveland series with a five-hitter that shut down the Indians, 1–0. In that game the Sox won at the eleventh hour over Stan Coveleski with one of the two hits he permitted in the tense duel, a Swede Risberg triple. The fellow who somehow found a way to win ball games all season long, Capt. Eddie Collins, then drove a fly ball far enough to score Risberg in the bottom of the ninth.

The box score of that game:

At Comiskey Park, Chicago, April 24, 1917

Cleveland	AB	R	H	PO	A	Chicago	AB	R	H	PO	A
Graney, lf	5	0	1	5	0	Leibold, rf	4	0	0	2	0
Chap'n, ss	3	0	1	0	1	Risberg, ss	3	1	1	1	4
Speaker, cf	3	0	1	4	0	E. Coll's,2b	2	0	0	2	0
Wa'g's, 2b	4	0	0	1	1	Jackson, lf	3	0	0	3	0
Guisto, 1b	3	0	0	10	0	Felsch, cf	3	0	0	1	1
Roth, rf	4	0	1	2	0	Gandil, 1b	3	0	0	7	1
Evans, 3b	4	0	1	0	4	Weaver, 3b	3	0	1	2	0
O'Neill, c	3	0	0	3	0	Schalk, c	3	0	0	6	0
Cv'ski, (LP)	3	0	0	0	5	Scott, (WP)	2	0	0	1	3
Totals	33	0	5	*25	11	Totals	26	1	2	27	9

*One out when winning run scored.

Cleveland	000 000 000	0–5–1
Chicago	000 000 001	1–2–4

2B: Weaver; 3B: Risberg; Sac. Hits: Chapman, E. Collins; Sac. Fly: E. Collins; LOB: Chicago 4, Cleveland 10; BB: Coveleski 2, Scott 3; K: Coveleski 3, Scott 6; Umpires: Evans and Nallin; Time of Game: 1:43.

The remaining five games of the homestand didn't go nearly as well as the first five that yielded four wins and a first place perch atop the American League with a 9 and 2 record. That was sufficient to put the Sox two games ahead of the Yankees, who had nudged into second place one-half game ahead of Boston's Carmine. But Cleveland, which had lost its first game in Chicago by that 1–0 Scott conquest of Coveleski, proceeded to win the next three straight, 4–1, 3–0

Hall of Famer Eddie Collins, the brains of the 1917 world champion White Sox. (Brace photograph) and 2–1, thus giving one of the league's top scoring machines a lesson in pitching mastery by allowing just three runs in 36 innings of play. That kind of offesive production could put a ball club on life-support in a hurry.

Then the Tigers came to town and split the last two games of a less than sensational ten-game set that by the end of the season's first month found the Pale Hose lagging behind the league's new frontrunners, the Red Sox, by a half-game. At that point, on May first, the standings read:

	Won	Lost	Percentage
Boston	9	4	.692
Chicago	10	6	.625
New York	7	5	.583
St. Louis	8	7	.533
Cleveland	8	9	.471
Philadelphia	6	8	.429
Detroit	5	9	.357
Washington	4	9	.308

On the last day of April Babe Ruth put together a 6 to 3 victory over the Athletics at Fenway, contributing a couple hits, as the Red Sox won their tenth. Five of those belonged to the league's premier lefthander, who by that time had jumped out to a 5 and 0 record. Boston fans, buoyed by their ball club's ascendancy into first place, felt sure that from now on it would only be a matter of time until their outright supremacy would crumble any Chicago hopes, making a shambles of the pennant race. The players knew better. The race between the two Sox teams would heat up as surely as summer was on the way.

During the opening furlong the numbers of some of the leading players in the American League looked like this:

Among the hitters as of May 5:

	GP	AB	R	H	BA
Tris Speaker, Clv	17	54	11	23	.426
George Sisler, StL	16	64	6	25	.391
Roger Peckinpaugh, NYY	15	53	5	17	.321
Tilly Walker, Bos	14	50	6	16	.320

Dick Hoblitzel, Bos	11	41	6	13	.317
Ty Cobb, Det	15	54	11	17	.315
Ray Chapman, Clv	19	68	13	21	.309
Baby Doll Jacobson, StL	14	46	6	14	.304
Shano Collins, Chi	10	34	5	10	.294
Buck Weaver, Chi	18	63	11	18	.286
Duffy Lewis, Bos	14	54	6	15	.278
Frank Baker, NYY	14	48	7	13	.270
Happy Felsch, Chi	18	65	8	17	.262
Eddie Collins, Chi	18	60	7	14	.233
Joe Jackson, Chi	17	61	4	14	.230

Among the pitchers as of May 5:

	GP	W	L	Pct.
Babe Ruth, Bos	5	5	0	1.000
Bernie Boland, Det	2	2	0	1.000
Ernie Shore, Bos	3	2	0	1.000
Urban Shocker, NYY	2	2	0	1.000
Lefty Williams, Chi	4	2	0	1.000
Dave Danforth, Chi	8	1	0	1.000
Dutch Leonard, Bos	4	3	1	.750
Alan Sothoron, StL	5	3	1	.750
Eddie Cicotte, Chi	4	2	1	.667
Red Faber, Chi	6	3	3	.500
Jim Scott, Chi	7	3	3	.500

The eastern teams in the National League suffered through an unusually damp early-spring, causing a pile-up of doubleheaders that would exact their toll during the summer months. So it was that John McGraw's Giants, with an 8 and 5 record in only 13 games, started off the campaign in the top spot, where McGraw expected them to be (as usual)—and—well rested. A month later they had added but 16 more games as the weather continued to dog both leagues. By the end of May they found themselves trailing the pace-setting Phillies, two behind Alexander's Philadelphia.

It wasn't only inclement weather

Fiery Buck Herzog, captain of John McGraw's Giants. (Brace photograph) that cramped the Giants' style. Buck Herzog, the peppery Giant Captain, who had started off the season hitting well and providing the kind of infectuous grit and hustle that set McGraw's ball clubs apart, was injured in New York's Pennsylvania Railroad Station, of all places, when, on April 25, he kicked at a piece of chewing gum on the marble floor, slipped, and fell heavily on his back. That put him out of commission for a spell, ultimately limiting his season to 114 games. Though he recovered, he turned in a sub-par season, for him, and, as it would also turn out, a sub-par world series.

But it was clear that 1916's best National League team at the end of the season, the Giants, would be the team to beat for pennant spoils in 1917. Heinie Zimmerman, off to a great start, and a much stronger pitching staff than the smart dope had projected, were on a course that aimed at the Fall Classic. A series against "The Busher," Pants Rowland, and his Pale Hose would make for an interesting tussle as far as John McGraw was concerned, but really didn't phase him in the least.

CHAPTER 3

Boston Confrontation I

The May portion of the Sox' 1917 schedule called for a short road trip to Cleveland and St. Louis, rounding out the first part of their season against teams in the American League's western sector. That was to be followed by the eastern clubs' first swing westward. Games with New York, Philadelphia, Boston and then Washington would fill out both the first lengthy homestand of the Comiskeymen and the rest of the month of May. How merry that month would be would depend on how much over the break-even mark the Sox would be after the four clubs had been in town. Additionally, the first series of the year against Boston would give the fans their first look at the 1916 World Series champs. The three-game set beginning on May 18 would enable everyone to draw a bead on that strong 1917 pitching staff which included Dutch Leonard, Ernie Shore, Carl Mays and the sensational young southpaw, the Babe himself. After that first head to head confrontation, it would be possible to make a much more definite estimtation about the overall strength of the Rowland lineup in comparison with the rest of the league. Were they *bona fide* contenders? By the end of the month some of those answers would be available.

The Sox' last homestand contest against the Tigers had

resulted not only in a 3–0 embarassment at the hands of southpaw Willie Mitchell, but the temporary loss of Red Faber, who took the April 29 defeat. Boss Rowland left the big righthander behind to recover from a muscle strain sustained while pitching. That was but one roster move. Pitcher Mellie Wolfgang, whose 1916 record of 4 and 6 with a career high 127 innings pitched and a 1.98 ERA merited another shot at making the staff, and utility players Joe Jenkins, Ted Jourdan, Freddie McMullin and Jack Fournier were also left behind. Among them, Fournier, a big Frenchman from the Pacific Northwest where he starred as a football player, had led the league in 1915 with a .491 slugging average. One of those good hit— no field, first basemen, he came north with the club as a reserve utility player. His starting days as a member of the Pale Hose were over, however, because of the acquisition of Chick Gandil. In fact big Jack Fournier was to make but one plate appearance, the sum and substance of his 1917 season, and that as a pinchhitter. He appeared in 27 games as a 1918 New York Yankee, dropped out of baseball for the 1919 season, and finally caught his stride as a National Leaguer first with St. Louis, and then with the Dodgers, finally winding up a 15-year career with the Braves in 1927 as a lifetime .313 hitter. It is very tempting to say that for all the turbulence and outright evil caused by his replacement, Chick Gandil, in the years ahead, it couldn't have been any worse with Big Jack, errors and all, around first base. It might have been better—a whole lot better.

One of the troubling developments of the recently completed homestand was a tepid, inconsistent offensive attack. As they opened the Cleveland series on the upcoming road trip the Rowlandmen would be running headlong into that same Indians pitching staff that had permitted a paltry three runs in their first encounter of the season. Pants Rowland had already shuffled his batting order a bit for the final game of the Detroit series, moving Buck Weaver into Swede Risberg's number two spot and dropping Risberg to seventh in the order, hoping to scare up more runs. He felt that would also be a good order to use against the Indians. The most welcome change, however, would be for the middle of the order to start swinging those big clubs with the authority everybody expected.

The Cleveland series, which opened on May 2, got the Sox off to a thumping start as they whaled away at the offerings of starter

Fritz Coumbe and relievers Al Gould and Clarence "Pop-Boy" Smith for three doubles and three triples in an 8–3 rout. The batting star of the game was Shano Collins, who came up with the first White Sox 4-hit day of the season. The win pulled them within percentage points of first place and that was very good news.

But on May 2 the big news in the major leagues was made back in Chicago, and not by Charles Comiskey or members of the White Sox front office. On the northside at Weeghman Park the famous double-no-hitter was being staged between the Cubs and the Reds. Through nine innings both the Bruins' Jim "Hippo" Vaughn and Cincinnati's Fred Toney had permitted not one solitary bingle. Then in the first overtime frame Jim Thorpe's famous swinging bunt scored Larry Kopf, who had broken up Vaughn's no-no with a clean single, with the winning run. Fred Toney closed out the bottom of the tenth without giving up a hit.

Elsewhere in the National League Ferdie Schupp, on his way to eight straight victories to open the season for John McGraw, fought Brooklyn's Larry Cheney to a 2–2, 14 inning draw and ex-Giant Red Ames of the Cardinals shut down the Pirates and youngster Burleigh Grimes with a 2-hit, 4–0 shutout.

The sensational no-hit news followed not too long after Eddie Cicotte's early April no-hitter. But no one on that day could know that there would soon be another pair of no-hitters. It seemed that 1917 might just turn out to be a year of extraordinary pitching news.

After their encouraging opener at League Park, the Chisox fell right back into their former punchless mode, the easy prey of the Tribe's Otis Lambeth, 2 to 1, mustering but six hits, four of them by Buck Weaver and Eddie Collins. At that, save for a two-run rally in in the bottom of the ninth, Jim Scott, the "Death Valley" man, might have won it 1 to 0. In the bottom of that fateful stanza, touched for nothing more boistrous than an infield scratch and a single that just made it through the infield, he finally gave way to Eddie Cicotte with the bases loaded only to have the usually reliable knuckleballer give up the winning run with a free pass that forced home Joe Evans with the tally that meant defeat.

The 1917 season, which was remarkable in many respects, was also a wonder in the one-run win and loss column. There were 52 one-run games, 30 of which were won by the Sox. Among those 52 games were eight 1–0 games, four of which we were won by the Pale Hose. Another ten games resulted in 2 to 1 scores like the May

3 finish at Cleveland. Of these the Sox lost three but won seven. If winning one-run games is a measure of a team's mental discipline and strength, the Sox had just enough of it to finish those kinds of exercises at a .577 winning clip. Of course, there is a huge difference between a one-run ball game that makes an immediate difference in the standings, or puts a ball club in first place, and a one-run tilt that is meaningless as far as championships are concerned.

There was one thing every city in both leagues had plenty of, and that was rain. It descended once again to wipe out the last of the three-game set in Cleveland, so the Sox moved on to St. Louis where they were to take on the Browns in a six-game series, a part of which would be two double headers.

Manager Fielder Jones chose to open the big series in the Mound City with lefty Ernie Koob who had beaten Red Faber in the season's second game. The young Michigander had posted an 11 and 8 record in 1916 that should really have been 12 and 7 but for his failure to touch third base on his way home in the 15th inning of a game with the Red Sox. That cost him what would have been the winning run. As it was, he lost that one in the 17th frame, 1 to 0. By the time 1917 was history, however, he was mired in the depths of a 6 and 14 record, and by 1920 his brief major league career was over.

But on May 5 of 1917 he was the toast of St. Louis for on that day he no-hit the White Sox, throwing a wet blanket on what hopes they harbored for getting their offense straightened around. The stocky 5'10" southpaw completely frustrated the Sox that day, coming up with an answer to the no-hitter they encountered in Chicago at the hands of Eddie Cicotte. This time it was Cicotte who was on the rough edge of a 1–0 *meisterwerk*. The winning run was unearned and was scored in the sixth, courtesy rookie Swede Risberg's bungling of a Jimmy Austin pop-up behind short. The big Swede's error put Austin on second and moments later George Sisler, never one to miss an opportunity to advance the Browns' cause, singled home the winning run. Consequently, Chicago's South Siders found themselves on that infamous slippery slope downward, having lost their eighth game in nineteen tries.

And just when it began to look as though things couldn't get worse—they did. The very next day the Sox ran headlong into a double header nightmare, falling with a thud before the St. Louis onslaught, the final effect of which was a tumble almost into the second division. It was a low spot, all right, the lowest position in the standings they would endure all year long, elevating Jones' Brownies to second place, while themsleves dropping into fourth place at 11 and 10.

How that came about was just as mindbending as the sudden nosedive of batting averages and clutch hitting that was making it downright easy for Pale Hose enemies to cut the *so-genannte* Comiskey Machine down to size.

The day after the Koob no-no, mind you, the Fielder Jones brigade cut down the Sox in the first of two, 8 to 4 in a game won by Allen Sothoron, who was starting to assemble the pieces of what surely would have earned him Rookie of the Year honors had they been awarded at that time. He got some help first from Eddie Plank and then from Bob Groom, who came on to pitch the last two innings for the Browns without a hit.

But more was to be heard from the tall fireballer, Mr. Robert Groom. Given the ball by manager Jones for the second fray of the afternoon, he proceeded, quite unbelievably, to subject the Pale Hose to yet another no-hitter, thus winding up eleven innings of no-hit pitching against the Chicagoans in the space of 24 hours. I. E. Sanborn, with the somewhat partial eye of a Chicago sports writer observed:

> There was no flaw in Groom's no-hit game. It was free from taint or suspicion which will always cling to the postmortem thing handed Koob yesterday by expunging a hit (Ed: the scorer of the Koob no-hitter, conferring with other writers in the press box after the game, reversed his decision on Buck Weaver, charging the St. Louis second baseman with an error to replace the hit originally awarded Weaver) that had already been recorded. The Rowlands not only did not get a hit off Groom, but did not get anything that looked as if it was going to be a hit. They had no chance to beat him except on his wildness, which they prevented from being costly by bad judgement on the bases [*Chicago Tribune*, May 7, 1917].

Remarkably, Groom's no-hitter was the fifth in the major leagues in a season that had barely nosed into the month of May. In sum there would be eight games in which pitchers would string together at least nine innings of no-hit pitching the summer of 1917. The list follows.

April 13	Eddie Cicotte, Chi, AL vs. St. Louis (11–0)
April 24	George Mogridge, NY, AL vs. Boston (2–1)
May 2	Jim Vaughn, Chi, NL vs. Cincinnati (0–1)
May 2	Fred Toney, Cin, NL vs. Chicago (1–0)
May 5	Ernie Koob, StL, AL vs. Chicago (1–0)
May 6	Bob Groom, StL, AL vs Chicago (3–0)
June 23	Ernie Shore*, Bos, AL vs. Washington (4–0)
July 10	Ray Caldwell†, NY, AL vs. St. Louis (7–5)

*The June 23 Shore no-hitter came after starter Babe Ruth was tossed because he had argued so vehemently (and profanely) over the umpire's calls on pitches to the leadoff hitter. Shore was rushed into the game and finished it and the Senators off with his no-no.

†Ray Caldwell's no-hit stretch came after entering as a reliever. Although touched for hits before and after his hitless performance, he did retire 29 consecutive batters, amounting to 9.2 innings.

With a suddenness no one along the southern shores of Lake Michigan was prepared for, the Sox awoke on the next day to find themselves looking up in the standings. Up there in first place, as most expected, was Boston, losers of but four in the 15 games they had played.

American League, May 7, 1917

	Won	Lost	Pct.
Boston	11	4	.733
St. Louis	11	8	.579
New York	9	7	.563
Chicago	11	10	.524
Cleveland	10	10	.500
Detroit	6	10	.375
Philadelphia	6	10	.375
Washington	6	11	.353

If there was to be a time of soul-testing for Rowland's club, as well as for his leadership of the Sox' fortunes in 1917, this was it. With three more games to go against the upstart Browns, now in second place, there was some serious business to transact. Nor was there much hope that others would be helping out, not even Walter Johnson, who had lost to Babe Ruth in Washington, 1–0, as The Babe not only squelched the Senators on two hits for his sixth straight, but drove in the winning run, to boot.

Pants Rowland stuck to his lineup. No changes. And he sent The Senator, Jim Scott to meet the Browns in the first of two. Scott pitched creditably, but when the Browns tied it up in the sixth with two out with the lead run on base, skipper Rowland pulled Eddie Cicotte out of the bullpen. Little Eddie finished off that inning without any further damage, and when the Sox pushed across a run in the eighth, he became a 4–3 winner as the Pale Hose broke a losing skein that had turned around a fine start with a horrible span of eight losses in ten games. And finally in the second game that day the heart of the order came through with a combined 7 for 14 to get the Sox past the Browns once again, this time by a 9–7 count. The very next day Eddie Cicotte came back, again in relief, to beat the Browns 4–2. That evened up the St. Louis series at 3–3, and as they headed back to Chicago for a lengthy homestand they were in third place, having dropped the Browns into fourth. The top of the heap looked just a bit nearer. As a matter of fact, they had seen the last of fourth place, and while it would take a month to move from third to the league's top spot, their flirtation with second division status had been put far behind them. More importantly, this ball club had stared down a stern testing and emerged toughened for the long grind ahead. And—it was under the firm control of Mr. Clarence Rowland.

Fans of the South Siders could hardly have been more pleased with the results of the long awaited 17-game homestand. By the time it was over the Sox had moved to within a game of the first place Red Sox, having ridden the crest of five and eight game winning streaks to push their homestand record to a gaudy 13–2–1 (there was a 1–1, May 26 game with the Senators). Every phase of the team's play picked up, from base-running to hitting to picking up the ball. The pitching, not much in doubt throughout the first 25 games, went from great to spectacular. And winning two out of three against Boston's Carmine didn't hurt the confidence level any, either. The Sox looked like they were for real.

But not at first. New York started out the first set of home games with two straight wins and in the four game series they gave up a measly four runs, beating the Sox 1–0 behind Bob Shawkey's five-hitter, and then whipping them 6–1 with Ray "Sum" Caldwell on the mound. At that point it looked as if a relapse was in the making, but Jim Scott came on to beat the Yankees 2–1 despite a puny three-hit attack, and Eddie Cicotte closed out the series with a taut,

1–0 squeaker that was won on a Hap Felsch single that scored Eddie Collins in the fourth inning *and* Cicotte's masterful two-hitter. Ex-Federal Leaguer Nick Cullop gave up only five hits himself, but Cicotte had proven once again that he was all sharp edges in close ball games, nudging his early season record upward to 5 and 2.

Then Connie Mack and his Athletics came to town. As of their first game with the Comiskeymen they stood at a 7 and 15 reading, having already plummeted to the American League basement. That's where they would wind up at season's end with but 55 wins to their credit, some 44½ games off the winning pace of the White Sox. Only the National League's Pittsburgh Pirates would finish out the 1917 season in worse shape.

Predictably, the Sox, on their way to a 15–7 season record against the Mackmen, polished them off four straight. including shellackings of 11–0, behind Joey Benz, and 7–0 in support of Cicotte.

The Indiana butcher boy they called Blitzen, Joey Benz, who had made it a habit of beating the A's and Senators during his career, recorded the first of his seven victories in 1917 by letting the Philadelphians down on four hits. Used by Pants Rowland as a spot starter, and in paricular against the Senators, the pixie-faced righthander did nothing to hurt his huge popularity with White Sox fans in his May 15 start. He was backed up by Buck Weaver's 5 for 5 day, the best multiple-hit performance of the summer. (Those who contributed 3 for 3, 4 for 4, and 4 for 5 days to the Pale Hose attack are listed in the table below.) A linedrive hitter, the wiry third baseman found the slants of Ellis Johnson and big Elmer Myers to his liking, contributing substantially both at the plate and afield as the Sox collected 16 hits in the massacre.

Game	*Outstanding Performer*
April 25: Cleveland 4, Chicago 1	Felsch, 3 for 3
July 1: Cleveland 5, Chicago 4	Felsch, 3 for 3
July 15:Washington 6, Chicago 5	Weaver, 3 for 3
September 1: St. Louis 6, Chicago 3	Jackson, 3 for 3
September 15: Detroit 4, Chicago 3	Jackson, 3 for 3
September 26: Washington 5, Chicago 4,	E. Collins, 3 for 3
May 2: Chicago 8, Cleveland 3	J. Collins, 4 for 5
June 27: Chicago 5, Detroit 2	Risberg, 4 for 4
July 6: Detroit 4, Chicago 1	Weaver, 4 for 4
July 23: Chicago 5, Boston 3	Felsch, 4 for 4

August 26: Chicago 8, New York 3   J. Collins, 4 for 4
September 29: New York 12, Chicago 8   E. Collins, 4 for 5
September 29: New York 12, Chicago 6   Jackson, 4 for 5
May 15: Chicago 11, Philadelphia 0   Weaver, 5 for 5

May 18, 1917, was far from "just another" day. In a proclamation signed by President Wilson, the United States was committed to conscripting young men between the ages of 21 and 30 for military service unless special circumstances would exempt them. The *New York Times* carried the full text of the presidential proclamation as a front page news item. That, of course, would have a direct effect not only on baseball players, but even among some of the team owners. One of these latter, Capt. Tillinghast L'Hommedieu Huston, a Spanish American War veteran, was summoned to active duty while with his Yankees in Chicago for the series concluded just days before. Til, as his friends called him, was the driving force behind military-type training for American League teams and had, as a matter of fact, watched both the Yanks and Sox drill prior to their game on May 13. From a baseball vantage point, however, he was best known as the co-owner of the franchise (Jake Ruppert was the other principal owner) who would be responsible for wresting Babe Ruth from the Red Sox, something for which his name would be forever cursed in Boston, along with the name of the man who sent the Babe on his way, owner Harry Frazee.

In baseball's much smaller world the day was significant because of the American League confrontation between the Sox of Red and White. For the battle ahead skipper Rowland had restored two of his ailing stars, Chick Gandil and Joe Jackson to the starting lineup. Red Faber, somewhat recovered from his recent ills, would probably still not be ready, however, for a while. The old Texan *bon vivant*, Reb Russell, was selected for the opening round of the big series. His opponent: Babe Ruth, in hot pursuit of his eighth straight win.

Amid rumors, supposedly starting out of the Cubs' camp out east that Rowland stood in jeopardy of losing his post to Bill "Rough" Carrigan, the recently deposed Red Sox manager, the Pale Hose readied for battle first by swearing their allegiance for their field general, and then by disposing of the Red Sox' ace, Ruth, before three innings were complete. Meanwhile Russell made short work of Boston's hitters, surrendering but two hits through the first eight innings, four overall, in Chicago's convincing 8–2 opening game win. The box score:

Boston at Comiskey Park, Chicago, May 18, 1917

Boston	AB	R	H	PO	A	Chicago	AB	R	H	PO	A
Hooper, rf	3	0	0	0	0	J. Collins, rf	4	1	2	3	0
Shorten, rf	1	0	0	0	0	Weaver, 3b	5	1	1	1	3
Barry, 2b	2	0	0	1	2	E. Collins, 2b	3	1	0	1	2
Janvrin, 2b	1	0	0	2	1	Jackson, lf	5	2	3	1	0
Gainer, 1b	4	1	1	10	1	Felsch, cf	4	1	2	5	0
Lewis, lf	4	0	0	3	0	Gandil, 1b	4	1	3	5	0
Walsh, cf	4	0	1	1	0	Jourdan, 1b	1	0	0	1	1
Gardner, 3b	4	1	1	3	3	Risberg, ss	4	1	0	3	1
Scott, ss	4	0	1	1	1	Schalk, c	3	0	2	7	0
Agnew, c	3	0	0	3	2	Russell, (WP)	4	0	2	0	1
Ruth, (LP)	1	0	0	0	0						
Bader. p	1	0	0	0	3						
Totals	32	2	4	24	13	Totals	37	8	15	28	8

Boston   010 000 001   2–4–2
Chicago   032 003 000   8–15–2

2B: Gardner, Scott, Felsch, Gainer; SB: Barrt; Sacrifice Hit: J. Collins; LOB: Boston 5, Chicago 11; BB: Russell 1, Ruth 3, Bader 2; K: Russell 5, Ruth 1, Bader 1; Hit by pitcher: Bader (by Russell); Wild Pitch: Bader; Umpires: Connolly, McCormick and Nallin; Time of Game: 2:07.

Concerning that rumor: Commisar Comiskey recognized it for what it was and dismissed it as a silly thing, and the rumor mill ground to a halt almost immediately. Nonetheless, the very appearance of that kind of gossip, and moreover, that it would appear in the press, was an indication of the tenuous hold Pants Rowland had on his position, at least in the minds of some who still didn't feel The Busher could get the job done.

With the strong start they made against the Red Sox, the homestanding Chicagoans went on to cop their next tilt by another 8–2 margin behind Claude Williams, who ran his winning streak to a season-opening four, featuring Eddie Collins' 3 for 4 and a home run by Buck Weaver. Lefty pitched the first six innings and Dave Danforth came on to finish up, fanning four in three innings of work to pick up the save.

Player-manager Jack Barry called on dour, submarine-balling Carl Mays to quiet Rowland's heavy lumber the next day in the series-ending game. And he did. There were no White Sox extra base blows as Mays scattered eight hits in the 2–1 win. En route to a sparkling 22 and 7 season with a 1.74 ERA that wound up second only to Eddie Cicotte's league-leading 1.53, he paced the Bosox win that not only renewed Boston's increasingly precarious hold on first place, but simultaneously dumped the Rowlandmen back into the league's third spot, plus putting their eight-game winning streak to bed. For the Red Sox and Mays, it was a good day's work and for the White Sox, it meant back to work getting hits with men on base when it counted.

On that same day in the National League the New York Giants climbed back into first place, having surrendered it to the fast moving Cubs back on May 15. However, a week later there was bad news not only on the south side of town, but on the north side, as well. The Cubs of Fred Mitchell lost their grip on the number one spot because of their loss to Eppa Rixey and the Phillies as the Giants were taking advantage of the hapless Pirates, 4–3, at the Polo Grounds. At that point the Cubs had won 22 of 34 while the McGraw forces had lost but eight of only 24 games played, the weather having put the National League's eastern clubs far in arrears of their scheduled allotment of games. Of the two Chicago teams, fast-food magnate Charley Weeghman's Cubbies were the more pleasant surprise up to that point, causing hopes to soar on the north side.

Washington's Senators came into Chicago for a five-game set that provided the Rowland charges with four wins and a tie. Far fewer than expected were on hand to see the final contest of the series, which would otherwise have been a sell-out because the pitching choices of the day were Walter Johnson and Eddie Cicotte. The "otherwise" was the weather, causing Chicago scribe Sanborn to open his coverage of the game this way:

> In the teeth of an icy nor-easter the White Sox beat Walter Johnson yesterday because Eddie V. G. Cicotte out-pitched him and made it four straight over Washington. Score: 4 to 1.
>
> With that gale adding extra zip to Johnson's blooie-blooie stuff and holding up everything hit into the air, the conditions were made for the blond star of Griffith's staff, realizing which Manager Rowland sent his best pitching bet against the enemy,

Submarine-baller Carl Mays won four out of six over the White Sox in 1917 and wound up with a fine 22 and 9 record for the season. (Transcendental Graphics)

with results wholly satisfactory to the 12,000 who braved pneumonia to see the battle.

The Sox tapped Johnson's smoke for seven safeties and earned two of their four tallies, the rest being handed them by Crane's eighth inning muff with the bases full. Cicotte held the Senators to five hits, one of which was a very doubtful guess by Umpire McCormick. It came at a critical time, nearly upset the ball game, and caused a storm of protest from everywhere, delaying proceedings until the Rowlands could recover from the shock. (*Chicago Tribune*, May 28, 1917)

Apparently the Sox recovered their composure and it was one of the Senators who later lost his, manhandling a Jackson pop-up in the eighth stanza that allowed the final two tallies to scamper home. Shoeless Joe's only hit that day was a similar Texas-Leaguer that was called a basehit although it might well have gone in the books as an error. The final, 4–2 reading left the Pale Hose with but one more game in their May homestand, a single contest with the Browns before leaving for a short trip east to start out the month of June. That game, by another 4–2 score, was put away by Hap Felsch who uncorked a prodigious blast over the left field wall that traveled on into the bleachers to score Buck Weaver and Eddie Collins, each of whom had singled in the first inning ahead of him.

Before reviewing Chicago's "merry month of," a word about the Washington icon, Walter Johnson, is in order. The Famer had nothing but praise for Shoeless Joe, calling him the very best natural hitter he *ever* faced, including the great Negro Leaguers like Pop Lloyd and Oscar Charleston against whom he worked during his star-studded career. That covers the same ground traveled by Ruth and Cobb, both of whom were equally lavish in their praise of the South Carolina wonder.

The question arises then, how did Jackson fare against Johnson during the White Sox' record-setting season of 1917. Here it is: Jackson and his Black Betsy recorded 17 official at bats that summer resulting in two singles for a .118 average. My my. After that first-inning hit in the May 27, 4–2 victory, The Big Train collared Jackson 15 consecutive times. Nor did he give Hap Felsch much more to look at, silencing the best number five hitter in the league with a 3 for 23 mark at .130. Beating Johnson (he wound up 1917 even-up at 3–3 against the Sox) was left to Eddie Collins, who got to Johnson for an 8 for 22 mark, .364, Nemo Leibold, who always hit Sir Walter rather well, and the rest of the Sox who scraped and scratched enough together between them to get past the big fellow now and then. But it was never easy and later on that summer it was almost impossible when, on August 10, his one-hitter (a Schalk single) at Griffith Stadium subdued Red Faber and his pennant-bound colleagues, 4–0.

In May, then, the White Sox won 16 of 24, tying once, for a .667 winning percentage. During that same month the Red Sox came away with a 17 and 6 record, also tieing one game with Washington. That's about dead even, although the Comiskey men had the edge in the big May 18–20 series, two games to one. Going into June the standings read:

American League	Won	Lost	Pct.
Boston	27	10	.730
Chicago	27	13	.675
New York	20	16	.556
Cleveland	22	21	.512
Detroit	15	21	.417
St. Louis	15	23	.395
Philadelphia	13	23	.361
Washington	13	25	.342

National League	Won	Lost	Pct.
New York	20	11	.645

Philadelphia	21	13	.618
Chicago	25	16	.610
St. Louis	19	17	.528
Brooklyn	13	17	.433
Cincinnati	17	24	.415
Boston	12	17	.414
Pittsburgh	13	25	.342

At approximately the 30–35-game mark, these were the hitting numbers registered by the top five White Sox, Red Sox and Giants:

Chicago	*GP*	*AB/H*	*BA*
Jackson	35	122/34	.279
Felsch	36	124/34	.275
Collins, J	20	84/21	.250
Weaver	36	131/32	.244
Leibold	26	83/20	.241
Boston			
Walker	23	85/27	.318
Hoblitzell	21	77/22	.286
Lewis	29	113/20	.265
Gardner	29	83/20	.241
Scott	29	101/23	.228
Hooper	25	101/23	.228
Giants			
G. Burns	29	105/40	.381
Kauff	27	99/33	.333
McCarty	24	68/22	.324
Zimmerman	25	100/31	.310
Herzog	15	52/15	.288

Although Rowland's machine was not consistently hitting on all cylinders, it was in the thick of the pennant chase, making do with outstanding pitching (opposition offenses garnered two runs or less in 22 of the 37 games played through the end of May), speed on the bases, and a defense that was gradually tightening its grip on enemy offenses. The insertion of Chick Gandil at first and Swede Risberg at short jacked up the inner defense despite the error-prone

Risberg's 13 miscues. Some of those errors came as the result of the big Swede's insistence on making throws or catches in next to impossible situations. But there was no denying the rookie's range, nor that he was making progress in knitting the defense up the middle. And it should be noted that the Sox had committed fewer errors as a team, 39 in the first 37 games, than any other team in the majors except the Cardinals (37).

Joe Jackson, who fought colds, a spiking, and a muscle pull through the early season, nonetheless played through those miseries to drive in game-winning runs and provide timely hitting despite a sub-par average that, even so, had shown recent signs of climbing to more Jackson-like numbers. Hap Felsch's explosive lumber had yet to settle into the groove that devastated American League pitching during the summer months. But again, he had done enough damage in the first six weeks of the campaign to instill a caution in the Boston and New York approach that caused them to work around him. Those two were buttressed principally by Eddie Collins and Buck Weaver, with Gandil chipping in several multi-hit ball games, to give the Pale Hose an adequate attack. It was reasonable to assume, if not inevitable, that the club's punch would soon make itself felt.

CHAPTER 4

On the Road

The White Sox opened their first longer road trip of the season on June 3 in Philadelphia to play the first of 14 games. Except for Red Faber, once again left behind, though in anticipation of joining the team during the course of the trip, the ball club was in its best physical condition since the the beginning of the season.

On that same day, June 3, Big Ed Walsh, former White Sox hero who had been released after the 1916 season, was slated to work out for John McGraw in New York. Although that didn't pan out, baseball's foremost spitballer got his reprieve a little later. John Stallings in Boston, in search of pitching help, did give Walsh the opportunity to pitch again, signing him to a contract on July 20. On August 2 he debuted with a five-inning start, scattering three hits and denying the visiting Chicago Cubs a run (what memories pitching against the Cubs must have stirred!), leaving the game with a 1–0 lead. The game was promptly tied after he left, denying him one last victory although the Braves won 4–3 in the tenth that day. Walsh's last complete game in the majors occured against Brooklyn on September 5 when Leon "Caddy" Cadore beat the Braves 8–1, shutting down the Stallings crew with five hits. A glorious career that won Hall of Fame honors came to an end that day, having left behind a trail of records and 195 victories, 57 of which were shutouts.

Two other titans of National League play joined Walsh in retirement during the 1917 season, Honus Wagner and another Chicago warrior of championship play both in the Windy City and with the Braves, Johnny Evers, who was described best in the words of Hughie Fullerton, Chicago sportswriter, as a nervous wreck waiting to happen. For all three it was time to let the younger ball players take a crack at the records they left behind.

Starting with a three-game set against the Athletics, which they swept, Pants Rowland's charges had climbed to within percentage points of the league lead with a 30 and 14 record. Boston, still in first with a 29 and 13 mark, opened a homestand of 15 games on May 31, but visiting Detroit and St. Louis settled in at Fenway Park as if they owned the place, beating the Red Sox five out of six, and then the Pale Hose came to town, beating them twice more before Boston regained enough composure to knock off Chicago in the last two games of their series. Consequently, by June 9 the South Siders had regained the league's top slot, hanging on through the next month until Boston edged back in front on July 5. Those weeks were indicative of the tussle that would mark the race at least through mid-August when the Comiskeymen forged ahead to stay.

To make certain the Athletics would not take the Sox in hand, as they had been doing to other teams in what proved, finally, to be their best stretch of the season, Rowland sent Eddie Cicotte to the hill to start out the series. It was a good move. Little Eddie responded with a three-hit shutout and Hap Felsch gave him all the support he needed with a base-clearing double that rattled the walls at Shibe Park. The final score was 3–0, and the Sox were on their way. Cicotte pushed his mark to 9 and 2, winning his seventh in a row. By the end of the season he would have chalked up seven shutouts and a league-leading ratio (a linear measurement that computes the number of hits plus walks plus hit batsmen allowed per nine innings pitched). Cicotte's ratio was 8.2 in a career-high 346.2 innings of work with a glimmering 1.53 ERA that ranks as one of the 50 best in the game's history. Compare this with the following list of the American League's top 15:

		Ratio
1)	Pedro Martinez, 2000	7.22
2)	Walter Johnson, 1913	7.26

3)	Addie Joss, 1908	7.31
4)	Ed Walsh, 1910	7.47
5)	Roger Nelson, 1972	7.89
6)	Dave McNally, 1968	7.91
7)	Ed Walsh, 1908	7.91
8)	Luis Tiant, 1968	7.98
9)	Cy Young, 1905	8.03
10)	Cy Young, 1910	8.07
11)	Russ Ford, 1910	8.17
12)	Eddie Cicotte, 1917	8.28
13)	Dutch Leonard, 1914	8.29
14)	Denny McLain, 1968	8.30
15)	Catfish Hunter, 1972	8.32

On the heels of their sweep in Philadelphia the Sox steamed into the nation's capital intent on maintaining their winning momentum. George Dumont was, of course, not of the same mindset, and proceeded to knock off Eddie Cicotte, Rowland's series starter, by a 3–0 count while doling out but four Sox singles. The 22 year old youngster they called Pea Soup, who threw his fast one almost as fast as Walter Johnson did, went on to a 5 and 14 record in 1917, his victory on June 6 the highlight of his season. Curiously, two wins of his meager total were shutouts.

If the Sox were impressed by Dumont's speed in the series opener, what would they have to say the next day when Sir Walter himself appeared for boss man Griffith's ball club? The answer: not much. Cut down to a ration of three hits this time, they were held scoreless again, bowing 1–0 in the last of the ninth, thus wasting a fine pitching effort by Reb Russell. So it was 0 for 18, that is, zero runs in 18 innings of frustration at Washington. And while on the subject of shutouts, Mr. Johnson, in an off-year, at least for him, added another eight to his all time record total of 110. And, little though they knew it in June, an even better Johnson-vintage "zero" was awaiting the chastised Sox later in the summer.

The very next day, however, it rained. Base hits. Like a desert caravan at long last encountering an oasis, the Sox fell upon "Grunting Jim" Shaw and Yancy Ayers for 16 hits, escorting Joey Benz to an 11 to 4 triumph. Joe Jackson exploded out of a 3 for 15 slump with a double, the only extra base hit of the day, and a pair of screeching singles, and Buck Weaver as well as Hap Felsch contributed three more safeties a piece in the melee.

Jackson's hitting was a welcome sight. There was no one quite like him in a batter's box, at least not among the Pale Hose, and more likely in all of baseball. Down around the .250 mark, Jackson and his Black Betsy were in the throes of an off year, and it took him all the way into September to get his average up to .300. And even that was grossly inferior to his customary ranking among the game's great hitters. His lifetime average at .356 over the course of 1332 major league ball games attests to that.

In 1917 Joe Jackson hit in spurts and while he was an ever present danger to the league's hurlers, he didn't connect as often as he had in the past or would in the future. Nonetheless his contribution to the Sox' pennant was substantial as he pitched in with great fielding and timely hitting especially in those crucial Red Sox games. The Shoeless One hit .311 against the carmine-hosed Bostons (28 for 90), with two doubles, three triples, and one monstrous homer beyond Fenway Park's centerfield flagpole off Carl Mays in a game on August 1 that put the Pale Hose back into first place.

Joe was acquired from the Cleveland Indians in 1915 and during his years with the White Sox he found the range for a .340 career batting average, still the number one White Sox average, all time. His complete Chicago record follows.

Year	GP	AB	R	H	EXBH	RBI	OB%	SA	BR	SB	BA	TPR
1915	45	158	21	43	11	36	.378	.399	6	6	.272	-0.2
1916	155	592	91	202	64	78	.393	.495	44	24	.341	3.6
1917	146	538	91	162	42	75	.375	.425	27	13	.301	3.1
1918*	17	65	9	23	5	20	.425	.492	6	3	.354	0.5
1919	139	516	79	181	52	96	.422	.506	41	9	.351	2.9
1920	146	570	105	218	74	121	.444	.589	58	9	.382	4.1
Totals	648	2439	396	829	248	426	.407	.498	182	64	.340	14.0

*Missed 123 of the 140 game World War I schedule in 1918 because he was employed in strategic defense.

EXBH—Extra base hits

BR—Batting Runs, a linear measurement calculating how many runs beyond a league-average player (league-average = zero), will be contributed by a batter to his team's offense.

TPR—Total Player Rating, the sum of a player's BR (batting runs), Fielding Runs, and Base Stealing Runs, each by sabermetric formuli, minus mathematical adjustment for the position he plays, and then divided by ten.

The Shoeless One, Joe Jackson, one of the game's all time premier hitters. (Dennis Colgin)

On June 9, while Chicago evened the Washington series at 2–2, Detroit won a thriller at Boston, 1–0, behind side-armer Howard Ehmke. The loss cost the Red Sox first place as the Comiskeymen eased into the lead.

Then, in a back-tracking over-nighter to Cleveland, they took on the Indians and beat them 10 to 4 as baby-faced Harry Leibold cracked a double and a triple to pace the 13-hit attack. Lefty Williams was the beneficiary of the Sox' robust hitting, winning his fifth straight.

The little fellow dubbed Nemo, after a comic-strip character, was brought to Chicago during the 1915 season from Cleveland, where he had played in the outfield with Joe Jackson the previous three seasons, and the Chicago tenure of both outfielders was almost identical, Leibold and Jackson both doing their outfielding at Comiskey Park some 5½ seasons. Leibold was cut loose after the

1920 season, winding up in Boston in a trade that brought Hall of
Famer Harry Hooper to Chicago. For Jackson, of course, 1921 was
the beginning of his "Elba Years." Shano Collins, with whom Nemo
Leibold was linked as the other half of Rowland's rightfield platoon,
was also a part of the same Hooper trade.

Standing just 5'6" and 155 pounds dripping wet, Nemo led off
for the Rowland charges, spraying hits (mostly singles) to all fields,
drawing walks and finding just about any and every way to get on
base, cranking his on base percentage up to .350-.375 on average.
A scrappy sort, he was to the the outfield, even from his right field
position, what Eddie Collins was to the infield, playing a shallow
sunfield that dared hitters to poke one over his head. During the
1917 season there were some pretty fair rightfielders at work, Harry
Hooper of the Bosox and Sam Rice of the Senators among them,
but none hustled more than Harry Leibold. His complete Chicago
record follows.

Year	GP	AB	R	H	EXBH	BB	K	OB%	SB	BA	TPR
1915	36	74	10	17	1	15	11	.360	1	.230	0.1
1916	45	82	5	20	3	7	7	.303	7	.244	-0.8
1917	125	428	59	101	18	74	34	.350	27	.236	-0.8
1918	116	440	57	110	21	63	32	.344	13	.250	0.2
1919	122	434	81	131	20	72	30	.404	17	.302	1.0
1920	108	413	61	91	20	55	30	.316	7	.220	-3.2
Totals	552	1871	273	470	83	286	144	.346	72	.251	-3.5

Finishing up their single-game Cleveland engagement just in
time to board the New York express, Nemo Leibold and Pants
Rowland and his White Sox contingent hurried off to the bustle and
klieg lights of The Big Apple where Wild Bill Donovan and his
Yankees were awaiting them. Four games were on tap. As of their
first playing date against the Pale Hose at the Polo Grounds on
June 11, the Yanks were still only five games behind the second
place Red Sox. A 3-out-of-4, or a sweep, would rearrange the standings in a hurry.

New York was in the baseball news for more than the upcoming Sox-Yankee series, however. That was because of John
McGraw—again—this time in the National League doghouse over
having exchanged a few words and probably several punches with

Umpire "Lord" Byron in a Cincinnati game. National League prexy, John K. Tener, a former major leaguer, slapped the belligerent McGraw with an indefinite suspension, causing Little Napoleon to name Buck Herzog, just back into the lineup after his Philadelphia mishap, as the Giants' interim manager. 28,000 turned out at Weeghman Field to see the New Yorkers open their series with the Cubs—*sans* Mc-Graw. The newsmaker in the series opener, however was neither McGraw nor his recently appointed field boss, Herzog. It was the diminutive Ferdinand Maurice de Soto Schupp (it was Cubs scribe Irving Sanborn who dug up that royal Schupp handle), working at the top of his game while letting the air out of the Cubs' tires with three dinky hits en route to a 4-zip shutout for his seventh straight against

Shown here stabbing a ball meant for extra bases, baby-faced Harry "Nemo" Leibold platooned in right field with Shano Collins. He came to the Sox in 1915 and was an ideal leadoff man. (Brace photograph)

as many defeats as the Cubs scored runs that day. He would be back in Chicago in another four months to take on the White Sox in their south side digs at Comiskey Park. On that occasion he would be accompanied by his manager, John McGraw, and work the second game of the World Series. It is that factor that etched every one of Ferdie Schupp's outings with the significance McGraw attached to each of his ace's assignments, and though the Giants' major domo wasn't on hand for Schupp's 4–0 victory, he knew full well how important his southpaw's contribution to the '17 Giants was.

The most the Yanks and Sox could wrest from their four game set from the wetherman, meanwhile, was a pair of games, neither of which bore the good news the fans back home were waiting for. In the first of their two, the Yanks, down 3 to 1 as they came to bat in the ninth, fought back with a Frank Baker moon shot that drove home the tying runs, sending the game into extra stanzas. The *Tribune*'s Jim Crusinberry explained the defeat that followed this way:

> Because J. Franklin Baker of home run fame piled a drive into the wing of the grandstand in the last half of the ninth inning, scoring two runs and tieing the count, the White Sox lost one of the hardest fought battles of the year when the Yanks pushed in the winning run in the twelfth inning. The final count was 4 to 3. If Baker hadn't poled that one in the ninth, the Sox would have been victors in regulation time, 3 to 1.
>
> It was about the fourth time in the last six or seven years that the Yankees have defeated Eddie Cicotte, the clever little knuckle baller of the Sox. Eddie fought 'em for the entire twelve rounds but it was his unlucky day. He ought to have won in nine innings. They should have won in the tenth. They had a chance in the eleventh. They should also have scored in the twelfth, but all the breaks went to New York [*Chicago Tribune,* June 13, 1917].

The Sox came back the very next day determined to blast the Yankees to kingdom come and unleashed a 19-hit barrage. 18 of those were singles, incidentally, none of which was good enough to chase home a winning tally. So the men of Donovan sent the Pale Hose packing, their tails between their legs, thankful for the little blessing of at least still sitting atop the American League roost. This is the way the tightened race was aligned after the disheartening June 13, 7 to 6 loss.

	Won	Lost	Pct.		Won	Lost	Pct.
Chicago	33	17	.660	Detroit	21	25	.457
Boston	30	16	.652	St. Louis	19	23	.404
New York	26	20	.565	Wash'ton	18	29	.383
Cleveland	26	26	.500	Philadel'ia	16	28	.364

Hopping the evening express to Boston, the Sox could only wonder what it might take to tame Ruth, Leonard, Hooper and Co. It would take more than what they offered in New York. Specifically, it would take better base-running, hits rather than double play ground balls and no bone-headedness afield that might result in still more unnecessary runs scampering across home plate.

Pants Rowland thought he had the answer, opening with the little portsider, Claude Williams. Rowland was right. Lefty answered the call with a four-hitter, standing the Red Sox on their ears, while upping the Sox lead to 2½ games. So good was Williams that it took the Carmine eight innings to crack the hit column. Though they managed a bingle or two, they were nonetheless unable to register a single tally, enabling Williams to score his eighth straight against nary a loss in the course of the still-young season. The extra base punch Lefty needed was provided by Buck Weaver, whose double off Herb Pennock with the sacks dripping in the fifth provided three runs after Joe Jackson had tripled home Eddie Collins to get things going in the previous inning.

Lefty Williams arrived in the White Sox camp back in 1916 having established his major league credentials in Salt Lake City of the Pacific Coast League after a brief stint with Detroit in 1913 and 1914. He was a winner right from the start, opening up with a 13 and 7 campaign in his rookie year. That he would start out the 1917 season with a nine game winning streak was a bonus not even Charley Comiskey dreamed possible. Pitching well, and often in good luck, the morose southpaw, among the most reserved and quiet players in the game, plowed through one challenge after another, finally finishing out the season with a great 17 and 8 mark. He would go on to win 23 for the '19 Sox, and become a member of the first pitching staff to boast four, 20-game winners with 22 W's in 1920. But as sudden as his success had been, just that quickly was he banished from the game. He was only 27 with a solid future ahead of him, but his involvement in The Great Fix brought all that to a shuddering halt. By the end of the 1920 season he had already won 82 games against but 48 losses. Here is his complete Chicago record.

Year	W	L	Pct.	GS	IP	GC	SH	SV	ERA	OBA	OB%	TPI
1916	13	7	.650	26	224.1	10	2	1	2.89.	.267	.327	-0.8
1917	17	8	.680	29	230	8	1	1	2.97	.252	.351	-1.7
1918*	6	4	.600	14	105.2	7	2	1	2.73	.209	.308	-0.5
1919	23	11	.676	40	297	27	5	1	2.64	.244	.289	1.5
1920	22	14	.611	38	299	38	0	0	3.91	.271	.332	-0.8
Totals	81	44	.648	147	856	90	10	4	3,02	.249	.303	-2.3

*Williams was employed in defense work during the 1918 season.

TPI—Total Pitcher Index, a sabermetric measure indicating the overall quality of a pitcher stated in numerical terms, a league-average pitcher rating a 0.0.

On June 16 the two teams got it going once again with Eddie Cicotte facing George Herman Ruth. That one turned out to be a riot. Literally. Both hurlers went the distance. Only one came away from the fray unscathed, and that was 'lil Eddie. The Pale Hose worked over the Babe for ten hits including doubles by Shano Collins and Jackson and a four-base blast by Buck Weaver. When it was all over, the Chicagos were on the long end of a 7 to 2 count. Between their hitting and the free-for-all that erupted during the game and after the players were leaving the field of play it took some time for the Boston folk, players included, to get over the White Sox' conquest. The hostilities, a by-product of the intense competition between the American League's defending champions and the contenders for the throne, set the tone for the remaining 18 games that made up the 22 scheduled for the season.

Animosities in Boston as well as in Chicago over the two pennant antagonists were a part of the pennant race. Nothing unusual there. What added to the fireworks this time, however, was the anger of the gambling element in town that erupted over their hometown heroes losing a ball game that the lords of the netherworlds figured would be a Boston victory over Chicago. So the Bosox lost ground in the pennant race and the boys with the heavy money lost a bundle. White-hot anger over the loss of all that wagered moolah precipitated the brawl that marred the afternoon of June 17. Another one like this might just break up the town. This is the way Crusinberry explained it:

Special to the *Chicago Tribune,* June 17, 1917.

Unless the American league or both major leagues take some decisive action to stamp out gambling in the ball parks in Boston, there are likely to be repetitions of the riot which occured at Fenway field yesterday when the White Sox and the Red Sox were playing.

Later investigation made it practically certain that the trouble was started by the horde of gamblers that assembles each day in the right field pavillion and carries on operations with as much vigor and vim as one would see in the wheat pit at the Chicago Board of Trade.

One of three southpaws on the 1917 championship team, Claude "Lefty" Williams went on to compile an 81–44 record to lead all White Sox pitchers in winning percentage at .648. (Dennis Colgin)

The same condition prevails at the National League (Boston Braves) park, and although gambling may take place more or less in all big league parks, there is no other city where it is allowed to flourish so openly.

The truth is that during the last two weeks the gamblers here have been stung, stung for a greater amount than in years. When they saw they were likely to get another trimming and that it might be averted by breaking up the ball game, they incited the fans to riot.

Before the Red Sox returned they had a record of nine straight victories and looked to be an odds-on bet for every

game. Consequently, the gamblers were offered odds in their
betting ring for every game in the St. Louis series, every game
of the Cleveland series, and every game of the Detroit series,
and were offering even money against the White Sox.

Instead of winning at home, the Red Sox have lost nine of
thirteen games played since their return from their western
tour. The crowd that stormed the field came from that portion
of the pavillion where the betting ring is formed each day.

Just why the betting ring is allowed in Boston and not tolerated in other cities never has been explained by the baseball
magnates, but it is supposed to carry a political angle which
has the hands of the magnates tied....

The fact that Harry Frazee, new owner of the Red Sox, tried
to prevent resuming play after the riot shows he needs some
coaching on the way to conduct baseball business, though he
may be a most successful theatrical man...

That there may be further trouble for the White Sox because
of the riot seems probable. It is said warrants for the arrest of
Weaver and McMullin and probably Schalk will be served in
the morning. Weaver and McMullin mixed with some of the
mob while trying to get off the field and Schalk had words with
one of the police officers."

In an accompanying article John Alcock reported that American League president Ban Johnson vowed to stomp out the Boston
ring just as he had done earlier in the year with the bookie crowd
in New York . Much like the bad penny, however, this issue and
these people were bound to show up again. And there was an almost
certain inevitability about the gradual ratcheting of underworld
"business" that would, in 1919–20, explode on the world of baseball with all of its accompanying havoc. The warning bells were
ringing loud and clear. With a national ban on race-track betting
in force, the gambling world turned its eye ever more intensely on
ball games everywhere. Another round, again involving the White
Sox, was ahead in September, and this time several of the White
Sox wouldn't be cast in the role of innocent bystanders.

With two down and two to go, the Sox were in a good position to take three, or possibly even four out of the Boston series.
Not to be. In front of a double header throng that was out in force
celebrating Bunker Hill day, the Red Sox won the battle of Fenway
Park with two, one-run decisions that sent the Pale Hose on their
way home still in first place but a scant game and a half in the lead

and tied with Boston at 19 in the loss column. The 8–7 loss in the twinbill's nightcap was particularly discouraging. Eddie Collins, with an error, and Swede Risberg with two, plus a wild pitch by Red Faber, who had returned to the hill for the first time since April 29, paved the way for a four-run Boston outburst in the bottom of the ninth that put this game away, converting what should have been a 7 to 4 White Sox win into an 8–7 Boston conquest. Championships are simply not won that way. About the only bright spot was the realization that during their road trip they had moved into the league's top spot and had captured eight of their fourteen road games. But there was room for some sober reflection over the ignominious loss to reliever Herb Pennock and his Boston buddies that concluded their swing through the league's eastern cities. The twin loss brought the tally on Boston-Chicago games to 4 and 3 in the White Sox' favor. It looked to be a long, difficult summer ahead and if these early season games were any indication, it would be a scramble to stay above the break-even mark in the 15 remaining games. With exactly 100 games left to play the hitting and pitching lined up this way:

Hitting, Team and Players (maximum 57 games played)

Team	GP	AB	R	H	Pct.
Chicago	56	1773	225	430	.243
Boston	54	1775	203	425	.240
St. Louis	54	1769	188	423	.239
New York	53	1783	198	413	.232

Players					
Babe Ruth, Bos	20	50	5	19	.380
Ty Cobb, Det	52	190	32	70	.368
Reb Russell, Chi	16	28	1	10	.357
Tris Speaker, Clv	57	204	30	70	.343
George Sisler, StL	52	210	16	63	.310
Ray Chapman, Clv	50	200	33	62	.310
Baby Doll Jacobson, StL	51	192	9	57	.297
Tilly Walker, Bos	40	139	18	40	.288
Joe Jackson, Chi	55	199	30	57	.287
Buck Weaver, Chi	56	211	40	60	.285
Frank Baker, NYY	51	189	24	51	.271
Hap Felsch, Chi	56	204	23	55	.270
Duffy Lewis, Bos	52	197	25	53	.269
Dick Hoblitzell, Bos	41	141	16	38	.269

Shano Collins, Chi	30	86	16	23	.267
Rog Peckinpaugh, NYY	53	188	18	49	.261
Eddie Collins, Chi	56	195	26	49	.251
Chick Gandil, Chi	51	186	13	45	.242
Harry Hooper, Bos	51	198	33	47	.237
Ray Schalk, Chi	51	157	17	32	.201
Swede Risberg, Chi	56	180	14	33	.183

Pitchers	GP	W	L	Pct.	K	BB
Lefty Williams, Chi	14	7	0	1.000	31	24
Urban Shocker, NYY	8	5	1	.833	27	27
Carl Mays, Bos	12	6	2	.750	30	32
Babe Ruth, Bos	16	11	4	.733	65	50
Stan Coveleski, Clv	17	8	4	.667	48	35
Reb Russell, Chi	16	6	3	.667	35	14
George Mogridge, NYY	9	4	2	.667	16	14
Alan Sothoron, StL	20	7	4	.636	33	30
Eddie Cicotte, Chi	20	10	6	.625	54	23
Jim Scott, Chi	13	5	3	.625	30	21
Ernie Shore, Bos	13	6	4	.600	24	24
Dutch Leonard, Bos	14	7	7	.500	58	23
Jim Bagby, Clv	20	7	7	.500	35	36
Dave Danforth, Chi	15	1	1	.500	18	30

The long trip home, complete with card games, talk about ball games and the big brawl in Boston, and the usual horseplay before dealing with upper and lower berths on the overnight special, brought the ball club back to Chicago to resume play for a two-series, ten-game set against Cleveland and Detroit, five a piece. It was time to put together a good home stand before heading back to play the same teams for another nine times. 19 ball games against two ball clubs: that would be enough of Speaker and Cobb after all that was over with!

CHAPTER 5

The Summer Chase

Sometimes ball games turn on miscues. One little misplay and the ol' ball game is lost. That one little misplay happened in the sixth inning of the opening game of a five-game series between the Sox and Cleveland. In that frame the Sox scored three runs, the last of which came home when second baseman Bill Wambsganns mishandled a Tris Speaker throw from the far reaches of right-center field where he had retrieved an Eddie Collins drive that went for three bases. Instead of heading off Collins and preventing him from scoring, the bobbled relay enabled swift Eddie to ramble on home. And that was the ball game. Lefty Williams, who posted his ninth straight win, went the distance in a game that was marked not only by Wambsganss' error, but by those of other reliable defenders, the likes of Nemo Leibold and the Indians' gifted mid-fielder Ray Chapman. Williams surrendered but four hits, two of them doubles by "Wamby," who otherwise just might have turned out to be the hero of the game. It was his second double that scored the Cleveland run pulling the Indians to within one of the Sox in the ninth. A hit at that juncture would have scored him with the tying run. But the southpaw-throwing Williams then clamped down to stem any further damage. Williams' victim was future Hall of

Famer Stan Coveleski who, even on his better days, seemed to find it difficult to beat the Pale Hose. And that little miscue did him in this time, as well, as the Indians went down 3 to 2.

So the June 20 opening game of the short homestand brought on summer with good gifts and a two-game lead over Boston, which on that same day split with the Yankees at the Polo Grounds. The Sox went on to win three of the next four, holding the Indians to but five runs in the five games. In one of them, played on the day after Williams' win, Jim Bagby beat Eddie Cicotte in an old-time pitching duel, 1–0. The winning tally was spliced together with a scratch hit by Ray Chapman on a close play at first, a single up the middle by Tris Speaker and a fielder's choice by one of the eleven players on 1917 major league rosters named Smith (this one was Cleveland's cleanup hitter for the day, Elmer John). The remainder of the game was a battle of trick pitches and changing speeds between Cicotte and Bagby, both of whom tolerated no offense, shutting each other out. But Cleveland had already put the game away in the first stanza, and 1–0 is the way it remained.

For Eddie Cicotte, it was his second 1–0 loss of the season. As the year wore on, he would also lose 3–0 (Washington), and 2–0 (the Senators again), and his last two losses of the season would be by 3–1 (Boston) and 2–1 (Philadelphia) scores. The box score of the 1–0 loss to Cleveland follows:

Cleveland at Chicago, June 21, 1917

Cleveland	AB	R	H	PO	A	Chicago	AB	R	H	PO	A
Graney, lf	4	0	0	1	0	Leibold, rf	3	0	0	2	0
Chapman, ss	4	1	1	2	4	Weaver, 3b	4	0	0	0	0
Speaker, cf	4	0	2	2	0	E. Collins, 2b	3	0	1	2	3
E. Smith, rf	3	0	1	3	0	Jackson, lf	3	0	1	5	0
W'gans, 2b	3	0	0	1	5	Felsch, cf	3	0	0	3	0
Guisto, 1b	4	0	0	9	1	Gandil, 1b	3	0	1	7	1
Evans, 3b	4	0	1	1	2	Risberg, ss	3	0	0	4	0
O'Neill, c	4	0	0	7	1	Schalk, c	2	0	0	2	0
Bagby, (WP)	4	0	0	1	0	Cicotte, (LP)	2	0	0	2	5
						Murphy, ph	1	0	0	0	0
Totals	34	1	5	27	13	Totals	27	0	3	27	9

Cleveland	100 000 000	1–5–0
Chicago	000 000 000	0–3–2

2B: E. Collins; SB: Speaker, E. Smith; Sac. hit: E. Smith; LOB: Cleveland 8, Chicago 2; DP: O'Neill and Chapman, Wambsganns, Chapman and Guisto; BB: Bagby 2, Cicotte 2; K: Bagby 4, Cicotte 2; Umpires: Connolly and Nallin; Time of Game: 1:36.

Countering the disappointment of the Cicotte loss was a Chicago answer to this 1–0 business with a Dave Danforth 3-hitter that rang up a similar 1–0 whitewashing. The lefthander, who was usually brought into the game by Rowland in a relief role and appeared a league-leading 50 times in 1917, as well as leading the league in saves with 9, was given a start to help relieve the logjam created by doubleheaders that were testing the Sox' staff to the limit. Not to be overlooked, either, was a route-going job by Red Faber, recording his first win since April 28. The big Iowan's 4 to 1 mastery of the Indians showed that he was ready to resume his spot in the starting rotation.

A day's respite provided by the weatherman, who decided that Detroit's Bengals were to be greeted with a downpour rather than an afternoon of baseball, apparently gave Pants Rowland too much time to get enthused about Red Faber's return to action. Why he chose to start the redhead after only two days rest will never be known, but the decision was a bad one. The result was a 9–2 victory for the Tigers in the opening game of the June 26 doubleheader, and for one of the few times during the 1917 season that a Rowland decision gave Chicagoans room to wonder about their manager's strategy. Faber lasted only three innings as the Tigers, led by a Cobb double and young Harry Heilmann's fourbagger, belabored relievers Joey Benz and Mellie Wolfgang, as well as starter Faber, for 16 hits.

There was a decided upturn in the nightcap when the Sox jumped on Tiger hurler Bill James for four early runs and hung on behind the slants of Lefty Williams to win out by a tight 4 to 3 margin. But it wasn't easy. An eleventh hour rally by Hughie Jennings' men chased Williams with one away in the ninth, scoring two before reliever Dave Danforth was able to douse Tiger hopes and pick up the save.

The series resumed the next day with the Sox' fourth doubleheader in a week. This time Cobb and Co. had to deal with Eddie Cicotte who went the route in a 5–2 victory, doling out only four hits, as he won his 11th game against five losses. The big Swede,

Charles Risberg, tripled and singled three times to round out a perfect, 4 for 4 game, giving some indication that his work with coach Kid Gleason might begin to pay off. It had thus far been a miserable spring at the plate for the rookie, his hitting hemmed in by failure after failure as he was trying to adjust to the superior talent of major league pitching.

In the second game Risberg again had a hand in the game's outcome, a thriller that the Sox snatched away from the Tigers, 3 to 2. Swede's unassisted double play in this one was the fielding play of the day. With Heilmann on second and Bobby Veach on third, Ossie Vitt scorched one that was headed for big trouble when the rangy Risberg speared Vitt's rope barehanded and beat Heilmann in the race to second base for a twinkilling that brought the house down.

In this Sox victory Rowland made the right moves. Giving Dave Danforth his second starting assignment as a part of the frontline rotation proved to be a good decision, and his insertion of Eddie Murphy once again as a pinch hitter for Danforth in the seventh turned out equally well as Murph's double drove home Chick Gandil and Risberg for the winning runs. The win made it three straight over the Tigers.

Despite an error-filled season, Swede Risberg was really a masterful shortstop. Cut in the Marty Marion mold, the rangy, long-armed Risberg arguably covered more ground in the middle of the diamond than any American Leaguer. In that respect Artie Fletcher of the Giants was his only competition. He was a fearless, strong-throwing infielder who made ridiculously difficult plays and made errors on ridiculously easy plays. Risberg's addition to the Sox lineup made it possible to shift a pretty smooth shortstopping machine by the name of Weaver to the hot corner, where old Buck became an even better third sacker. The Swede was good enough right from the start to keep another fine fielder on the bench, relegated to utility status, Fred McMullin. All three of these fellows would, of course, be heard from in dark and troubling terms in the very near future as memebrs of the Black Sox corps of game-fixers. As a matter of fact, before the summer of 1917 would be out, they would, in one way or another, already be involved in the betting scandals of 1917—and with the same Tigers that were in town for the five game series in June.

There are those who claim that Charley Comiskey's best move

in bringing the 1917 White Sox together was the late February acquisition of Chick Gandil from the Cleveland Indians. An even better case can be made for his January purchase of Pacific Coast Leaguer Risberg. It was the move that made possible the Weaver switch to third, enabling Risberg to take over the key midfield position. How that all played out later on would have its eventual chapter in baseball's history book, but in 1917 the keystone combination of Collins and Risberg was intact, pennant bound, and an overwhelming Chicago favorite. Here is the Risberg record.

Year	GP	AB	R	H	2B	3B	SA	BB	SB	OB%	BA	TPR
1917	149	474	59	96	20	8	.285	59	16	.297	.203	-4.8
1918	82	273	36	70	12	3	.333	23	5	.321	.256	-0.8
1919	119	414	48	106	19	6	.345	35	19	.317	.256	-1.6
1920	126	458	53	122	21	10	.369	31	12	.316	.266	-1.0
Totals	476	1619	196	394	72	27	.332	148	52	.311	.243	-8.2

Scheduled for yet another twinbill, the Sox and Tigers escaped two and played one, another thunderstorm slicing up the afternoon just after the Tigers had annexed a sloppily played ball game, 6 to 5, in ten innings. Five errors, three by the Sox, bone-headed base running by both clubs, and more than one arguable decision by umpires Dick Nallin, George Moriarty and Tommy Connolly messed up what turned out to be the last game of the homestand. Nonetheless, there was a third inning play that in retrospect after the final contest of the Fall Classic awaiting fandom in October must have had Eddie Collins wondering what the fates had in mind.

What happened was a dress rehearsal for Collins' sprint to home plate at the Polo Grounds in the fourth inning of the Sox' World Series-winning game on October 15, which must have been the bluest Monday of John McGraw's life. Here's how that happened. With one out Eddie Collins tripled. That brought up Joe Jackson who slammed a sizzler right back to pitcher Bernie Boland who then trapped Collins, always the aggressive base runner, by throwing to third baseman Ossie Vitt rather than to first to get Jackson. And the race was on. Collins, with his head start, was chased by Vitt right across home plate before finally being caught up with by Vitt near the Sox' dugout. The only difference in the "dress rehearsal" was

Charles "Swede" Risberg, far-ranging, strong-armed and fearless, stepped into the shortstop position in 1917 enabling Buck Weaver to take over at third base, solidifying the Pale Hose infield. (Dennis Colgin)

that it was in the third inning, and that the Tigers won the ball game despite the run Eddie Collins scored. But then, that's what rehearsals are for, right?!

The Sox, their loss that afternoon notwithstanding, finished their brief Cleveland-Detroit homestand with a seven and three mark. They were still in command of the American League parade, and still ahead of Boston, who had cut into the Sox lead, paring it down to 2½ games with a double-header triumph over New York.

While all this was going on in the American League, Ferdie Schupp was unravelling a potential no-hitter at the expense of Boston's Braves, and at least through seven frames he was successful before the Giants were forced to withstand a brief Boston flurry in the eighth, finally winning 3–2, and thus maintaining a one-game lead over the Phillies. It was Schupp's ninth win of the season against but two losses. McGraw's other two lefties, Rube Benton (5 and 3) and Slim Sallee (4 and 4), along with Pol Perritt and Fred Anderson, 9 and 8 between them, were Schupp's chief pitching support. At the end of June this is the way the National League shaped up:

	Won	*Lost*	*Pct.*
New York	38	22	.633
Philadelphia	37	24	.607
Chicago	39	32	.549
St. Louis	34	31	.523
Cincinnati	34	37	.479
Brooklyn	27	33	.450
Boston	23	35	.397
Pittsburgh	21	40	.344

In the resumption of their prolonged Cleveland-Detroit warfare, the Sox returned to the Forest City where they got their eight-game road trip off to a rousing start with a 3 to 1 victory behind Red Faber. Rowland's sturdy righthander combined with Eddie Collins to provide most of the wherewithal as Collins rammed a weird shot through short that eluded leftfielder Jack Graney, bouncing over his head, and then, unbelievably, took another odd bounce that escaped Tris Speaker. Before the ball was run down and returned to the infield Collins was perched on third with a clean, though mind-boggling triple that had scored Buck Weaver with what turned out to be the winning run. All this happened at the expense of—who else?!—Stan Coveleski, once again trumped by his own personal Sox jinx.

While that was going on owner Comiskey was busy delivering a check in the amount of some two thousand plus dollars to the Red Cross in support of the war effort. That raised the total to over seven thousand all told (there would be much more as the war went on), which along with donations to other wartime agencies, cartons of baseball gear and uniforms to service training camps, still other donations to service support groups, special admissions rates for service men, and the expenses involved in outfitting his players for military exercises through the season, raised the expenses of running his ball club for the 1917 season to astronomical numbers. Although the Old Roman was not alone in that regard, he was in the vanguard of baseball people in support of the war effort. Nor was this his only venture into the world of civic philanthropy. He had for a long time been most supportive of Chicago's up-and-forward drive to become one of the nation's leading sports and cultural centers.

And that brings up an interesting question: why was he such a fusspot over such essential items as player salaries, player facilities, and clubhouse amenities? Although his overall salary commitment was no worse than that of other franchises, there is no questioning the fact that the golden era of Comiskey baseball in Chicago brought bales of money into the club's coffers. Where other ball clubs had already abandoned the practice of charging their players for laundering services, Comiskey's players were still paying for it themselves. In fact, the term Black Sox was in vogue before the scandals of 1919–20. Black was actually the way their sox looked after having gone through who knows how many games before soap and water got any where near them. That may have been due to personal habits and preferences, but there was only so much to go around and ball players, being ball players, spent what there was on personally arranged priorities. Sox and uniforms were way down the list.

As to how much there was available, Richard Lindberg, in his *Stealing First in a Two-Team Town* (Sagamore Publishing, Champaign, 1994. p. 104) lists these 1919–20 salaries, at the height of the championship era: Eddie Collins, finishing up his 1915, multi-year contract, at $15,000; Ray Schalk, $12,000; and the third of the three Hall of Famers on the Comiskey roster, Red Faber, $6,600. Others included Joe Jackson, $8,000 for 1920; Eddie Cicotte, $9,075 plus a $3,285 bonus; Swede Risberg, $3,435; pinch hitter Eddie Murphy, $4,800 plus a $1,200 renewal bonus; Shano Collins, $4,800 plus a $1,200 renewal bonus; Buck Weaver, $7,644; and Happy Felsch, at $7,400.

While he was willing to foot the bill for guests to and at his famous North Woods lodge in Wisconsin, which included players on the guest list as well as members of the renowned Woodland Bards, a group of died-in-the-wool Sox fans with a cultural, that is to say poetic bent, his blind spot on player remuneration was ever in the way of outright respect and friendships with his ball players with the possible exception of a few, including Ed Walsh, Ray Schalk and Red Faber, each of whom seemed to have had a special place in the Old Roman's heart.

Some might call that a psychological quirk, or the inner working of a complicated personality, or even the mark of an insecure employer. Most called it what it more than likely was: the mark of a parsimonious, peevishly close-to-the-vest franchise owner who ran his club on a dime and spent millions on personal and civic pursuits. If that latter was actually true, and most observers even during Comiskey's time subscribed to that characterization, it could not help but have its singular effect on the playing field. And as the deadball era drew to a close, it did, ringing down the curtain on an era synonymous with scuffed baseballs, one-run games, mythical pitching feats, and—baseball supremacy on the south side of Chicago. Once the 1920 season crumbled into ashes for Comiskey and Co., it was time for Taps on the south side.

But as July, 1917, approached, the Sox prepared to win another ball game in Cleveland, and what was uppermost in their minds was a fellow by the name of Jim Bagby, who had really shut them down a little over a week earlier in Chicago. This time around the score wasn't 1–0, it was 11 to 1, and the winner wasn't Chicago. Only one run sullied an otherwise brilliant afternoon on the hill for Mr. Bagby as he coasted to victory behind a 12-hit barrage that blew away Sox hurlers Claude Williams, the starter and loser, and Jim Scott and Joey Benz. It was undoubtedly the easiest of the tall Cleveland righthander's 23 wins that season.

Something had to be done about that. And further, the pennant race was melting down on the Sox to a point where there was little or no comfort zone left between themselves and the Bosox. That "something" didn't happen the next day, not even with Eddie Cicotte on the firing line. On July's first day he contributed mightily to his own demise by throwing away two potential outs in the same inning as the Sox lost their second straight to the Indians 4 to 3. That tightened things up in the pennant chase in a hurry. The standings as of July 1's ball games:

	Won	Lost	Pct.
Chicago	43	24	.642
Boston	41	24	.631
New York	35	29	.547
Detroit	33	32	.508
Cleveland	35	34	.507
Washington	25	39	.391
St. Louis	26	41	.388
Philadelphia	23	38	.377

The Sox finally put an end to bad baseball, defeats and their frustration at the hands of Jim Bagby and troublesome Tris Speaker by edging the Indians 4 to 3 behind Dave Danforth and Red Faber. In this particular game Danforth, in his third straight start, won out with the help of Pants Rowland's frontliner, Red Faber, who came on in the seventh and final frame (the teams by agreement played only seven innings in order to catch trains for different destinations) to squelch a Cleveland rally in 1–2–3 order, thus winding up the series in a 2–2 standoff with the Tribe.

Over in Detroit, meanwhile, Reb Russell and the Tigers were awaiting the start of another five-game set which included the annual and colorful 4th of July festivities, a double header on the

5th, and single games on the 6th and 7th. The aforementioned Russell, resting his still bothersome elbow in Chicago during the Cleveland trip, would no doubt see action in the series with the Tigers.

The White Sox skipper's choice for the series opener was Red Faber, who had so convincingly closed the door on the Indians the day before. This time Rowland's strategy didn't backfire as the pale Hose derailed the Detroiters 5–1, extending their lead over Boston to two games as the Red Sox were splitting with the Athletics, who took the measure of Babe Ruth in the twinbill opener, 3 to 0, behind the five-hit, shutout pitching of Elmer Myers.

That night Buck Weaver and Jim Scott, who was married to a sister of Weaver's, already began celebrating the 4th by taking in the vaudeville performance of the Four Cook Sisters. Their attendance was tantamount to a command appearance inasmuch Buck's wife had been one of the entertaining Cook Sisters. On the crest of their victory that afternoon they began their holiday celebrating in great style, something that mattered much in the life of the Sox' gritty third sacker.

During the national pastime's earlier days, Independence Day was celebrated with morning and afternoon games, those famed 4th of July doubleheaders. In 1917 the celebration had special meaning. It wasn't only that the contending White Sox were in town. Just days before a huge contingent of General Pershing's troops had landed in France. The Great War had become a real and frightening presence, much on the minds of the many Americans who also happened to be baseball fans. Though they didn't dwell on it, major league ball players knew there was much more to the military drills they were doing than parading around to entertain the fans. Of a certainty, the 1917 and 1918 July 4th doubleheaders would have very special overtones, very special meanings. Such was the setting at what Detroit fans for years called The Corner, the place where Bengal heroes thrilled their Motor City followers, first at rickety old Bennett Field at the intersection of Michigan and Trumbull Avenues, and then the renamed and refurbished Navin Field, and then, in turn, renamed Briggs Stadium before finally giving way to its final renaming, Tiger Stadium, after which it was reincarnated in the modern trappings of the the ball club's present day stadium, the recently constructed Comerica Park.

On 1917's 4th of July, big Bill James was primed to take on the Sox' Eddie Cicotte, a native Detroiter, in the morning game, with

Willie Mitchell, the southern squire from Pleasant Grove, Mississippi, slated to take on Lefty Williams in the afternoon tilt. Unfortunately for the locals, things did not go well for their Tigers. About the only thing they had to cheer about was Ty Cobb's hitting in both games, extending his streak to 34 games which began to threaten the Willie Keeler mark of 44 set back in 1897.

Scribe Jim Crusineberry penned these words about the two ball games for the July 5, *Chicago Tribune* sports pages:

In an act which fitted the day, the Chicago White Sox declared their own independence today of the old hoodoo, which formerly hung to them here, by beating the Tigers twice, nosing out the morning contest, 4 to 3, and the afternoon battle by the same count. In each instance the boys from Chicago came from behind....

Although 1917 was Ty Cobb's best season (he led the American League in eight major departments) it wasn't good enough to lead the Tigers to a pennant. (Dennis Colgin)

The day was very satisfactory to the Sox in every way. First, the weather was perfect, something seldom enjoyed on this historic holiday.

Then—the crowds were grand—there were 11,532 persons who paid to see the morning show, and there were 17,300 who bought tickets and attended in the afternoon. The latter crowd filled the park to capacity and spilled out in the corners of the outfield to the extent of about 600.

The hero roles for the day were handed to Eddie Cicotte and Claude Williams, and both of them played their parts heroically....

Joe Jackson, Hap Felsch and John Collins and one or two other of our boys cut in on the hero stuff, too.... In the afternoon the Collins boys cut in, *especially Shano* [emphasis added; see following], who poled the triple which won the game in the seventh.

Chicago White Sox at Detroit, July 4, 1917, second game

Chicago	AB	R	H	PO	A	Detroit	AB	R	H	PO	A
J. Col's, rf	5	2	3	2	0	Bush, ss	4	1	1	2	5
Weaver, 3b	3	0	1	2	1	Young, 2b	3	0	0	1	1
E. Col's, 2b	3	0	2	2	2	Cobb, cf	3	0	1	5	0
Jackson, lf	4	0	0	1	0	Veach, lf	4	0	0	2	0
Felsch, cf	3	1	0	5	1	Heilm'n, rf	4	0	0	2	0
Gandil, 1b	4	0	0	7	0	Burns, 1b	4	0	1	10	0
Risberg, ss	4	0	0	2	3	Vitt, 3b	4	1	2	1	1
Schalk, c	4	1	1	6	1	Spencer, c	3	0	1	3	0
Wms, (WP)	4	0	1	0	0	Mitch'l (LP)	1	1	1	0	1
						Cun'ham, p	1	0	0	1	0
						Boland, p	0	0	0	0	2
						Stanage, ph1		0	0	0	0
						Crawf'd, ph1		0	0	0	0
						R. Jones, pr0		0	0	0	0
Totals	34	4	8	27	8	Totals	33	3	7	27	10

Chicago	001 200 100	4–8–2
Detroit	003 000 000	3–7–0

2B: J. Collins; 3B: Bush, Williams, J. Collins; SB: E. Collins; Sac. Hit: Young; Sac. Fly: Weaver; LOB: Detroit 7, Chicago 7; DP: Felsch and Gandil; BB: Williams 3, Williams 2; K: Williams 3, Cunningham 1, Boland 2; Hit Batsmen: Felsch, by Mitchell; Umpires: Owens and Evans, Time of Game: 1:53.

Entering the top of the seventh, the game was knotted at 3. That was when Shano Collins tripled home Ray Schalk with the winning run. The younger of the Collins men also doubled in the ninth, but to no avail.

A word about this unsung warrior is in order. Shano, as his teammates called him, had been around in a Sox uniform since 1910, and with Jim Scott had the team's top seniority rights. Used both in the outfield and at first base, he was a hardened pro in every respect, without a whimper in him though he was asked to sit in many a ball game for the sake of platooning not only with Nemo Leibold, but with other first basemen the Sox employed from time to time.

But Shano, it seemed, was always there, a steadying influence on the ball club, ready to go whenever asked. A strong-armed, better than average outfielder, he seldom, if ever, threw to the wrong base, and was possessed of strong fundamentals, especially on the offense. He was the fellow who would deliver the game-winning hit that clinched the pennant in Boston later in 1917. A Welshman, his nickname was derived from the Gaelic equivalent of John, which is Sean. As Americans are prone to do, they twisted Sean around to Shano, and it stuck, a name that was always used in genuine respect.

More would be heard from this Collins throughout the course of the summer. As much as Nemo Leibold contributed to the Sox' 1917 success, Pants Rowland was fortunate to be able to call on this team-oriented ball player, and said so. His Chicago record follows:

Year	AB	R	H	RBI	EXBH	BB	SB	OB%	SA	FR*	BA	TPR
1910	315	29	62	24	19	25	10	.258	.289	4	.197	-1.1
1911	370	48	97	48	32	20	14	.309	,403	4	.262	0.0
1912	575	75	168	81	46	29	26	.330	.397	3	.292	0.1
1913	535	53	128	47	36	32	22	.286	.327	1	.239	-2.4
1914	598	61	164	65	46	27	30	.312	.376	6	.274	-0.3
1915	576	73	148	85	43	28	38	.298	.368	2	.257	-1.0
1916	527	74	128	42	40	59	16	.323	.342	8	.243	-0.1
1917	252	38	59	14	17	10	14	.269	.321	-2	.234	-1.4
1918	365	30	100	56	30	17	7	.310	.392	14	.274	1.2
1919	179	21	50	16	10	7	3	.317	.363	1	.279	-0.5
1920	495	70	150	63	32	23	12	.339	.392	-9	,303	-1.8
Totals	4787	572	1254	541	351	277	192	.305	.361	32	.262	-7.3

*FR: Fielding Runs, a sabermetric measurement which calculates how many runs a player saves beyond what an average (average calculated at 0 for any given year) player might contribute to his team's defensive effort.

What was more entertaining, Ty Cobb's base running, hitting that so often resulted in slashing drives to every part of the diamond between the chalked lines, his bullying tactics from the sidelines or on the bases, his dashes to the far off fences that regularly resulted in spectacular catches, his bunting, his white-hot fire in arguments with players and umpires, or still other of his many antics? The man was quite a show all by himself and saw to it that no matter the opponent, it would be nine innings of hell-bent-for-leather base-ball—every out, every inning, every game.

Among the countless "Cobb-moments" during the 1917 season, during which, by the way, he turned in his greatest single season in a 24-year, upper echelon Hall of Fame career, was one that occured in the eighth inning of the Sox' loss to the Tigers following their 4th of July conquests. One of those legendary fade-away Cobb slides was the beginning of a little episode between Cobb and Buck Weaver. The Georgia Peach reached third safely on a Bobby Veach single that Hap Felsch picked up and then threw to Weaver, who thought he had Cobb dead to rights. Swerving out of line to make his slide, Cobb eluded Weaver's tag and umpire Billy Evans called him safe over the heated protests of several White Sox players.

Buck Weaver, as volatile as Cobb, was so upset with the whole thing that he took the ball, still in his hand, and rolled it about twenty feet behind third base, just daring Cobb to make a dash for home. When Buck didn't move, it proved too much of a temptation for the high-strung Cobb. He broke for the plate trying to draw a throw, but swerved and headed back to third. Weaver took a dive to block him off the base but Evans once again gave Cobb the safe signal. By this time just about everybody on hand, including Weaver, recognized the incident for what it was, sheer comedy on the baseball diamond. With a chuckle he then threw the ball to Reb Russell, at that time on the mound for the Sox, the incident was over, and play resumed.

Another Cobb accomplishment in the Tigers' 11 to 6 win was his first base hit that day, which marked the 35th straight game in which he had hit safely, and because he failed to hit safely in his next game, 35 is where his mark stood. It would be the fifth longest streak in American League history (Cobb's 40 game streak would rank third to Joe DiMaggio's famed 56), adding to his many hitting achievements.

The Sox didn't fare any better than Buck Weaver, losing not only that game, but the next, and with it their league lead. So the Detroit series was, after an auspicious start, right next to a disaster. In the final game of the series Hooks Dauss knocked off Red Faber, 4 to 1, in a game that featured Tiger outfielder Bobby Veach's double and triple, and despite racking up 12 hits off Dauss, the Sox were able to push but one run over the plate, ending the series on a particularly low note and sending the subdued Comiskeymen back to Chicago with a thing or two to think about.

One of the things Pants Rowland was thinking about was what had been accomplished during the first half of the season. Just where was his ball club at and what might he expect during the second

A solid hitter, dependable right fielder, and a good baserunner, Shano Collins was a Pale Hose favorite for a full decade before being traded to the Red Sox in 1920 in the deal that brought Hall of Famer Harry Hooper to Chicago. (Brace photograph)

half of the season? The standings were a good place place to start.
With 73 games behind his ball club this is the way the top five clubs
shaped up:

July 6: 1917 and 1916

1917	W	L	Pct.	GB
Boston	46	25	.648	
Chicago	47	26	.644	1
New York	36	32	.522	8.5
Cleveland	39	37	.513	9.5
Detroit	36	35	.507	10

1916	W	L	Pct.	GB
New York	42	27	.609	
Cleveland	40	30	.571	2.5
Boston	38	31	.551	4
Chicago	37	31	.544	4.5
Detroit	36	36	.500	7.5

Rowland would note, first, that his Sox were ten wins ahead
of his 1916 team's pace, trailing Boston both years, but in 1917 second behind the frontrunning Bosox. A mere four percentage points
separated the two teams, though the Pale Hose were down a half
game in the loss column.

The gap between the two pace setters and the next three teams
was sufficient to merit far lesser concern than the remaining 15
games on the schedule with the Red Sox who had, between June
28 and July 5, blazed a nine out of ten trail leading to first place.
While it would be impossible to keep up that kind of streak, it
nonetheless indicated in no uncertain terms that the defending
champions had hit their stride and would absolutely refuse to go
silently into the night. That made the series with them at Comiskey
Park in just two weeks huge. On deck would be a five-game set that
would conclude their upcoming 18-game home stand.

But while Rowland, and no doubt bossman Comiskey with
him, might have wished that the Chisox would have been more
consistent and would have played at that higher level they both felt
the ball club was capable of, the bigger concern was no doubt up
there in Beantown, where manager Jack Barry & Co. were by this

time trying to adjust to one of the stubborn facts of life issuing from the shores of Lake Michigan, that the Pale Hose were every bit as good as the 1916 ball club—and probably a notch or two better— than the Chicagos that fought them to within a two-game margin for the previous year's laurels. The race gave every prospect of heating up, as opposed to a second half run-away, thus keeping both clubs preoccupied with their own race for pennant spoils and leaving little time to take a peek at what was happening elsewhere— over in the National League, for example.

The aim for the second half of the season, then, was to play at a better clip than merely "good-enough-to-win." Put another way: Rowland would insist on more concentration and more consistency, thereby putting the ball club in a position to raise its level of play no matter the opposition.

As of the July halfway point the numbers of some of the players from the primary contending teams in both leagues were as follows:

The American League Hitters

	GP	AB	R	H	SB	BA
Babe Ruth, Bos	22	53	5	19	0	.358
Reb Russell, Chi	20	32	2	11	0	.344
Del "The Sherriff" Gainer, Bos	22	78	10	21	0	.288
Buck Weaver, Chi	78	274	47	77	17	.281
Duffy Lewis, Bos	69	260	31	73	3	.281
Hap Felsch, Chi	71	260	28	72	7	.277
Larry Gardner, Bos	78	253	24	70	5	.277
Joe Jackson, Chi	72	264	36	72	4	.270
R. C. "Doc" Hoblitzell, Bos	58	196	23	52	6	.265
Eddie Collins, Chi	73	254	88	66	12	.260
Shano Collins, Chi	40	112	20	29	5	.259
C. "Tilly" Walker, Bos	59	201	26	51	4	.254
Harry Hooper, Bos	60	265	42	65	11	.245
Ev "Deacon" Scott, Bos	71	241	28	55	16	.241
Chick Gandil, Chi	67	243	17	58	6	.239
C. "Pinch" Thomas, Bos	44	113	16	27	0	.239
Nemo Leibold, Chi	57	181	23	42	10	.232
Samuel "Slam" Agnew, Bos	34	100	7	24	1	.218
Cracker Schalk, Chi	64	194	28	40	4	.206
Swede Risberg, Chi	70	230	18	47	6	.204
Jack Barry, Bos	55	175	25	32	7	.183
Eddie Murphy, Chi	24	24	4	4	0	.167

The sturdy righthander from Cascade, Iowa, Red Faber, struggled
through the first half of the 1917 season, but when he caught his stride
he was a tower of strength in Pants Rowland's pitching rotation, winding up the season with those three World Series victories that brought
a world's championship to Chicago's South Side. (Brace photograph)

The American League Pitchers

	GP	W	L	K	BB	Pct.
Lefty Williams, Chi	19	10	3	33	34	.769
Carl Mays, Bos	16	9	3	47	89	.750
Babe Ruth, Bos	18	11	5	68	53	.688
Reb Russell, Ch	19	6	3	35	17	.667
Joey "Blitzen" Benz, Chi	12	4	2	14	12	.667
Dave Danforth, Chi	21	4	2	31	41	.667
Eddie Cicotte, Chi	24	12	7	70	86	.632
"Death Valley Jim" Scott, Chi	14	5	3	30	21	.625
Ernie Shore, Bos	17	8	5	84	32	.615
Dutch Leonard, Bos	17	10	7	72	31	.588
Herb Pennock, Bos	12	4	3	22	15	.571
U. "Red" Faber, Chi	13	6	5	28	26	.545
George "Rube" Foster, Bos	5	2	2	4	14	.500

The National League Hitters

	GP	AB	R	H	SB	BA
Heinie Zimmerman, NY	63	248	34	75	6	.309
Bennie Kauff, NY	65	232	42	69	5	.297
"Tioga George" Burns, NY	65	253	45	74	3	.292
Lew McCarty, NY	35	100	11	29	4	.290
Geo. "Possum" Whitted, Phl	62	230	35	69	16	.289
"Reindeer Bill" Killifer, Phl	60	204	16	58	8	.284
Geo. "Dode" Paskert, Phl	65	256	44	68	4	.266
"Beauty" Bancroft, Phl	53	202	27	53	9	.262
Milt Stock, Phl	66	248	82	64	11	.258
Fred Luderus, Phl	66	218	26	56	10	.257
Bert Niehoff, Phl	63	217	17	56	9	.257
Dave Robertson, NY	65	252	29	64	11	.254
W. "Union Man" Holke, NY	65	225	27	56	8	.249
Pete Alexander, Phl	20	61	10	15	5	.246
Buck Herzog, NY	53	191	35	46	7	.241
Artie Fletcher, NY	65	237	33	56	8	.236

The National League Pitchers

	GP	W	L	K	BB	Pct.
Ferdie Schupp, NY	15	9	2	69	33	.818
Rube Benton, NY	13	6	2	31	10	.750
Chas. "Jeff" Tesreau, NY	15	7	3	46	23	.700
Pete Alexander, Phl	19	13	6	94	28	.684
Wm. "Pol" Perritt, NY	14	5	3	31	19	.625
Eppa Rixey, Phl	18	10	7	48	33	.588
Erskine Mayer, Phl	13	4	3	37	16	.571
Harry "Slim" Sallee	14	5	4	20	12	.556
Fred Anderson, NY	14	7	6	40	22	.538
Joe Oeschger, Phl	13	6	6	46	33	.500
Jim Middleton, NY	11	1	1	9	8	.500

CHAPTER **6**

Boston Confrontation II

If there was to be an immediate upswing in the team's intensity and execution of play, the Philadelphia Athletics series of four games beginning on July 7 certainly gave no indication. The league's worst ball club came into Comiskey Park and promptly gave the White Sox a three-out-of-four lesson in how to win ball games. In only one game did the Sox approximate a winner and that was behind Eddie Cicotte, as they beat the A's in the second game of the series, 8 to 4, and even in that one it was more a case of Philadelphia ineptitude that paved the way to victory than Chisox "brilliance."

While this was going on, the Red Sox, fortunately for the Pale Hose, were dropping three straight at Cleveland. But The Carmine found themselves when they got to Detroit, and, on July 11, with Babe Ruth on the mound, they beat the Tigers, scoring the game's only run in the top of the ninth. In a spectacularly pitched game Ruth smothered the Bengals' attack, surrendering but one hit, a Donie Bush smash back to the box that Ruth deflected but couldn't recover in time to convert into a putout. It was the closest the big fellow ever came to a no-hitter, and that particular win nudged the Beantowners back into first place. On the morning of July 12 the standings looked like this:

	W	L	Pct.		W	L	Pct.
Boston	47	28	.627	Detroit	38	38	.500
Chicago	48	29	.623	Washington	31	43	.419
Cleveland	43	37	.538	Philadelphia	28	45	.384
New York	38	34	.528	St. Louis	30	49	.380

So there it was. With the Red Sox due in Chicago after the series with Washington, which was directly ahead, Rowland's charges were faced with the necessity of finding ways and means to get back into the lead while Boston was in Detroit and then St. Louis. Their work was cut out for them. It was high time to get down to business, and *not* as usual.

The good news was Joe Jackson and the bad news was Walter Johnson as the Sox began their series with the Senators. After missing the past five games, a rested Jackson was restored to the lineup for the series opener, and he responded with a 2 for 5 day, including a double that helped the Sox mount a 4 to 2 lead going into the ninth. That was when Walter Johnson came to the Senators' rescue with a pinch hit appearance during the Washington ninth inning rally. And then, as Clark Griffith's replacement for starter Jim Shaw in the Sox' half of the ninth, he brought the bad news with him. Though the Sox managed a run off Sir Walter, the comeback threat ended when Jackson bounced one of Johnson's offerings meekly back to the mound and was thrown out. The final score was 6 to 5, Johnson had added another W to his outsized list, and the Senators pushed the Comiskeymen a full game behind the Red Sox, who had won two in St. Louis.

Consequently, as they neared July's mid-point, there was still no convincing sign that the Sox were ready to make a move and put together the big push that would really separate them from the rest of the league. That made two impending doubleheaders with the Senators and a five game set with Jack Barry's men a very crucial series of games.

At that very critical point the Sox drew a line in the dirt, and, starting with a twinbill conquest on July 17, the first of which was an Eddie Cicotte one-hitter over the Senators, they worked their way through an eleven game stretch during which they only lost one and tied one to go with nine wins while playing some of their best ball of the season to that date. By the end of their homestand on July 23, they had forged to a 4½ game lead, their first big bulge of the pennant race, and their first sustained exhibition of championship level baseball of the season.

The Cicotte masterpiece came at the expense of George Dumont, who had earlier shut out the Sox, as the Sox scored all they needed with a run in the second inning. They added four in the third to whip the Senators 5 to 0. That one set the pace for what was to follow against both Washington and Boston. James Crusinberry summed up the Cicotte triumph (Chicago Tribune, July 18, 1917):

> Pennant hopes, confidence, enthusiasm and loyalty all were restored to Chicago's baseball fans yesterday when the White Sox won two corking games of ball from Washington while the Boston Red Sox lost to St. Louis. The result permitted the Sox to leap far out and take a firm grasp on first place in the flag race. The scores were 5 to 0 and 3 to 2, the second combat requiring eleven innings before Walter Johnson could be downed.
>
> Not this season have the south siders displayed more class than they did at this long matinee. They looked and acted like champions from start to finish. There was superb fielding, superlative pitching, timely and driving base hits and general all around efficiency.

A Ray Schalk double scored what would be the winning run in the first game, sending home Chick Gandil with the go-ahead tally. Although the big news in that 5–0 Cicotte victory was little Eddie's one-hitter, which prompted Sox fans to bring him back for a justly deserved curtain-call at the end of the game, it was the other half of the midget-sized battery that once again turned in a steady game behind the plate plus that run-scoring two-base blow.

By 1917 Ray Schalk was a five-year veteran, a pepper-pot whose enthusiasm for the game was unbounded. More significantly, he was, almost from the beginning of his career, a part of the White Sox brain-trust, involved in strategy and team leadership. And, as might have been expected considering his status in the organization, he wound up 17 years of distinguished service as the South Siders' skipper in 1927 and 1928. Later, during the 1930 and '31 seasons he continued to serve Charley Comiskey as a coach for manager Donie Bush. After his July 4, 1928, resignation as manager,

Shown warming up here, Eddie Cicotte was skipper Rowland's ace, a
starter, reliever and stopper. (Dennis Colgin)

that old Mr. Stingy, Commisar Comiskey came down with one of
his frequent salary fevers and wound up paying Schalk a mere
$6,000, at the end of the '20's, mind you, to assist Bush. That, it
should be pointed out, followed the $25,000 salary Comiskey paid

Schalk as a player manager, after which the future Hall of Famer offered to have his salary cut back to $15,000 inasmuch as he was no longer managing. Instead, after thinking the whole thing over, Comiskey made the paltry $6,000 offer, which, unblieveably, Schalk actually accepted.

There are many who consider Ray Schalk's Hall of Fame credentials very weak, suggesting that the lifelong Chicagoan really doesn't belong in the company of baseball's elite. No pitcher who ever was caught by Ray Schalk ever said that, nor did many ball players who played against him. A .250 hitter (his punch-and-judy hitting is usually cited as the prime reason he doesn't belong at Cooperstown), his reputation as a Hall of Famer was made "behind the mask." Beginning in 1915 under Pants Rowland, he ran a stretch of seven or eight seasons where there was no question but that he was baseball's best and brainiest behind home plate.

While the 1917 season did nothing to enhance his offensive credentials, he did chip in with timely hitting in some of the key Boston encounters, and beyond that quarterbacked the Chicago defense, as much a factor in throttling the enemy attack from behind the plate as Eddie Collins was in the infield.

It might be a bit of a stretch to say that Ray Schalk ranks among the top ten backstops in the game's history. What *can* be said without reservation is that he was without peer, a catcher ahead of his time, during his years behind the plate for the White Sox. His Chicago record follows.

YR	GP	AB	R	H	EXBH	BB	OB%	SA	SB	FR	BA	TPR
1912	23	63	7	18	2	3	.357	.317	2	4	.286	0.5
1913	129	401	38	98	21	27	.297	.314	14	-1	.244	-0.1
1914	135	392	30	106	15	38	.347	.314	24	6	.270	2.1
1915	135	413	46	110	19	62	.366	.327	15	-3	.266	1.0
1916	129	410	36	95	21	41	.311	.305	30	9	.232	1.5
1917	140	424	48	96	19	59	.331	.292	19	5	.226	1.5
1918	108	333	35	73	9	36	.301	.255	12	-4	.219	-0.8
1919	131	394	57	111	12	51	.367	.320	11	1	.282	1.1
1920	151	485	64	131	31	68	.362	.348	10	-1	.270	0.7
1921	128	416	32	105	28	40	.328	.329	3	8	.252	-0.4
1922	142	442	57	124	29	67	.379	.371	12	20	.281	3.0
1923	123	382	42	87	15	39	.228	.277	6	5	.228	-1.1
1924	57	153	15	30	7	21	.301	.268	1	6	.196	-0.3
1925	125	343	44	94	19	57	.382	.332	11	3	.274	0.7
1926	82	226	26	60	10	27	.349	.314	5	-6	.265	-0.8

1927	16	26	2	6	2	2	.286	.308	0	1	.231	0.0
1928	2	1	0	1	0	0	1.000	1.000	1	1	1.000	0.1
Totals	1755	5304	579	1345	259	638	.340	.316	176	53	.253	8.7

Spitballer Joey Benz and Dave Danforth combined to finish off the Washington series with a twinbill victory, boosting the Chicago lead to 2½ games over the Bosox, who disposed of the Browns behind a Carl Mays gem, in a 1 to 0 four-hitter. The unfortunate loser was the same Ernie Koob who had earlier no-hit the Pale Hose. This time he was victimized by an untimely error that cost him the 1–0 loss.

In the daily notes appended to the *Chicago Tribune*'s coverage of White Sox games, the importance of the Boston series, due to start on July 19, was highlighted:

The crucial series with the Boston Red Sox begins today. Only one game this time. The definition of crucial is "supremely critical."

Diminutive pepperpot, hustling receiver and a member of the Pale Hose braintrust, Hall of Famer Ray "Cracker" Schalk. (Dennis Colgin)

And that, of course, set the series in its proper perspective. Since Carl Mays had pitched the closer in the Browns series at St. Louis, manager Jack Barry's other staff ace, Babe Ruth, got the call for the opener. Pants Rowland's selection was Lefty Williams, 10 and 5, who had fallen on hard times, losing four of his last five starts after a 9 and 0 start. Ruth, 3 and 5 after a 10 and 1 start, had most recently knocked off the Browns, 4 to 2, in ten innings at St. Louis. In that game he contributed a double and two singles to boost his batting average to a hefty .368, the leading hitter among pitchers in both leagues.

In the middle of the working week on Thursday, the White Sox faithful bought up all the available seats in anticipation of a great ball game, and although the outcome wasn't to their liking, they got it. Behind the Bambino, who withstood a ninth inning rally that fell one short, the Red Sox won the series opener 3 to 2 in a game that started with first baseman Del Gainer's stunning two-run blow into the left field bleachers to give the Bostons a 2–0 lead before White Sox fans were fully settled in their seats. After that first inning explosion Lefty Williams matched Ruth pitch for pitch and kept the pale Hose in the game, but surrendered the hill to Mellie Wolfgang for the last two Bosox at bats, while the hometown idols were held at bay by The Bambino. Consequently, the Red Sox pulled to within a game and a half in a well-played, championship level contest.

Evidence of championship play came in the Boston half of the seventh. Ev Scott led off with an infield hit. That was followed by catcher Sam Agnew's single through the infield, sending Scott to third. Ruth then forced Agnew, Scott staying at third. Then center fielder Jimmy Walsh drew a free pass to fill the bases. That brought on an attempted squeeze play with manager Jack Barry at the plate. Anticipating the play, Ray Schalk snatched the Barry bunt in front of home plate, stepped on home and fired to Chick Gandil at first for the DP. That stalled the Boston express in its tracks and the score remained 3 to 1.

And more. Just an inning later, with Mellie Wolfgang on in relief of Williams, third baseman Larry Gardner filled out a perfect day at the plate with a well placed bunt for his fourth hit. Wolfgang fired an off-balance throw past Chick Gandil which was run down by Shano Collins, who picked it up and fired a strike to Swede Risberg, nailing Gardner at second. Del Gainer, who had walked ahead of the Gardner bunt, went around to third on the play. That brought up Harry Hooper who flied out to Shano. The younger Collins then blew Gainer away, trying to score after the fly, with a perfect shot to Ray Schalk who tagged him out. The Red Sox once again came away empty, the score hanging on that 3 to 1 margin.

Unfortunately, the Rowlandmen could only come up with a single, ninth inning run and Babe Ruth, equal to the challenge, shut down Chicago victory hopes with the final 3 to 2 count. That cut into Chicago's league lead by a full game. Another Boston triumph the next day would really pull a black pall over July.

Boston Red Sox at Comiskey Park, July 19, 1917

Boston	AB	R	H	PO	A	Chicago	AB	R	H	PO	A
Walsh, cf	3	0	0	4	1	J. Collins, rf	5	0	0	3	2
Barry, 2b	3	1	0	2	2	Weaver, 3b	4	0	0	0	1
Gainer, 1b	3	1	1	8	0	E. Collins, 2b	3	0	1	3	1
Gardner, 3b	4	1	4	0	3	Jackson, lf	4	1	1	1	0
Hooper, rf	4	0	1	4	0	Felsch, cf	4	0	1	1	0
Lewis, lf	4	0	0	2	0	Gandil, 1b	3	0	1	5	1
Scott, ss	4	0	2	2	2	Risberg, ss	4	1	1	5	1
Agnew, c	4	0	2	4	0	Schalk, c	4	0	2	9	2
Ruth, (WP)	4	0	0	1	1	Williams, (LP)	1	0	0	0	0
						McMullin, ph	1	0	1	0	0
						Wolfgang, p	0	0	0	0	0
						Murphy, pr	0	0	0	0	0
						Jenkins, ph	1	0	0	0	0
Totals	33	3	10	27	9	Totals	34	2	8	27	8

Boston	200 001 000	3–10–0
Chicago	001 000 001	2–8–1

2B: Gardner 2, Felsch; 3B: Risberg; Home Run: Gainer; SB: Gardner; LOB: Boston 6, Chicago 8; DP: Schalk and Gandil, J. Collins and Schalk; BB: Williams 2, Ruth 3: Wolfgang 1; K: Williams 5, Ruth 3; Umpires: Dinneen and O'Loughlin; Time of Game: 1:52

Manager Jack Barry's choice for mound duty in the second game of the series, George Foster, was somewhat of a surprise. Nonetheless, the short and stocky righthander they called Rube, who had strung together 14 and 8, 19 and 8, and 17–7 seasons prior to 1917, was well rested, and in the spacious acreage of Comiskey Park he was expected to be very effective. Pants Rowland countered, more likely out of dire necessity, with Eddie Cicotte, whose last effort was his scintillating one-hitter against the Senators. Barry also moved Doc Hoblitzell, lefthanded hitting first baseman into the third slot of the batting order against righthander Cicotte. He replaced Del Gainer, who had been in the lineup against portsider Claude Williams the previous day.

This time it was Boston errors that marred the game. The Chicagos were the ones who benefitted, this time playing errorless baseball, as they made the Red Sox earn the pair of runs they managed to wrangle from Eddie Cicotte's superior effort. Foster, who worked creditably into the seventh, was the loser when the Chicagoans hustled four markers across the plate, partly due to bad throws and otherwise sloppy defensive play by the Red Sox. Herb Pennock, rushed onto the scene in an effort to stem the Pale Hose tide, was almost immediately victimized by a Schalk and Cicotte double steal that put them on second and third. That didn't

Babe Ruth broke even against the Sox in 1917 with a 3 and 3 record. Overall, he was a 24 game winner and led the American League with 35 complete games. The big fellow never did anything in half-measures. (Dennis Colgin)

help the Beantowners' cause any. After jamming up the base paths with a walk to Eddie Collins, The General, Joe Jackson, came along to crack one of his patented line drives into right scoring both Schalk and Cicotte. Pennock was sent packing and Sam Jones came on to finish up the game that evened up the series. Little Eddie won his 16th as compared to 6 losses to pace both major leagues. The final score read 5 to 2 and at the end of the day the White Sox found themselves 2½ games better than The Carmine in the standings.

The Red Sox vs. the White Sox at Comiskey Park, July 20, 1917

Boston	AB	R	H	PO	A	Chicago	AB	R	H	PO	A
Walsh, cf	4	0	0	6	0	Leibold, rf	3	0	1	1	0
Barry, 2b	4	0	1	0	1	Weaver, 3b	4	0	0	0	1
Hoblitzel, 1b	4	0	0	7	2	E. Collins, 2b	2	1	0	1	3
Gardner, 3b	4	1	1	0	3	Jackson, lf	4	0	1	1	0
Hooper, rf	3	1	0	1	0	Felsch, cf	3	0	1	4	1
Lewis, lf	2	0	1	1	0	Gandil, 1b	4	0	0	12	0
Scott, ss	3	0	1	2	3	Risberg, ss	4	1	0	0	4
Thomas, c	3	0	0	5	0	Schalk, c	3	2	1	8	1
Foster, (LP)	2	0	0	2	0	Cicotte, (WP)	2	1	1	0	1
Pennock, p	0	0	0	0	0						
Jones, p	1	0	0	0	0						
Totals	30	2	4	24	9	Totals	29	5	5	27	11

Boston	000 010 100	2–4–3
Chicago	000 010 40x	5–5–1

3B: Scott; DP: Felsch and Schalk; BB: Cicotte 1, Foster 3, Pennock 1; K: Cicotte 6, Foster 2; Wild Pitch: Jones; Umpires: O'Loughlin and Dinneen; Time of Game: 2:10

The third game of the pivotal Bosox-Chisox series didn't have a winner. Struggling stubbornly through 15 innings with neither side minded to give in, the decision-maker in this one proved to be umpire Bill Dinneen, who called an end to the extra inning drama that kept another capacity crowd in their seats until, in Dinneen's judgement, it was too long into the early evening to play any more baseball. Between the first pitch and the last out first sacker Chick Gandil had recorded 21 putouts, White Sox infielders had collaborated on some 28 assists, and were charged with six errors, and despite all the hitting, seven walks and a hit batsman in the 15 innings the White Sox left only six men on base and Boston, ten.

Each time Boston came up with a run, or in the case of the

sixth frame, three, the Chicagoans answered with the same number, so that by the time Ump Dinneen called it, each side had tallied five times, thus postponing to another day any direct change in the league standings. Chicago's Hall of Fame battery, Red Faber and Ray Schalk started out. Faber was followed by Chief Rowland's premier reliever, Dave Danforth, who came on in the seventh, finally retiring in favor of Lefty Williams, who finished up.

For Boston, Dutch Leonard, starting the game at 9 and 10, went the first ten, followed by the irrepressible Ruth, who pitched the last five stanzas. Though Mr. G. H. Ruth would also be admitted to the Hall of Fame, it was not to be as a pitcher. He did hit a few home runs later in his career to elevate him to Cooperstown Status, but that was down the line a few years and in a different uniform. As a result, two Famers from each ball club battled through the long afternoon, Faber and Schalk for Chicago and Harry Hooper and The Babe for Boston. None of them put their teams in a position to win, though Ruth came close to losing the whole bag of groceries by allowing a Swede Risberg three-bagger that resulted in tying the score in the 14th inning. But he quickly retired the side without any further damage. So after three games the two teams stood at 1–1–1, about as even at that point as two peas in a pod.

Boston at Chicago, July 21, 1917

Boston	AB	R	H	PO	A	Chicago	AB	R	H	PO	A
Walsh, cf	6	0	2	3	0	J. Collins, rf	7	2	3	1	0
Barry, 2b	6	1	1	1	2	Weaver, 3b	5	1	1	6	5
Hoblitzel, 1b	3	1	1	6	0	E. Collins, 2b	6	0	1	1	5
Gardner, 3b	5	1	0	1	3	Jackson, lf	5	1	1	4	1
Hooper, rf	6	1	2	3	0	Felsch, cf	6	0	2	4	0
Lewis, lf	7	0	2	7	0	Gandil, 1b	6	0	1	21	0
Scott, ss	5	0	1	4	3	Risberg, ss	5	1	1	4	7
Thomas, c	3	0	0	6	2	Schalk, c	5	0	1	4	4
Leonard, p	4	0	0	0	3	Faber, p	1	0	0	0	1
Walker, ph	1	0	0	0	0	Danforth, p	2	0	0	0	3
Agnew, c	1	0	0	4	1	Williams, p	0	0	0	0	3
Gainer, 1b	4	0	1	9	1	McMullin, ph	1	0	0	0	0
Ruth, p	2	1	0	1	1	Lynn, ph	1	0	0	0	0
						Murphy, pr	0	0	0	0	0
Totals	53	5	10	45	16	Totals	50	5	11	45	29

| Boston | 010 003 000 000 010 | 5–10–0 |
| Chicago | 000 103 000 000 010 | 5–11–5 |

2B: Scott 1, J. Collins 2, Gainer, Walsh; 3B: Jackson, Walsh, Risberg; SB: E. Collins 2, Thomas; Sac. Hits: Hooper, Gardner, Weaver, Barry; Sac. Fly: Gardner; LOB: Chicago 6, Boston 10; DP: Barry, Scott, Gainer and Agnew; BB: Faber 1, Leonard 2, Ruth 2, Danforth 2; K: Leonard 3, Danforth 2, Ruth 2; Hit by Pitcher: Shalk, by Leonard; Umpires: Dinneen and O'Loughlin; Time of Game: 3:55

It's probably never quite right to say that on a certain day one ball player or another was "the whole show" because baseball is a

The Boston pitching staff, coming back intact after pacing the Red Sox to the 1916 world's championship, included, L to R: Rube Foster (8 and 7 in 1917); Carl Mays, who posted his first 20-game season in 1917; Ernie Shore, author of that famous perfect game against the Senators on June 23, 1917, a game remembered more for Babe Ruth being bounced after complaining about calls to the first batter of the game—it was Shore who came in and then retired 27 straight; Babe Ruth (326.1 IP and 2.01 ERA in 1917); and Hub Leonard (16 game winner, 2.17 ERA in 1917). (Brace photograph)

team game that is affected by so many different players and circumstances. But on July 22, two fellows came close. They were the
ol' Texan, Reb Russell, and the young 'un, shortfielder Swede Risberg, who combined with the sore-armed southpaw to lead the Pale
Hose to a 2 to 0 conquest of the Red Sox, putting the Chisox 3½
up on Boston. It was a heart-throbber, and the final outcome would
have meant that either the Chicagos would end up the series with
a comfortable lead as they prepared to hit the road for 23 games
in foreign ports of call—or—Boston, with a win, could position
itself with still another win in the series closer to leave town within
two games of the frontrunning Chisox.

The Reb and Swede show dashed any hopes the Red Sox and
their loyal following might have had to leave the Windy City still
hot on the heels of the Comiskeymen. After the 2 to 0 licking they
absorbed at the hands of the two principals, Russell and Risberg,
that would have to wait.

In the first place, Sir Ewell, the affable southerner, threw his
variety of fluff, benders and feathers, along with an occasional
quickie, so effectively that the big sticks of the Bostons wilted in a
feeble, four hit effort that netted nothing but frustration. Risberg,
principally, and Russell secondarily, were the movers and shakers
of the day. After Riz doubled in the second inning, Ray Schalk
bunted safely to move the big Swede all the way over to third, after
which he scored the first run on a pop fly in foul territory by Russell that Larry Gardner ran down. Gardner's throw to the plate was
right on the money and arrived well ahead of Risberg. But Swede
put such a jarring slide on catcher Sam Agnew that the ball popped
loose and the Sox had the only run they really needed.

Another capacity throng braved threatening weather to see this
one. Their numbers, upwards of 25–26,000, swelled the season
count, well on its way to league leadership in that department also.
That's what pennant contenders will stir up as they battle for the
lead. Fenway Park, the home of Boston's defending champs would
be waiting with its own full house. The series there would be played
in just a matter of a few days.

Red Sox at Chicago, July 22, 1917

Boston	AB	R	H	PO	A	Chicago	AB	R	H	PO	A
Walsh, cf	4	0	0	0	0	Leibold, rf	4	0	3	1	0
Barry, 2b	4	0	1	0	3	Weaver, 3b	2	0	0	0	0
Gainer, 1b	4	0	0	9	0	E. Collins, 2b	4	0	1	3	1
Gardner, 3b	3	0	1	4	2	Jackson, lf	4	0	2	3	0
Hooper, rf	3	0	0	0	0	Felsch, cf	4	0	1	1	0
Lewis, lf	3	0	0	3	1	Gandil, 1b	4	1	3	10	1
Scott, ss	3	0	0	5	0	Risberg, ss	4	1	2	3	7
Agnew, c	2	0	0	2	1	Schalk, c	3	0	1	5	1
Janvrin, ph	1	0	1	0	0	Russell, (WP)	2	0	0	1	1
Thomas, c	0	0	0	0	0						
Mays, (LP)	2	0	1	1	3						
Walker, ph	1	0	0	0	0						
Bader, p	0	0	0	0	1						
Totals	30	0	4	24	11	Totals	31	2	13	27	11

Boston	000 000 000	0–4–1
Chicago	010 001 00x	2–13–0

2B: Risberg, Leibold; SB: Barry, Gandil, Felsch; Sac. Hits: Weaver 2; Sac. Fly: Russell; LOB: Boston 3, Chicago 9; DP: Mays and Gainer, Lewis, Bader and Scott; BB: Mays 1, Russell 0; K: Mays 1, Russell 0; Wild Pitch: Mays; Umpires: O'Loughlin and Dinneen; Time of Game: 1:59

The 2–0 triumph put the White Sox within a victory of winning the series three games to one, thus enabling them to wind up their hometand with a 13–6–1 mark, fortifying them for the road trip ahead. For that final series game Rowland would send Lefty Williams against Boston's tall and talented righthander, Ernie Shore. In contrast to the White Sox' victorious home stand, the Red Sox awaited the final game of their road trip with a disappointing 6 and 9 record, dropping from a half-game lead before they left Beantown to a 3½ game deficit. Although that's one of the things that so often awaits a travelling ball club, championship ball clubs usually play at least on a break-even level on the road, hoping to win two out of three in their home stadium. Boston's road was uphill after this road trip.

Enter The Happy One. Oscar Emil Felsch, the muscular, free-wheeling Milwaukeean who, during the exciting 1916 battle with the Red Sox for supremacy of the Junior Circuit had recorded his first

.300 season while leading the league in fielding percentage, found the offerings of Ernie Shore and Sam Jones just what the doctor ordered to spruce up his 1917 batting average. In the process of recording a 4 for 4 day, which included a double and a triple, he doused Boston's last remaining hope to regain some of the ground that was lost in this pivotal series. The final score was 5 to 3 and every one of the Felsch blows figured in the White Sox' victory.

Felsch and Co. moved out to a 3–0 lead by the time three rounds had been completed, giving starter Lefty Williams the cushion he needed to withstand a pesky, steady stream of Red Sox baserunners. Boston's attack, which had been blunted at first, broke through with a pair of tallies in the top of the fourth, tightening up the ball game, but the Pale Hose extended their lead to 5–2 in the sixth with a combination of Felsch, Risberg and Schalk singles.

Behind some flashy fielding, featuring Chick Gandil, among others, Williams stayed afloat on into the eighth. An unassisted double-up bailed Lefty out of trouble right off the bat in the opening inning when, with playing-manager Jack Barry on third and Del Gainer on first, Larry Gardner scorched a Williams hook that Gandil speared. Chick doubled Gainer, off with the crack of the bat, by stepping on first. During the course of the game other fielding gems were contributed by Ray Schalk, Nemo Leibold and Buck Weaver, all contributing to a flawless defensive exhibition.

But Williams didn't make it through the eighth. With a run already scored, Boston loaded the bases with two out. Looking at a potential disaster, Rowland sent Williams to the dugout, and without hesitation replaced him with his ace, Cicotte, to face Dick Hoblitzell, who had been sent up to hit in the ninth spot of the batting order. Manager Barry had the right idea, but Cicotte foiled another of those "best laid plans" by disposing of The Doc, ending the threat. There were no further Boston shenanigans and the ninth ended harmlessly without a run, Cicotte picking up the save, Williams the win, and Boston the frustration that accompanied a 4½ game deficit as they headed homeward.

Boston Red Sox vs. Chicago White Sox at Comiskey Park, July 23, 1917

Boston	AB	R	H	PO	A	*Chicago*	AB	R	H	PO	A
Walsh, cf	4	0	1	1	0	Leibold, rf	4	0	0	1	0
Barry, 2b	3	0	1	0	8	Weaver, 3b	4	1	1	4	3

	AB	R	H	PO	A		AB	R	H	PO	A
Gainer, 1b	4	0	1	13	1	E. Collins, 2b	4	0	1	1	2
Agnew, c	1	0	0	1	0	Jackson, lf	3	1	0	1	1
Gardner, 3b	4	2	1	2	1	Felsch, cf	4	2	4	3	0
Hooper, rf	4	1	1	0	1	Gandil, 1b	4	0	1	9	0
Lewis, lf	4	0	2	3	1	Risberg, ss	2	1	1	0	0
Scott, ss	4	0	2	0	1	Schalk, c	3	0	1	8	0
McNally, pr	0	0	0	0	0	Wil'ms, (WP)	3	0	0	0	1
Bader, p	0	0	0	0	1	Cicotte, (SV)	0	0	0	0	0
Thomas, c	3	0	0	1	1						
Janvrin, ss	0	0	0	1	0						
Shore, (LP)	2	0	0	1	1						
Walker, ph	1	0	1	0	0						
Jones, p	0	0	0	0	0						
Cady, ph	0	0	0	0	0						
Hoblitzel, 1b	1	0	0	1	0						
Totals	35	3	10	24	16	Totals	31	5	9	27	7

Boston	000 200 010	3–10–0
Chicago	013 001 00x	5–9–0

2B: Felsch, Scott, Walsh; 3B: Felsch; SB: E. Collins, Weaver; LOB: Chicago 4, Boston 9; DP: Gandil unassisted, Thomas and Garner; BB: Williams 3, Shore 2; K: Shore 1, Cicotte 1, Williams 5; Hit by Pitcher: Gardner, by Williams; Wild Pitch: Shore; Umpires: Dinnean and O'Loughlin; Time of Game: 2:00

Hap Felsch's perfect day closed out his Boston series average at .429 on 9 hits in 21 official at bats. The Bosox' cleanup hitter, Larry Gardner, was next in line with a .350 average (7 for 20). White Sox pitching held Boston hitters to a .210 batting average, while the Boston hurlers were hit for a .263 average by the Chisox. Among the series pitchers Babe Ruth emerged as the best of the Bostons, giving up but a pair of runs in the series opener as well as turning in a scoreless, five-inning relief stint in the 15-inning marathon. In that same game, Red Faber and Dave Danforth combined to yield but one earned run in 13 innings. But the pitching star of the series was Reb Russell, whose four-hit shutout in game four put the Pale Hose out in front two games to one.

Defensively, the two clubs commited a dozen errors in 51 innings of play, Chicago contributing seven of them. That was countered by some exceptional defensive work, most notably in the last game of the series by Chicago's stout play, not only in getting to the ball, but in throwing it with deadly accuracy.

As both clubs sped eastward on overnight trains, Boston

headed homeward to host the Browns, and Chicago to New York to take on the Yanks at the Polo Grounds, both Jack Barry and Pants Rowland were assessing the ins and outs of the five-game encounter at Comiskey Park. There was time enough, with a scheduled day off, to think about series openers later, although it had already been determined that Eddie Cicotte and Red Faber would open the Yankee series doubleheader at the Polo Grounds, while up there in the Back Bay, Jack Barry would open against the Browns with Dutch Leonard.

The overriding fact of life coming out of the series was Chicago's convincing and superior play in every phase of the game. Not only did they overcome a fine effort on the part of Babe Ruth and his Boston compadres in the opening game, they just got stronger with each passing inning of play. Whatever was called for was there, be it laying the ball down to advance a runner, relaying to nail a baserunner, coming up with a clutch hit, stealing a base (there

Little Napoleon, John McGraw. After rebuilding his team in 1916, McGraw's Giants were the acknowledged National League frontrunners in 1917 and they won the pennant by a comfortable margin. It was the fifth for Mr. Giants during the Deadball Era.

were eight of them for the Chisox, two of them in the Schalk-Cicotte double steal that resulted in a go-ahead run), or mixing speed with breaking ball pitching in just the right combination of pitching assignments. In a word, the White Sox played at championship levels with few low spots to ruin their otherwise stellar performance.

Whether that made the Commisar, Hizonor Comiskey, so happy that he decided to go west to watch the wonders of Old Faithful (he departed for Yellowstone with relatives immediately after the last out of the series) is not known, but of a certainty, Commy, Rowland and Gleason must have felt a great deal better about the team's chances after the Boston series. By dint of their outstanding play in the Boston series, the Sox had signalled that they were about to change the script that unfolded in 1916. They had the Red Sox on the run.

The National League race, meantime, was grinding along, as much as foul weather would permit, to a point where John McGraw's Giants had stretched their league lead to 8½ games over Christy Mathewson's Cincinnati Reds, the current runnersup. During the first three weeks in July they ran over their opponents without mercy, the customary habit of a McGraw winner, with a 15 out of 20 stretch, as they finished up their homestand with a 6–2 win over the hapless Pirates. Four teams were above the .500 level at that point, as follows:

	Won	Lost	Pct.
New York	53	27	.663
Cincinnati	52	43	.598
St. Louis	48	40	.545
Philadelphia	42	37	.532

As they prepared to head west, Ferdie Schupp sported an 11 and 4 record, Slim Sallee had upped his record to 9 and 4, Pol Perritt raised his to 8 and 4, and Rube Benton checked in with an 8–3 mark. The McGraw bandwagon was rolling. Having developed depth on the mound, and with an upswing in Giant hitting, they were positioning themselves to withstand the inordinate number of doubleheaders that were necessary to make up their sharp deficit in games played. But with August right around the corner, National League teams were on notice that if they had pennant aspirations, they had better get around to doing something about it. Fast.

CHAPTER 7

Frontrunning Pale Hose

The race for American League supremacy was on in dead earnest. Boston and Chicago, in anticipation of their upcoming four game set at Fenway Park, eyed one another warily from a distance, the Red Sox at home against the Browns and the Chisox at the Polo Grounds against the Yanks. Both clubs finished their assignments for the day in winning form, Boston by a 5 to 4 margin over St. Louis and the White Sox twice victorious in a sweep of Wild Bill Donovan's New Yorkers. That put Chicago's cushion at five games, a highwater mark for the season to that point.

Was that too good to be true? Well, yes. The very next day, as the New York Times reported that Uncle Sam's folks were "not awake to the peril confronting them" and, with the War Department requesting a monstrous $2,500,000,000 for coastal defense, beefed up Army appropriations and for loans abroad, the White Sox took it on the chin, losing to Frank Baker and the Yankees in 14 innings, 6 to 5. Both news items served as reality checks, especially in Chicago. And while the New York marathon unfolded on an oppressively hot day in Gotham, so did a doubleheader victory in Boston. That jerked the Pale Hose lead back to 3½ games pronto.

On July 27 the Sox picked up a half game on Boston, idled by

rain in Beantown, as they beat the Yankees in a close ball game, at
least through six innings, that was finally put away with a three-run
surge in the top of the eighth. One of the more interesting events
of the day was a run the Rowlandmen didn't score, reported by the
New York Times this way:

> The latest edition of umpires, George Moriarty,* got into a jam
> with the Sox players in the eighth inning when he made a deci-
> sion calling Eddie Collins out at the platter. On this play
> (Urban) Shocker was sprawled across the base line as Collins
> came sliding home. He dropped the ball, a throw from (catcher
> Roxy) Walters, but, as he had Collins blocked, he recovered
> the ball and tagged him. It seems that a short time ago Billy
> Evans had a play like this in Chicago and called the runner safe
> because Schalk had blocked the runner by occupying all the
> available space on the base line, thereby halting all traffic.
>   Manager Rowland and Kid Gleason, his first assistant, tried
> to point out to Moriarty was just opposite to the precedent
> established by his partner in umperical crime, Evans. Although
> Moriarty has been umpiring only a short time he has already
> acquired a tin ear, and all the Chicago conversation went for
> naught. The White Sox orators insisted that it wasn't because
> they lost the darned old run that they were kicking at it, it was
> the principle of the thing.

Of course, that didn't work, and as things turned out the Sox
didn't need the run. Reb Russell picked up the 9 to 6 victory, his
eleventh against but four losses, though he needed late-inning relief
help from Eddie Cicotte. After the 14-inning heart-breaker of the
day before, skipper Rowland was taking no chances with this one,
working under the theory that the wider the margin between his
ball club and Boston he could take to the next series, the greater
the club's chances of surviving it with a decent lead.

In the third inning of the Sox' 9–5 triumph Reb Russell, noted
previously as one of the better hitting hurlers in the game, tripled.
After Nemo Leibold was retired on a grounder, switch-hitting Buck
Weaver blasted one of Ray "Sum" Caldwell's righthanded offerings

---

*George Moriarty, in his rookie season of American League umpiring, had just finished
his major league career during the 1916 season. Pants Rowland and Kid Gleason knew
him well—as a member of the White Sox during his final playing days.

into the right center field bleachers, putting the Sox up two. It was one of 12 safe blows he registered in the five-game series, demonstrating both at the plate and afield what he could do playing at full tilt.

This was clearly a Weaver series. He hit .444, turning in ten putouts and 16 assists in a flawless *tour de force* that didn't go without notice in New York. It seemed that just when the Yanks had things settled down, or were about to score, Weaver was there to upset the Bronx applecart. And, it should be noted that Weaver's minor miracles in this series were performed, at least in part, from short, not third, after Swede Risberg had collided with a concrete barrier chasing a pop fly in the third game of the series. (Risberg did, however, come back to finish the New York series.) Buck moved in at short with Freddy McMullin taking over at third, making spectacular stops and catches that were greeted by New York applause on several occasions.

George Daniel Weaver, far better known as simply Buck, was the best third baseman in The Bigs during the 1917 season, certainly, and throughout the 1910s, arguably. The hawk-faced infielder was one of baseball's more gritty, rough-and-tumble ball players whose spikes were every bit as sharply filed as Ty Cobb's. That said, it should be pointed out that he was nattily attired in "the latest" of the day, and further, that he was no stranger to the bustling nightlife of the league's cities. It was Weaver, who, incidentally, helped Shoeless Joe upgrade his wardrobe and appearance and get his teeth straightened and glossed up, who was in the vanguard of the Sox' "city-slicker" brigade. He had made the around-the-world tour of 1913–14, enjoyed it immensely, and never forgot it. The man was never quite content with ordinary surroundings or the hum-drum of work-a-day life even though he spent many years after the Black Sox scandal as a daily grind pharmacist in Chicago, his days of flash and sparkle by that time long gone.

Acquired for the 1912 season, "The Ginger Kid," as he was often called, hit searing line drives, threw runners out with screaming throws across the infield and, while playing third base, was absolutely death on bunted balls. So feared was he in that respect that no less than Ty Cobb refused to lay the ball down the third base line—or anywhere near it—when the Tigers and White Sox teed it up. Nor did he head into any base Weaver was covering spikes up. Buck had filed his before every Tiger series, just in case.

As one of the Sox of longer tenure the flashy infielder rode at the front of the bus where players of seniority were accustomed to ride. By 1917 he was a veteran of five seasons, having served under three managers. Though his average had dipped to .227 in 1916, he was on his way to a more robust season in 1917, finishing at .284 in 112 ball games. (Not too far ahead in August he would be sidelined for better than five weeks with a nasty finger injury, thus accounting for more than 40 games riding the bench while his hand was healing.)

The Weaver years in Chicago came to an end with Comiskey's September 28, 1920, suspension of "The Eight Men Out." When Judge Landis banned Weaver and the other seven players for life, his nine year career was over. His Chicago record:

Year	GP	AB	R	H	BB	EXBH	OBP	SA	SB	FR	BA	TPR
1912	147	523	55	117	9	30	.245	.300	12	-6	.224	-2.7
1913	151	533	51	145	15	29	.302	.356	20	34	.272	3.9
1914	136	541	64	133	20	31	.279	.327	14	5	.246	-0.4
1915	148	536	83	151	32	32	.316	.355	24	1	.268	0.6
1916	151	582	78	132	30	36	.280	,309	22	7	.227	-0.5
1917	118	447	64	127	27	24	.332	.362	19	9	.284	1.8
1918	112	420	37	126	11	17	.323	.352	20	0	.300	0.7
1919	140	571	89	169	11	45	.315	.401	22	0	.296	0.3
1920	151	629	102	208	28	44	.365	.420	19	-10	.331	-0.1
Totals	1254	4809	623	1308	183	288	.307	.355	172	39	.272	3.6

However well Buck Weaver may have been playing in the New York series, it was to no avail on the final day at the Polo Grounds when the Yankees crushed Pale Hose spirits, knocking off Red Faber and Jim Scott by one-run margins, 5 to 4 and 4 to 3. While that despressing development was taking place, Boston, up to a mischievous afternoon of their own, twice turned aside the St. Louis Browns, both times by a 3–2 margin. For the Chicagoans it was a very bad afternoon, all things considered, their lead chopped to a pair of games—and even up in the loss column—with another showdown staring them in the face at Fenway Park.

So what started out so grandly with a twin-whipping of the Yanks in the series opener ended up the same way it started, only with the Yanks on the payoff end of a twinbill sweep on the back end of the six game set. One thing had to be better in Boston: the weather. Playing two games in 90+ degree heat with humidity to

The smiling fellow in this picture, Buck Weaver, "The Ginger Kid," was tough as barbed wire, the only player Ty Cobb wouldn't bunt or run on with spikes high. (Transcendental Graphics)

match was about all either ball club could bear in New York's torrid mid-summer heat wave.

On the morning of the series opener in Beantown the New
York Limited hurried the White Sox northward for a day off to
gather themselves for the skirmish ahead. Apparently no one had
told the weatherman just how far up the coast Boston was, because
what he had waiting for everyone in Bunker Hill Land was more
of the same merciless heat that wilted New Yorkers—and, the White
Sox.

Manager Jack Barry had 22-year-old Babe Ruth rested and
ready for Chicago's invasion. At 15 and 6 he was two behind Eddie
Cicotte's league-leading 17, and his 95 whiffs were four ahead of
teammate Dutch Leonard's 91, leading American League pitchers.
By season's end the big fellow would have won 24, paced league
hurlers in complete games with 35 and would place third in
hits/game at 6.73. To make it a left hander's affair, Pants Rowland
sent Claude Williams to the hill. What worked for Barry didn't work
for Rowland and the Pale Hose went down 3 to 1, able to muster
but four hits good for a single tally in the second stanza. That wasn't
nearly enough, as the Bosox put the game away already in the bottom of the opening inning with a two run spurt that turned out to
be sufficient not only to win, but to edge within a game of the White
Sox, causing the standings to look like this:

	Won	Lost	Pct.
Chicago	61	36	.629
Boston	58	35	.624

Chicago at Fenway Park, July 30, 1917

Chicago	AB	R	H	PO	A	Boston	AB	R	H	PO	A
J. Collins, rf	4	0	0	3	0	Walsh, cf	3	1	1	0	0
Weaver, 3b	3	0	0	1	0	Barry, 2b	2	0	2	3	5
E. Collins, 2b	4	0	0	3	3	Gainer, 1b	4	1	1	11	0
Jackson, lf	4	1	1	5	1	Gardner, 3b	3	0	0	1	2
Felsch, cf	2	0	1	2	0	Hooper, rf	3	0	1	1	0
Gandil, 1b	3	0	0	9	0	Lewis, lf	3	0	1	5	0
Risberg, ss	3	0	1	1	2	Scott, ss	3	0	0	2	4
Schalk, c	2	0	1	1	0	Agnew, c	3	1	1	4	1
Will'ms, (LP)	0	0	0	0	1	Ruth, (WP)	2	0	1	0	3

McMul'n, ph	1	0	0	0	0					
Danforth, p	2	0	0	0	1					
Totals	28	1	4	24	8	Totals	26	3	8	27	15

Chicago 010 000 000 1–4–2
Boston 120 000 00x 3–8–2

2B: Gainer; 3B: Jackson; Sac. Hits: Barry, Ruth; Sac. Flies: Felsch, Barry; LOB: Boston 4, Chicago 4; DP: Scott, Barry and Gainer, E. Collins, Risberg and Gandil, Gardner, Barry and Gainer; Jackson and E. Collins; BB: Williams 1, Danforth 1, Ruth 3; K: Danforth 1, Ruth 4; Umpires: Dinneen and O'Loughlin; Time of Game: 1:55

The heat was on. Another loss and the Sox would find themselves once again looking up. That's exactly what happened as July used up its last, steaming day in Massachusetts. This time the score was 5 to 2, the Beantowners once again scoring all that was needed in their very first at bat, pushing three across at the expense of the Pale Hose ace, Eddie Cicotte. Eddie went down to his seventh defeat, snapping a six-game winning streak. On this red hot day in the Back Bay, the red-hosed Bostons touched up the Sox' best hurler for 11 hits, pounding him around without respect for his tricky offerings or for his lofty status among the league's pitchers. Consequently, they commandeered the league lead, nudging ahead of the Comiskey forces by six one-hundreths of a percentage point. They were two less in the win column than the Chicagos, but also two less in the important loss column. The time had come, as far as Rowland and Co. were concerned, to redraw that line in the dirt.

White Sox at Red Sox, July 31, 1917

Chicago	*AB*	*R*	*H*	*PO*	*A*	*Boston*	*AB*	*R*	*H*	*PO*	*A*
J. Collins, rf	4	1	1	2	0	Walsh, cf	4	1	1	4	0
Weaver, 3b	3	0	1	0	2	Barry, 2b	3	1	1	1	3
E. Collins, 2b	3	1	1	1	3	Hobliz'l, 1b	4	1	2	11	0
Jackson, lf	3	0	0	1	0	Gardner, 3b	4	0	2	1	3
Felsch, cf	4	0	2	3	1	Hooper, rf	4	1	1	1	0
Gandil, 1b	4	0	2	12	1	Lewis, lf	4	1	3	4	0
Risberg, ss	3	0	0	0	1	Scott, ss	2	0	1	1	4
Schalk, c	3	0	0	5	1	Thomas, c	4	0	1	4	1
Cicotte, (LP)	2	0	0	0	2	Leon'd, (WP)	3	0	1	0	2
Lynn, ph	1	0	0	0	0						

| Williams, p | 0 | 0 | 0 | 0 | 1 | | | | | |
| Totals | 30 | 2 | 7 | 24 | 12 | Totals | 32 | 5 | 13 | 27 | 13 |

Chicago	200 000 000	2–7–0
Boston	300 100 10x	5–13–0

2B: Weaver, Lewis, Leonard, Felsch; HR: Hooper; Sac. Hits: Weaver, E. Collins, Scott (2), Barry; Left on Base: Boston 7, Chicago 4; DP: Scott, Barry and Hoblitzel, Schalk unassisted, Felsch and Gandil; BB: Cicotte 1, Leonard 1; K: Cicotte 3, Leonard 4; Umpires: O'Loughlin and Dinneen; Time of Game: 1:58

He had whitewashed the Bosox in the Chicago series, hadn't he? Why not once more! Ol' Tex, Ewell Russell, impish smile and all, was Pants Rowland's choice to rub a little winning magic on his battered forces in an attempt to bring a halt to Boston's momentum. The series might still be saved, and the White Sox might yet be able to leave Beantown with a game lead—IF they were able to bring this latter day Boston massacre under control. So The Rebel got the ball. Arrayed against him as August debuted was none less than submariner Carl Mays, doing as well as if not a mite better than staffmate Babe Ruth.

Well now, White Sox fans, Mr. Russell did all that was asked of him. And more. With a monstrous triple to deep center that might easily have been an inside the park home run had he not been held up at third (anyone else in the lineup would have been given the green light), and a single, he not only did his pitching thing, but added the usual batting tricks that accompanied his outings. For you Red Sox fans, discouraged by having had such a brief taste of the first place wine, there would be another game on August 2 and still another series with the Chicago outfit later in the month. There was still time for reckoning, still time make up for the indignities heaped upon the hometown nine by Russell's dominating six-hit shutout. After the 4–0 conquest, the standings were:

	Won	*Lost*	*Pct.*
Chicago	62	37	.626
Boston	59	36	.622

In this game, the third well-played contest of the series, there was a role reversal. This time it was the Pale Hose that scored the first runs in a two-run opening round of fire. Those two were enough inasmuch as Reb's stuff was sufficient to get by very nicely through nine goose-egg innings.

That is not to say that it was strictly an afternoon concert by a one-man band. Russell did get help. For starters, there was more of summer's searing heat. That plus some of the Reb's own special linament kept his tendinitis in check, enabling him to toss up those big benders and nothing balls at just the right mixture of speeds with change-ups and tantalizing strikes that were to be found on the black edges of the plate. Then too, there were some troublemakers in the middle of the batting order who not only offensively, but defensively, pitched in to help the Texan along. In the first inning The General, Joe Jackson, laced a shot past the center field flag pole and legged it all the way around the bases, scoring Eddie Collins, who had doubled, ahead of him. Later, Hap Felsch took a triple away from Tilly Walker with a dazzling running catch of Walker's shot to right center. Buck Weaver and Swede Risberg chipped in with some highway robbery of their own on smashes that were headed for extra base territory.

It all came together in a scintillating afternoon of championship baseball. And it came at *the* most critical point of the 1917 season. For those inclined to search out the one game in the season that made all the difference in the championship race, it would be unnecessary to look beyond this one. This was the game that restored White Sox spirits, as well as a measure of supremacy. Further, that supremacy was restored at the expense of the defending champion Red Sox right under Bostonian noses. While it is true that the race would remain tight through mid-August, and that once more, on August 17 to be exact, the Comiskeymen would have to renew their hold on the league's top spot, this very ball game at Fenway Park was the one that stemmed Boston's determined rush to repeat as American League champ when it was most needed.

During the course of the next several weeks both teams would record identical 9 and 7 records, bringing them back into head to head competition in Chicago for a four game series that would test each ball club's mettle all over again. However, had the Red Sox swept their Fenway Park series, or had they won three of four, it would have meant that a break-even series at Comiskey, at very least, would enable them to leave Chicago without as much game to game, inning to inning pressure than might otherwise have mounted. But Reb Russell and his Chicago teammates changed all that. What is more, it was the Texan, who in that Chicago series later in August, would, remarkably, go through the same shutout routine to trample Boston hopes once again. By that time Reb was well on his way to the best winning percentage the American League had to offer, .750, fashioned on a 15 and 5 record for the season. The Carmine finally did catch up with him, but it was too little and too late even though there must have been great satisfaction in once and for all stomping on this pestiforous White Sox nuisance, handing him his fifth loss of the season on September 24. Following is the Russell record.

Year	GP	W	L	Pct.	SH	IP	BB	K	OBA	OB%	PB*	TPI
1913#	51	22	16	.579	8	316	79	122	.219	.273	3	4.2
1914	38	8	12	.368	1	167.1	33	79	.268	.308	4	-0.1
1915	41	11	10	.524	3	229.1	47	90	.249	.292	4	1.1
1916	56	18	11	.621	5	264.1	42	112	.220	.254	-4	0.6
1917	35	15	5	,750	5	189.1	32	54	.245	.279	5	2.2
1918	19	7	5	.583	2	124.2	33	38	.252	.302	-1	-0.2
1919	1	0	0	.000	0	0	0	0	1.000	1.000	0	0.0
Totals	241	81	59	.576	24	1291.1	267	495	.238	.281	11	7.8

*PB—Pitcher as Batter: Sabermetric measure, a linear measurement expressed in the number of Batting Runs a pitcher contributes to his team's offense. (Batting Runs indicate the number of runs contributed by a hitter in excess, or less than the number of runs by a league-average player [0].

#—In *Total Baseball Encyclopedia* baseball historian Bill Deane lists pitchers who would have merited a Rookie of the Year Award (p. 208, 2001 ed.): Reb Russell was named for the honor for the 1913 season.

On August 2 The Big Red, Urban Faber, brought his spitball and other hard-breaking stuff to Fenway to take on Ernie Shore in the final game of the four-game set. The aim of the two clubs was clear: Boston was out to win another, making it three out of four; Chicago was determined to win another before heading to Philadelphia, thus stretching its lead to two full games despite its dead-even status with Boston in the loss column.

Only one team could have its way. That team was Chicago, as the White Sox unearthed another star to pitch *and* hit the Red Sox into submission by a 7 to 1 count that at first blush might appear to have been a cakewalk. Not so. This one tightened up to the extent that Red Faber's 3 to 1 lead in the eighth inning was right next to torn apart by a determined Red Sox rally that wound up with loaded bases and the go-ahead run coming to the plate in the person of the Boston skipper, Jack Barry, with none out. Pants Rowland hurried on to take the ball from Faber and hand it over to the star of the game, Dauntless David Danforth, the American League's most active relief pitcher. There followed three outs that cut the heart out of the Bostons. The first two came in succession via the strike-out route, leaving the fate of the Red Sox in the hands of their third sacker and cleanup hitter, the dangerous Larry Gardner. Danforth, with his breaking stuff doing its devious best, caused Gardner to pop up, choking the rally and preserving the two-run lead going into the top of the ninth.

Saving the Sox from impending doom was apparently not all that Dave Danforth had in mind for this particular day. In the ninth the Pale Hose promptly tore loose a singles attack that loaded the bases. "The Knight of Kennett Square," Herb Pennock, rattled by the suddenness of the attack, then issued a free pass to Ray Schalk, which not only kept the bases jammed up with White Sox runners, but sent one of them, Hap Felsch, across the plate to make it 4 to 1. That brought up Mr. Danforth, who whaled the daylights out of a Pennock offering that soared over center fielder Tilly Walker's head, scoring three more.

The only order of business left was to get past the Red Sox in the bottom of the ninth. Re-enter Dauntless Dave, who added another pair of whiffs to his stint, sitting the Red Sox down in 1–2–3 order.

If ever two clutch, back-to-back pitching gems were more needed by the White Sox, it would take a story right out of *Grimm's Fairy Tales* to tell the tale. Red Faber got the win, but Dave Danforth got the hero's mantle and Chicago left town two games up on The Carmine.

Here's what Chicago's victory did to the standings at the end of the day:

	Won	Lost	Pct.
Chicago	63	37	.630
Boston	59	37	.615

Texan Reb Russell was one of the better hitting pitchers in the majors during his years with the Chisox. When his arm gave out he turned to outfielding and hit .368 with the 1922 Pirates. He was a Comiskey Park favorite. (Dennis Colgin)

There was, at the same time, some business being transacted by John McGraw's Giants, first with a four game set in Chicago, and then five more in Pittsburgh. Copping six of the nine, the Giants pumped up their win-count to 60 ball games as compared to but 30 losses. That put them 11½ games ahead of Philadelphia, which had recaptured the National League's second spot in what had already turned out to be a scrap for the league's second place money.

Just a year earlier the McGrawmen, reorganized with a lineup that had added principally Buck Herzog and Heinie Zimmerman, began putting the pieces together to wind up the season with the kind of momentum needed to put the Giants back into pennant contention. They were right on target to do just that and the incredible glories of September, 1916, turned out to be so special that even the Little Napoleon had trouble believing it. Surveying the world's championship possibilities, he knew just what to expect. It would be one of the Sox teams, and of the two, he preferred the red hosed Sox over the white because of the prestige that attached to knocking off the defending champion. It was apparent to all involved that he was not at all thrilled with the prospect of a Chicago-New York World Series even as the last month of the season was unfolding.

At the beginning of August (as of games of the 2nd) the top players among hitters and pitchers of the four frontrunners had posted the following records:

The Hitters

New York, NL	AB	R	H	BA	Phil., NL	AB	R	H	BA
Bennie Kauff	324	56	100	.309	G. Cravath	326	51	98	.301
George Burns	353	69	107	.303	B. Killefer	236	19	73	.285
H. Zimmerman	345	41	103	.299	M. Stock	335	47	93	.278
Bill Rariden	141	13	41	.291	G. Whitted	315	42	86	.273
Walter Holke	312	35	83	.266	F. Luderus	217	31	81	.273
D. Robertson	327	38	85	.260	D. Paskert	333	54	85	.255

Chicago, AL	AB	R	H	BA	Boston, AL	AB	R	H	BA
E. Reb Russell	46	4	15	.326	G. H. Ruth	75	6	28	.373
Buck Weaver	379	58	110	.290	Duffy Lewis	341	34	96	.282
Happy Felsch	373	45	108	.290	L. Gardner	349	34	97	.278
Chick Gandil	360	30	98	.272	D. Gainer	112	15	29	.259
Eddie Collins	359	57	97	.270	H. Hooper	360	56	92	.266
Joe Jackson	346	53	92	.266	R. Hoblitzell	258	34	65	.252

Left: The Babe's record after his July 19, 1917, win at Comiskey Park was 14 and 6. He was well on his way to 25–30 victories. (Dennis Colgin). *Right:* Henry Zimmerman, better known as Heinie Zim, was the National League's leading run-producer (102 RBI) for the 1917 Giants. One of McGraw's mainstays, he had starred for the Cubs (1907–1916) before returning to Chicago for the 1917 World Series.

The Pitchers

New York, NL	Won	Lost	Pct.	K/BB
Rube Benton	9	2	.818	39/12
Ferdie Schupp	13	5	.722	103/50
Slim Sallee	9	4	.692	29/19
Pol Perritt	9	4	.692	41/28
Jeff Tesreau	10	5	.667	59/34
Fred Anderson	7	7	.500	46/26

Philadelphia, NL	Won	Lost	Pct.	K/BB
G. Alexander	18	8	.692	122/31
Eppa Rixey	11	11	.500	66/47
Jim Lavender	6	6	.500	46/29
Erskine Mayer	5	5	.500	48/22

Chicago, AL	Won	Lost	Pct.	K/BB
E. Reb Russell	11	4	.738	44/22
Joey Benz	5	2	.714	18/17
Eddie Cicotte	17	8	.680	91/51
Dave Danforth	5	3	.625	48/58
Lefty Williams	11	6	.611	59/53
U. "Red" Faber	9	8	.529	44/48
Jim Scott	5	5	.500	32/30

Boston, AL	Won	Lost	Pct.	K/BB
Babe Ruth	16	6	.727	90/75
Carl Mays	12	6	.667	64/55
Herb Pennock	5	3	.625	28/18
Dutch Leonard	12	10	.545	95/48
Ernie Shore	9	8	.529	39/37
George Foster	3	4	.429	12/24

Team Fielding	GP	PO	A	E	FA
Chicago, AL	102	2789	1164	121	.970
Boston, AL	99	2686	1318	126	.969
New York, NL	90	2438	1191	129	.966
Philadelphia, NL	89	2398	1222	139	.963

CHAPTER 8

Boston Confrontation III

The pale-hosed Comiskeymen were rolling. They greeted August with a pair of wins in Boston, and then set their sights on Philadelphia, hopeful that a five-game set there would yield as many as four, or even five victories, enabling them to put some distance between themselves and Jack Barry's Bosox. There weren't many who would have thought that unlikely—not the way they were playing.

The Sox invasion of Philadelphia at Shibe Park started out well. Skipper Rowland looked to the veteran Jim Scott to give his fatigued pitching staff a bit of a respite, and he got it. Scotty turned in a route-going job that doused any hopes the A's might have had of beating the American League's frontrunners. Not only did the A's fail to win, they didn't even score, as Scott, another of the Sox' stable of breaking-ball pitchers, fired a sharp, 4 to 0 six-hitter that put the Chicagoans three games up on Boston, frustrated once again by Jim Bagby who was on his way to a 23-win season. Bagby led Cleveland to a 2–1 triumph over Babe Ruth and the Bosox.

The victory was James Scott's 26th and final career shutout. Known variously as "Death Valley Jim," The "Wyoming Nimrod" (so-named by sportswriter Irving Sanborn), and the more familiar

Scotty, Jim Scott had been around about as long as anyone else on the '17 Sox team, having thrown his first pitch in Pale Hose livery back in 1909. Now into his last major league season, he had been moved into an occasional starter and relief role behind the "Big Four" of Rowland's pitching staff.

Scott was born in Deadwood, South Dakota, and raised in Wyoming, and that strange monicker of his came right out of the Old West where "Death Valley Scotty" was one of the more fabled pioneer characters. He was a strapping 6'2" 230-pounder who fit that tough, Old West image, but turned instead to athletic pursuits, specializing in throwing screwballs and spitters. Charlie Comiskey's grapevine caught up with him and brought him to Chicago for a successful 1–0 debut in 1909 in a game covered by one of the sports world's legendary reporters, Ring Lardner, who raved about Scott's pitching and his potential as a big leaguer. Although the big fellow didn't quite measure up to the superstar status Lardner thought he saw in that April 9 sparkler against the St. Louis Browns, his career did have its big moments.

A two-time 20-game winner, Scott was at his very best, through nine innings, at least, on May 14, 1914, when he throttled Washington Senator bats without a run—or a hit. Unfortunately, his teammates were unable to score either, so the game went into extra innings. That was his undoing. In the tenth frame Washington came up with the only run of the game, fashioned on a single by Chick Gandil, at that time the Senators' first baseman, and a double by outfielder Howie Shanks. Scotty's no-hitter and a victory vanished into the thin air of an early spring day in Washington D.C. To balance that disappointment, however, he did have the satisfaction of winning a pair of one-hitters, and, after a 20–20 season in 1913, of making the round-the-world excursion of the Comiskey-McGraw tour in 1913–14. Further, en route to a World Series winner's check, he had a hand in putting an end to Ty Cobb's 35-game hitting streak, getting the Georgia Peach on his final try on July 6 in Detroit in relief of Red Faber in a 4 to 1 Tiger victory.

One of a number of interesting personalities on the last White Sox world's championship team, Jim Scott finished his career on August 17, 1917, with a start against the same A's he had white-washed two weeks earlier. In a matter of days after that no-decision appearance (the Sox lost that game 9 to 7, Eddie Cicotte absorbing the loss in relief) Scotty became the first major leaguer called to active duty, joining Hank Gowdy, the first enlistee, in the ranks of Uncle Sam's military. Pitcher Scott ultimately became Captain Scott, serving on the Western Front in France in 1918. His post-career and post-service years involved him in several ventures including a return to baseball in the capacity of a major league umpire, and finally, a move to California where he died at Jacumba on the Mexican border, near the site of a religious cult he led in his later years. His record as a White Sox hurler, not quite as captivating as the story of his life, follows.

Year	GP	IP	W/L	GS	GC	SH	BB	K	OB%	PR	ERA	TPI
1909	36	250.1	12–12	29	19	4	93	135	.310	5	2.30	-0.2
1910	41	229.2	8–18	23	14	2	86	135	.303	2	2.43	0.4
1911	39	202.0	14–11	26	14	3	81	128	.311	24	2.63	1.5
1912	6	37.2	2–2	4	2	1	15	23	.342	5	2.15	0.2
1913	48	312.1	20–20	38	25	4	86	158	.281	36	1.90	3.9
1914	43	253.1	14–18	33	12	2	75	138	.306	-3	2.84	-0.4
1915	48	296.1	24–11	35	23	7	78	120	.292	30	2.03	3.4
1916	32	165.1	7–14	21	8	1	53	71	.321	2	2.72	-0.4
1917	24	125.0	6–7	17	6	2	42	37	.341	11	1.87	1.0
Totals	317	1872	107–113	226	123	26	609	945	.305	111	2.32	9.4

On August 5, the Rowlandmen edged their lead upward by another half game to 3½ over Boston by dint of a twinbill victory over the Mackmen while Boston's Dutch Leonard beat Stan Coveleski, Tris Speaker & Co. winning a single game from Cleveland 3 to 2 in 11 innings. It began to look as though Chicago just might move on to decisive control of the pennant race.

But just a minute. That was not to be—not quite yet, anyway. During the next 16 days, covering a span of 17 games, the White Sox won eight while losing nine, including a split in the four-game series ending on August 22 with the Barrymen, giving Boston every opportunity to overtake their league lead. It was, at best, a mediocre stretch of baseball and couldn't have come at a more inopportune time. But the Bosox weren't much better, winning only 10 of 18 during that same period. On August 22, in Chicago, in the last of a four-game set between the two pennant contenders, the Red Sox beat the homestanding Pale Hose behind Dutch Leonard to once again whittle the White Sox' lead to two games. Had Boston gone on a tear during that stretch, winning perhaps 12 or 14 of

Ed Walsh, still with the White Sox in 1915 when this photograph was taken, stands with handsome Jim Scott, a.k.a. "Death Valley Jim," Eddie Cicotte, Joey Benz and Reb Russell. Scott was a 20-game winner in 1913 and 1915. Note the quaint collection of "railbirds" in the stands. (Brace photograph)

those 18 games it would have been an entirely different pennant race. For Boston this turned out to be akin to the handwriting on the wall, the decisive turning point of the 1917 pennant race. It left Jack Barry & Co. to deal with the inevitability of winding up in second place, along with the end of the Bosox' championship reign, and it was closer at hand than Bostonians were ready to admit.

Directly ahead was a White Sox hurricane that swept away everything in sight as Comiskey's charges put the race on ice with one of the more awesome displays of team power and versatility in baseball history. Between August 23 and September 21, when Red Faber pitched Chicago's pennant-clinching victory in Boston, the Pale Hose won a staggering 23 ball games in 26 tries. The South Siders had turned killer, winning 18 out of 19 between August 23 and September 14, and the baseball world now would have to acknowledge that John McGraw's mighty Giants had better tend to their knittin' if they intended to bring the world's championship back to Coogan's Bluff. It would even be conceivable that Pants Rowland's hinterlanders would be favored to deprive New York of another World Series victory. That would all play out in due course.

The first order of business, however, was the final third of the 1917 schedule. And the way the White Sox proceeded to manhandle the first segment of the final chapter of the campaign gave no positive sign that they were capable of coming away with The Big Prize.

But despite the team's inconsistency, there were some bright spots, just enough of them to withstand panic. The first of these was a nailbiter on August 9 at Washington when the Sox edged the Senators 3 to 2 as Joey Benz, 6 and 2 as a result of the victory, with relief help from Dave Danforth, stopped the men of Clark Griffith with a combined four hit effort. But in the next two games, a doubleheader feature, two of the Sox' big guns, Red Faber and Eddie Cicotte, went down to superior Washington pitching, first, from Walter Johnson, who slammed the door on the Sox with another of his 110 career shutouts, this one a masterful one-hitter, while bedeviling the Chisox with a 3 for 3 day on two doubles and a single.

Johnson's masterpiece was followed by Jim Shaw's 3 to 2 triumph over Eddie Cicotte, who suffered his ninth defeat. Eddie, who won his 18th in relief of Joey Benz at Philadelphia on August 4, would wind up at a sticking point on 18, losing not only to Shaw, but to the A's Rube Schauer and then to Carl Mays before recapturing his winning ways on August 23 in a glossy 6–0 shutout over the same Jim Shaw who had beaten him earlier in the month. Cicotte was now poised to win his 20th of the season, which came in his next appearance, against Bob Shawkey, as he defeated the Yanks at Comiskey Park on the 27th. Could he move on to 30? That remained to be seen.

Johnson's 4 to 0 triumph wasn't the only Chicago misfortune that day. More devastating was Buck Weaver's injury, sustained while trying to tag out Eddie Ainsmith. The big Washington backstop had moved around from first on Johnson's single in the third inning and slid into third, knocking the ball from Weaver's hand as he tried to tag Ainsmith. As a result of the violent contact during the tag, the index finger on Weaver's glove hand was broken, putting him out of the lineup indefinitely. As a matter of fact, it wouldn't be until September 24 that the switch-hitting infielder would get back into the lineup. That brought Pants Rowland's utility infielder, Fred McMullin, to the fore, quickly inserted into the number two slot in the batting order, and installed at third in Weaver's place. Weaver would be missed for a number of reasons, and it would remain to be seen just how costly the injury might be.

Walter Johnson (left), shown here in a relaxing moment with Ty Cobb, authored eight shutouts in 1917. The one-hitter he threw at the Sox on August 10 was one of five duing his peerless career. (Dennis Colgin)

There was another troubling item to consider. Manager Rowland's pitching staff, dangerously thin in numbers even for a

Deadball Era staff, would soon be deprived of Jim Scott's services with his departure to the Armed Forces, and Reb Russell was beginning to show the wear and tear on his already balky throwing arm. Though he was enjoying a superb season, filled with shutouts and clutch victories, it was a major nightmare to think what might happen if he were to be shelved at this crucial point in the season. Juggling starters who also relieved and relievers like Dave Danforth, who also started, would have to be refined to a rare art if Pants Rowland were to be successful in bringing his ball club home a pennant winner. Ultimately, the gritty Sox pitching corps piled up the following appearance numbers:

	GS	OG	SV	IP
Cicotte	35	14	4	346.2
Faber	29	14	3	248.0*
Williams	29	16	1	230.0
Russell	24	11	3	189.1
Danforth	9	41	9	173.1
Scott	17	7	1	125.0
Benz	13	6	0	94.2

*Red Faber was out of the lineup six weeks. He did not start a game between April 29 and June 22.

Eddie Cicotte's numbers, of course, are awesome. The chunky little scuffed ball artist would turn in a Cy Young Award season before it was all over, the major and indispensable factor in manager Rowland's pitching scheme. And yet, he was but one of seven who exceeded 300 in the number of innings pitched during the 1917 campaign. Pete Alexander's 388.0 led this elite group followed by Cicotte and Cincinnati's Fred Toney (339.1). Other 300+ hurlers included the Reds' 20-game winner Pete Schneider (333.2), Babe Ruth (326.1) and Walter Johnson (326.0). Seen from the vantage point of contemporary statistic tables, these numbers are almost beyond credibility, yet even those 1917 numbers pale by comparison with those of earlier days in the game's history. Such was the result of the evolving nature of the game, its players and the strategies involved.

On August 12 the White Sox opened a four game engagement in the Forest City at Cleveland's Dunn Field, better known as

League Park. A throng of better than 20,000 turned out to cheer
the hometown Indians, at that point in third place and still harboring
hopes of a pennant. Manager Lee Fohl sent out his ace, Jim Bagby,
to meet the Sox' Jim Scott, whose last start turned into a bracing
4 to 0 conquest of Connie Mack's A's nine days earlier. Scotty left
the fray in the ninth inning because his pitching hand was numbed
while batting (he had cued a ball off the end of his bat that had a
numbing effect on both hands) to the extent that he couldn't grip
the ball adequately to resume pitching. Rowland promptly brought
Dave Danforth in from the bullpen to do the Sox' pitching. What
Jim Scott left behind was a 3 to 2 lead. That evaporated after Danforth issued a free pass to catcher Hank DeBerry, sent in to pinch
hit for Bagby, and a double by Jack Graney that scored DeBerry,
sending the game into extra innings.

The two teams fought through another three scoreless innings
in a well-pitched duel between Smokey Joe Wood, of 1912 Boston
fame, and the accomplished Sox reliever Dave Danforth, 1917's
premier relief pitcher. Three innings tired Wood, so Fohl replaced
him with Joe Boehling for the 13th frame to face the business end
of the Chicago batting order, beginning with The General, Joe
Jackson, who greeted Boehling with one of his patented line drives to put the lead run on base. But the crafty Boehling worked
things around to where Jackson was on third with two out and
Swede Risberg up. It was not beyond reasonable hope that the
light-hitting Risberg might be disposed of without further damage. But the big Swede dashed Cleveland hopes by bunting up the
line on the first pitch. Jackson, off with the pitch, scored easily on
the suicide squeeze. That raised the Sox count to four and left
matters up to Danforth and his assortment of doctored pitches,
the most famous, or infamous, depending on one's loyalties, of
which was his "Sailor Pitch" that tailed in on the hitter. Hotly
debated, and always argued, that pitch, as well as others that Texan
Danforth offered up, was sure to cause managers, coaches and
fans to scream protests. There were no protests, however, in the
bottom of the thirteenth, Cleveland's last chance to do something
about Chicago's 4–3 lead. Reliever Danforth took the steam out
of Cleveland's attack by picking off pinch-runner Fritz Coumbe
with one away. Bill Wambsganss then popped out and Terry
Turner fanned on, who knows, one of those trick pitches to bring
an end to the day. The box score:

Chicago	AB	R	H	PO	A	Cleveland	AB	R	H	PO	A
Leibold, lf	6	0	1	5	0	Graney, lf	5	0	2	3	1
McMul'n, 3b	5	1	2	1	2	Chapman, ss	6	1	3	2	7
E. Collins, 2b	3	1	1	3	3	Speaker, cf	5	1	2	2	0
Jackson, rf	5	1	2	2	0	Smith, rf	6	0	0	0	0
Felsch, cf	6	0	2	4	0	Harris, 1b	4	0	2	21	1
Gandil, 1b	6	0	3	11	1	Wambsg's, 2b	6	0	0	4	6
Risberg, ss	4	0	0	4	6	Evans, 3b	3	0	0	1	8
Schalk, c	6	1	1	7	1	Turner, 3b	2	0	0	1	0
Scott, p	3	0	0	2	1	Billings, c	2	0	0	2	0
Danforth, (WP)	2	0	0	0	2	O'Neill, c	3	0	1	3	0
						Bagby, p	3	0	0	0	2
						Lambeth, p	0	0	0	0	0
						Wood, p	1	0	0	0	2
						Boehling, (LP)	0	0	0	0	0
						Roth, ph	1	0	0	0	0
						DeBerry, ph	0	0	0	0	0
						Howard, pr	0	1	0	0	0
						Coumbe, pr	0	0	0	0	0
Totals	46	4	12	39	16	Totals	47	3	10	39	27

```
Chicago      001 001 010 000 1    4–12–5
Cleveland    000 002 001 000 0    3–10–1
```

2B: Schalk, Speaker, Harris, Graney, Chapman; SB: Howard; Sac. Hits: Jackson, E. Collins, Risberg 2; LOB: Chicago 11, Cleveland 10; DP: Evans, Wambsganss and Harris, Scott, Risberg and Gandil; BB: Scott 2, Danforth 3, Bagby 2, Lambeth 2; K: Scott 2, Wood 2, Boehling 1; Passed Ball: Schalk; Umpires: Nallin and Owen; Time of Game: 3:15.

Pants Rowland called on Dave Danforth out of the bullpen more than 40 times during the 1917 season. That number exceeded anything that went before it, and although the day of the relief pitcher, so designated and used accordingly in major league ball games, was still to gain favor among managers and baseball strategists (it was during the '20's that a number of teams actually began to rely on late inning relief), Rowland, for one, was committed to the idea. He picked up Danforth for the 1916 season after the athletically gifted Texan had languished in the minors several seasons following his 1911, 4 and 1 debut with Connie Mack's A's. That 1911 season under Mack and among Athletic greats like pitchers Eddie Plank and Chief Bender, who, along with Eddie Collins, Frank Baker and Jack Barry, sparked a world championship year for the A's, having defeated New York's Giants in the World Series, was an eye-opener for the rookie. Danforth's 1911 debut on August 1 and the following two months, combined with the World Series, was an education in and of itself, and the experience was not lost on "Dauntless Dave," as he was known. Though he spent the next four seasons bouncing around minor league ball parks, Danforth savored his Philadelphia experience while learning his trade, and brought to the 1917 Chicago champions a winning touch as well as the experience of a winner. The only other member of the Pale Hose with championship laurels, and indeed a great one, was Eddie Collins, another member of the 1911–14 champs in Philadelphia, reunited with his former 1911 teammate in '17.

The White Sox picked up Danforth after his 1915 season with Louisville where he perfected one of the many trick pitches in his arsenal, the infamous "shine ball," a pitch that tailed in sharply on the hitter. It was a pitch also used by Eddie Cicotte, though Danforth's pitch broke in different and more disturbing ways than Cicotte's. In any case, it was one of the many offerings used by White Sox pitchers that set skippers, coaches and players screaming, a constant source of irritation when Chicago came to town. Scuffing and darkening balls was a part of the daily routine for the White Sox staff and Dave Danforth contributed his share. And, of course, until 1920 it was all legal.

Danforth's 1917 debut with the White Sox was on April 13. He had won a spot in Pants Rowland's five-man rotation, and beat the Detroit Tigers 8 to 6. He started again against St. Louis four days later, winning 6 to 5. Rowland noticed, however, that there was a difference in Danforth's pitches, as well as in his defiant, fearless attitude, especially in clutch situations. While employing some of the same scuffed and darkened ball pitches used by the rest of the staff, Danforth's offerings broke more sharply—and far more unpredictably. Ray Schalk was always more alert and positioned himself more defensively with Danforth on the mound. These differences set Rowland thinking about extensive use of the Danforth repertoire out of the pen. The result was a spot starter and relief role, and during the course of the 1916 season that role was polished to the extent that the Sox knew this would be Danforth's primary role during the 1917 season. Rowland's strategy worked well, resulting, finally, in Danforth's league-leading numbers in appearances, 50, and saves, 9, both of which led all major league pitchers.

The Great War, rules changes, Pants Rowland's departure in favor of Bill Gleason as Chicago's 1919 manager, and the cata-

Twenty doubles, 17 triples and 5 homers helped produce Joe Jackson's .429 slugging average to lead the Pale Hose in 1917. Deceptively fast, he stole over 200 bases during his 13-year career. (Dennis Colgin)

clysmic changes in Chicago baseball following The Scandals, inpacted Dave Danforth's stay with the Sox, limiting his tenure to four seasons. Dauntless Dave's Chicago record follows.

Year	GP	SV	W/L	Pct.	IP	H	HR	OBA	OB%	K/BB	ERA	TPI
1916	28	2	6–5	.545	93.2	87	1	.259	.338	49/37	3.27	-0.6
1917	50	9	11–6	.647	173.0	155	1	.244	.325	79/74	2.65	-0.3
1918	39	2	6–15	.286	139.0	148	1	.288	.345	48/40	3.43	-1.8
1919	15	1	1–2	.333	41.2	58	1	.333	.405	17/20	7.78	-1.5
Totals	132	14	24–28	.462	447.1	448	4	.281	.335	281/335	3.31	-4.2

After Dave Danforth's win in relief of Jim Scott over the Indians on August 12 in the opener of the four game Cleveland set, the Chisox went on to win the series, taking two out of the next three games. That brought them back to Chicago for a 21-game homestand beginning on August 17 against the Mackmen. Winning two of three in that series, they next faced the men from Massachusetts' Back Bay, the Red Sox. Going into that series of four, the American League's first division standings were:

	Won	Lost	Pct.	GB
Chicago	72	44	.621	–
Boston	68	44	.607	2
Cleveland	63	56	.529	10½
Detroit	59	56	.513	12½

The White Sox, thus, found themselves in essentially the same spot as they had been a few weeks earlier when they travelled to Boston for their four game series at Fenway Park. During that series it took a pair of brilliant outings by Reb Russell and Red Faber to salvage an even break in that engagement after having lost the first two encounters. This time, however, playing in their own back yard, the Chisox were presented with a choice opportunity to put some real heat on the Red Sox.

Red Faber, Eddie Cicotte, Reb Russell and Lefty Williams, in that order, were summoned to meet the Bostons, Cicotte having been selected in the number two spot of the rotation as a safety valve to even up the series behind Faber should the latter encounter trouble with the Bosox, a recurring problem with the big Chicago spitballer. The Faber-Boston clash (Jack Barry selected Rube Foster to work against Chicago) opened an August 20 doubleheader, and Faber's slants in the first game were razor sharp. In the habit of walking about as many as he fanned over the course of his Hall of Fame career, Big Red this time walked only one, K'd two, and silenced Red Sox bats with but four hits in a 7–0 shutout that was interrupted by a sixth inning downpour that actually made a travesty of the rest of the afternoon's entertainment. After more than an hour's delay the teams returned to action, "afloat on the seas of Comiskey Park" as *Chicago Tribune* reporter Irv Sanborn put it. But as it turned out Red Faber was just as good asea as he was

Lefty Dave Danforth was Pants Rowland's handy man among Chisox moundsmen. In 1917 he started 9 games, threw one shutout, relieved in 41 games and posted a sparkling 11 and 6 record, including a league-leading 9 saves. The Sox could hardly have won the pennant without him. *(The Sporting News)*

before The Deluge that descended in the sixth inning. The Faber exhibition no doubt had Rowland wondering what he was ever worried about as the Pale Hose nudged their lead to three full games with ace Eddie Cicotte on deck and a chance to move up by four.

In the nightcap, under dark, overcast skies and more threatened rain, the two teams groped their way through eight innings that eventually turned out to be enough for the day, the Bostons up on the Chicagos and Eddie Cicotte, 3 to 1. That left the two heavyweights, groggy from an afternoon of slugging away at one another, just where they started before the first pitch was thrown that day by Red Faber.

Urban Faber, the big, rawboned Iowa spitballer, had been around the Chicago scene since November of 1913, when Czar Comiskey purchased him from the Des Moines club of the Western League, where he had turned in his second straight 20-game season. He had attracted attention earlier, having thrown the first perfect game in minor league history in 1910. But he was to attract far more attention on the round-the-world tour of the Sox and Giants in the winter of 1913–14 when as a last minute addition to the entourage, sans passport and wardrobe, he set sail for the Orient to earn his ticket to the big leagues as a pitcher loaned to McGraw's touring Giants team. After travelling credentials and other necessities were straightened out the young man went on to impress bossman Comiskey sufficiently to invite him to spring training. His first major league manager, Nixey Callahan, was also impressed, and he brought 25-year-old Faber, by now a mature competitor in his own right, along with him to start out the season. Four days into the 1914 campaign Big Red won the first major league game of his career (there were to be another 253, many of them for some unimaginably inept Chicago ball clubs) on April 17, starting out a 10 and 9 season on the right foot. It was the first of his 20 seasons in a White Sox uniform, the most memorable of which was 1917, at least from the standpoint of pitching on a team that had won it all. There were other high points to be sure, and that one, black, low point in 1919 when he not only suffered through the notorious scandal that turned the White Sox franchise inside out, but was unable to do anything about it on the field of play because of an ankle injury that prevented him from appearing in the Series.

Red Faber went on to achieve icon status on Chicago's South Side, one of three future Hall of Famers in the 1917 Sox lineup. His batterymate, Ray Schalk, always insisted that if Faber had pitched for some of the other steady winners in the league, he would have won upwards of 400 ball games. Maybe so. The fact is, his total of 254 was good enough to gain entry into baseball's elite showcase at Cooperstown, and he certainly didn't do his candidacy for those special honors any harm with his extraordinary performance in the 1917 World Series, explained later and in some detail.

The 20-season Faber log, every inning of it in a White Sox uniform, follows.

Year	GP	GS	CG	IP	SH	SV	W/L	Pct.	OBA	K/BB	ERA	TPI
1914	40	20	11	181.1	2	4	10–9	.526	.239	88/64	2.68	0.3
1915	50	32	22	299.2	2	2	24–14	.632	.240	182/99	2.55	2.1
1916	35	25	15	205.1	3	1	17–9	.654	.228	87/61	2.02	2.0
1917	41	29	16	248.0	3	3	16–13	.552	.247	84/85	1.92	2.2
1918	11	9	5	80.2	1	1	4–1	.800	.245	26/23	1.23	0.8
1919	25	20	9	162.1	0	0	11–9	.550	.287	45/45	3.83	-1.3
1920	40	39	28	319.0	2	1	23–13	.639	.277	108/88	2.99	2.3
1921	43	39	32	330.2	4	1	25–15	.625	.242	124/87	2.48	7.0
1922	43	38	31	353.0	4	2	21–17	.553	.252	148/83	2.80	4.9
1923	32	31	15	232.1	2	0	14–11	.560	.259	91/62	3.41	1.9
1924	21	20	9	161.1	0	0	9–11	.450	.282	47/58	3.85	0.2
1925	34	32	16	238.0	1	0	12–11	.522	.289	71/59	3.78	0.6
1926	27	25	13	184.2	1	0	15–9	.625	.281	65/57	3.56	0.4
1927	18	15	6	110.2	0	0	4–7	.364	.312	39/41	4.55	-0.2
1928	27	27	16	201.1	2	0	13–9	.591	.286	43/68	3.75	0.4
1929	31	31	15	234.0	1	0	13–13	.500	.273	68/61	3.88	0.9
1930	29	26	10	169.0	0	1	8–13	.381	.283	62/49	4.21	0.6
1931	44	19	5	184.0	1	1	10–14	.417	.285	49/57	3.82	0.6
1932	42	5	0	106.0	0	6	2–11	.154	.290	26/38	3.74	1.0
1933	36	2	0	86.1	0	5	3–4	.429	.266	18/28	3.44	0.3
Totals	669	484	274	4087.2	29	28	254–213	.544	.266	1471/1213	3.15	27.0

Chicago's league-leading nine had its work cut out for itself on August 21. A loss would trim its paper-thin lead to a single game, making it possible for the Red Sox to even up the American League race on the morrow. On the other hand, a win would put Beantown three games in arrears, thus ensuring that the Boston series would end with the Pale Hose still in command of the league. The last time Sox manager Rowland encountered that situation his club was at Fenway Park and he called on Reb Russell to stem the tide. Why not again!

The Texan hadn't started a game in two weeks. Well rested, that quirky arm of his would either be ready for a good workout at this point or—well, that was something Rowland would rather not think about. So Reb got the ball.

The result on this occasion was almost a carbon copy of the August 1 encounter. This time the White Sox scored only two, which was two less than the number that backed up southpaw Russell's victory that day. Once again Boston failed to cross home plate, bowing to a super effort not only by Russell, but by a hustling Chisox defense showcasing fielding gems by Swede Risberg, Eddie Collins and Hap Felsch, who, in the seventh committed outfield larceny on a Duffy Lewis drive ticketed for at least three bases. But the play of the game took place in the first Boston at bat.

The *Chicago Tribune* reported it as the "Break of the Game":

> Barry was on third and Lewis on first with two outs in the first
> inning. They got there by clean, solid singles, and the fans were
> wondering if Russell would last. Hooper smashed a fast
> bounder past Russell over second base and Barry raced for the
> plate on it. Risberg went back, stopped the ball as it shot past
> him, and, while running toward center field, tossed it behind
> him toward second. R's aim was perfect and Collins was on
> base to catch the ball, forcing out Lewis. If that hit had gone
> through, the Red Sox might have won the game in that inning.
> Risberg's play took a lot of pep out of them.

The one run Chicago needed came in the sixth inning on one
of Capt. Eddie Collins' three hits, scoring Fred McMullin. They
registered another off loser Babe Ruth, whose work on the mound
almost equalled that of Russell's, in the next frame when—guess
who—Mr. Russell himself singled home Swede Risberg. The win
raised Russell's record to 13 and 4 and the loss dropped Ruth to 18
and 8. Equally important, the Pale Hose that day inched their league
lead back up to three games. It was Reb Russell and a league lead
deja vu, per August 1.

During the next month Reb Russell would "pitch in" here and
there, winning two more and losing one for a season's mark of 15
and 5, good for league leadership in winning percentage at .750. It
should be pointed out, further, that in three of his losses during that
magic summer of '17 his supporting cast went scoreless, the last of
these a 3 to 0 loss to Babe Ruth on September 24.

More determined than ever, and probably fuming over "that
Russell fellow" with his collection of nothing-balls, the Beantowners came back the next day to trounce the White Sox 5 to 1 as their
Old Reliable, Dutch Leonard, beat Lefty Williams, surrendering but
six singles, while Del Gainer and Larry Gardner, with three hits
apiece, led the Carmine attack. Consequently, Boston came out of
the series with a split in games and no worse in the standings than
a two game deficit. More encouraging from their standpoint was a
flat-footed tie in games lost, 46, for each club.

On the same day that Boston and Chicago concluded their
skirmishes for first place honors, there were close encounters of
another kind in the National League, where Wilbert Robinson's
Dodgers dueled Hans Wagner and his Pirate teammates in Pitts-

burgh. There, in the Steel City, the two clubs matched outs for a record-setting 22 innings before the day's work was over. Scoring in the top of the 22nd, the Dodgers finally won out, 6 to 5. Jake Daubert, Brooklyn first sacker, recorded 27 putouts *himself,* enough for a game of regulation length. It was somehow preordained by the baseball gods that Pittsburgh, in the midst of an abysmally terrible season, would lose a ball game after expending all the energy demanded by 22 innings of play. As if to add an exclamation mark, the losing pitcher that day, Elmer Jacobs (6 and 19 on the season), toiled through the last 17 stanzas of the game while the winner, Rube Marquard, pitched only the last two innings to win it.

In six full seasons with Chicago, Reb Russell won 80, of which 22 were won during a Rookie of the Year season in 1913, when he pitched in 52 games to lead the American League. (Dennis Colgin)

The Giants, meanwhile, beat Christy Mathewson's Reds behind the shutout pitching of lefty Rube Benton, who improved his record to 12 and 4 as the men of McGraw continued their domination of the National League, riding the crest of a ten game lead. Pennant bound, Little Napoleon continued to rely on his potent left handed threesome of Ferdie Schupp, 16 and 6 at that point, Slim Sallee at 13 and 4, and Benton.

There were other battles going on—of a much more serious nature. While major league teams were continuing to go through their military drills to entertain fans before ball games, warfare in earnest was exploding on a number of fronts across Europe. On this day, August 22, *The New York Times* reported from its foreign desk at Petrograd (St. Petersburg) that German troops were driving toward Riga, ousting Russian troops from their advanced northern European strongholds. On the Western Front British troops captured German positions on the Ypres-Menin Road. Indeed, the war, grinding on with its monotonous repitition of capturing and recapturing cities, fortresses, trenches and strategic positions along far flung battlelines, had settled down into a prolonged slaughter that showed no signs of letup either in its ferocity or in its alarming number of casulties. That would have its singular effect on every part and parcel of American life, including the national pastime which, in 1918, would get to a point of considering seriously the cancellation of the major league baseball schedule.

CHAPTER 9

In Command

Without doubt the greatest spectacle of its kind ever seen in a baseball park was staged yesterday by President Comiskey in the observance of Military Day at the White Sox battle field. Approximately 7,500 soldiers and sailors, including nearly 300 officers, accepted Comiskey's invitation to watch the competitive drill of the Sox and Senators, and completely overshadowed all the rest of the occasion. Incidentally, the Rowlands won a ball game by a score of 6 to 0, and kept pace with the Red Sox in the pennant race.

Parades, martial music, flag raisings, and the other military features completely swamped the national pastime, although every man of the many who so soon expect to be in France, rooted lustily for the White Sox and cheered vehemently the Sox players' exhibition of drilling before the game...

The spectacle began with a review of the Second Infantry, I.N.G., led by Col. J. J. Garity. Headed by their band, the 1,900 soliders circled the field, and there were so many of them that, marching four abreast, the first company reached the entrance gate before the last had passed through onto the field...

When Sergt. Smiley led the White Sox out for their drill, with each player clad in regulation khaki and carrying a Springfield rifle, few recognized them at first, thinking they were part of

one of the regiments present. When it was discovered they
were ball players all hands joined in a cheer. The Rowlands
made a much more impressive showing than the Senators on
account of their better equipment, but they have strong competitors in some of the other teams for the Ban Johnson prize
of $500, particularly New York [*The Chicago Tribune*, August
24, 1917].

Military parading, filled stands, red-white-blue bunting deco-
rating the stands, and dignitaries notwithstanding, the star of this
particular afternoon, concerning baseball at any rate, was diminutive Eddie Cicotte, who spread eight Senator safeties around so art-
fully that the Senators came up empty as the Sox cuffed Jim Shaw
and his Washington partners around for a 6 to 0 shutout, Little
Eddie's sixth on the season, raising his mark to 19 and 11. And it
was well that the Sox tended to business. The Red Sox were winning a ball game of their own, downing the Browns in St. Louis
behind Carl Mays, 4 to 2. The day, then, left the Sox one notch
closer to their $500 military prize and still two games ahead of the
Bosox.

But there was additional significance attached to this victory,
for it was the beginning of the Sox' strongest and most decisive
surge of the season. A single afternoon's victory doth not a winning streak make—but you have to start somewhere, and that's what
the Pale Hose did on August 23. They embarked, with this conquest, on a madcap tear through their next nine engagements before
dropping another one, only to resume their streak after a St. Louis
defeat as September began, with another streak of nine before losing at Detroit in the middle of September. It was Cicotte's shutout
win that got the parade moving as the Sox slashed through an 18
for 19 streak, putting the pennant out of everyone's reach.

During that same period the carmine-hosed Boston team won,
but not nearly enough to keep up, victorious in twelve of nineteen
matches, while tying two more. As of September 15, then, they
trailed Chicago 7½ games, losing 5½ in the process. Though the
White Sox finished out the season at an 8 and 8 clip, Boston could
do no better than 8 and 9. What began on August 23 with their 6
to 0 conquest of the Senators was the beginning of the trip to the
end of the rainbow, and with it the gold of an American League
pennant.

During a winning streak the team prospers, of course, but so do individual players. Batting averages and that host of other offensive marks tend to move upward toward respectable levels and those already sporting high marks tend to extend themselves up into league-leadership and record-making standards. Those streaks usually put a number of exceptional performances front and center, as well. The White Sox' streak to the pennant was no exception.

On August 25 the White Sox and Senators completed their series in Chicago in an unusual afternoon that featured no earned runs, five stolen bases off Walter Johnson, something unheard of against the Great One, and another pregame military drill, this time parading the Eighth Illinois infantry, a precision unit composed of Black Infantrymen under the command of Col. Dennison, among other units in front of another standing room only throng. And all this on a day set aside to honor Clark Griffith, the old White Sox pitcher who managed the Sox to the American League's first pennant in 1901, and presently in charge of the Senators.

The exceptional baseball performance on this day was Red Faber's dominating pitching, winning the second of what would become a six game winning streak, as his ERA continued to drop and hitters found it harder and harder to solve his moist array of breaking balls. That would prove to be the icing on Pants Rowland's cake, paving the way to a World Series conquest that was much the doing of Mr. Faber. After having struggled most of the spring and well into the summer, Big Red simply got stronger and more effective with each passing game as August made its way into September. That was especially welcome, what with Jim Scott gone and Reb Russell in need of extended rest between starts or even relief roles. The 4 to 1 triumph over the Senators raised Faber's mark to 12–11 in a season that would wind up at 16 and 13 with an outstanding 1.92 ERA.

Seventeen games had gone into the record books as the Rowlandmen prepared to go up against the Yankees on August 28. On August 10, the day Walter Johnson shut them out on a one-hitter, and regretably, the day Buck Weaver's finger was broken, the Pale Hose were 2½ games up on the Bosox. Eighteen days later, still without Weaver, the Sox' lead was at two games, and though there is no doubt about the fact that "The Ginger Kid" was missed, it was also true—and equally fortunate—that Freddie McMullin was around to stand in until the peppery Weaver got back. The versatile util-

Too bad this fellow kept the wrong company. Freddie McMullin cast his lot with Chick Gandil and his cohorts. That cost him a major league career just when he was about to become a starting infielder. His stand-in work for Buck Weaver during Weaver's convalescence in August/September of 1917 was a major factor in the Sox' explosive streak of 20 victories in 22 games late in the season. (Dennis Colgin)

ity player certainly hadn't disrupted the club's inner defenses. As a matter of fact he had played well enough to cause manager Rowland to think about keeping McMullin right at third, moving Weaver in at his old shortstop digs and benching Swede Risberg. There would be another few days to get through, giving him time to mull over that move.

On August 28 the Sox made it three in a row over the visiting Yanks, McMullin chipping in with a 2 for 3 day, including an RBI and a sacrifice plus a pair of putouts that helped along in the tight, 4–3 victory. That pushed the Chisox lead to 3½ over Boston, idled by rain in Detroit.

Fred McMullin was a square-jawed Irishman from Scammon, Kansas, one of seven in a family that moved to Los Angeles when he entered high school. The Tigers signed him in 1914 and he debuted with Detroit on August 27, appearing in but one game. Among his teammates was Lefty Williams, who would also join him on the White Sox roster in 1916. McMullin still needed seasoning, so he spent the 1915 season back in Los Angeles, playing for the Angels in the Pacific Coast League. One of his teammates there was "Sleepy" Bill Burns, who would later surface in the 1919–20 scandals which, tragically, caught up in galewind force with McMullin and swept him out of major league baseball altogether. In one of those stranger-than-life twists, he returned to Los Angeles after his banishment, working for many years in the Office of the U.S. Marshal as an effective law enforcement officer. The McMullin White Sox years are profiled, following:

Year	GP	AB	R	H	3B	SB	BB	K	BA	OBA	SLG	TPR
1916	68	187	8	48	0	9	19	30	.257	.332	.273	-0.6
1917	59	194	35	46	1	9	27	17	.237	.339	.258	-1.7
1918	70	235	32	65	0	7	25	26	.277	.356	.319	0.2
1919	60	170	31	50	4	4	11	18	.294	.355	.388	0.3
1920	46	127	14	25	4	1	9	13	.197	.255	.268	-1.5
Totals	303	913	120	234	9	30	91	104	.256	.333	.302	-3.3

As September neared, these were the numbers posted by the leaders of the contending ball clubs:

The Pitchers in the National League

	GP	Won	Lost	Pct.	K	BB
Bender, Phl	17	6	1	.857	82	21
Sallee, NY	27	15	5	.750	40	24
Benton, NY	25	12	4	.750	45	20
Schupp, NY	28	17	6	.739	123	59
Tesreau, NY	26	11	6	.647	72	43
Alexander, Phil	35	21	12	.636	147	45
Perritt, NY	28	11	7	.611	49	32
Oeschger, Phil	35	11	11	.500	100	56

The Pitchers in the American League

Russell, Chi	31	15	4	.789	50	26
Mays, Bos	27	17	6	.739	74	66
Danforth, Chi	41	8	3	.727	62	67
Benz, Chi	17	5	2	.714	20	21
Ruth, Bos	33	18	10	.643	113	94
Cicotte, Chi	42	21	12	.636	120	70
Williams, Chi	34	14	8	.636	64	67
Pennock, Bos	20	5	3	.625	29	22
Leonard, Bos	30	15	12	.556	123	63
Shore, Bos	24	10	9	.526	43	40
Faber, Chi	30	12	11	.522	66	63

The Hitters of the American League:

	GP	AB	R	H	SB	BA
Cobb, Det	124	480	90	188	88	.392
Ruth, Bos	40	96	8	83	0	.348
Speaker, Clv	120	439	74	152	15	.346
Russell, Chi	30	32	8	10	0	.313

Felsch, Chi	128	479	58	142	18	.296
Lewis, Bos	118	434	45	128	7	.295
Baker, NY	119	452	45	132	14	.292
Jackson, Chi	123	452	74	125	10	.277
Weaver, Chi	108	412	60	114	20	.277
E. Collins, Chi	130	465	73	128	31	.275
Gandil, Chi	125	464	39	126	12	.272
Gardner, Bos	124	427	44	114	10	.267
Hoblitzell, Bos	97	333	39	86	8	.258
Hooper, Bos	120	444	66	111	17	.250
Scott, Bos	124	413	31	94	7	.228
Schalk, Chi	116	355	40	77	14	.217

The Hitters of the National League

Kauff, NY	119	437	71	136	18	.311
Zimmerman, NY	117	453	51	136	9	.300
G. Burns, NY	119	470	84	140	33	.298
Killefer, Phl	100	323	24	98	3	.288
Whitted, Phl	113	419	53	120	8	.286
Holke, NY	119	413	48	118	15	.286
Cravath, Phl	118	426	61	121	4	.284
Rariden, NY	78	204	18	56	3	.275
Robertson, NY	114	428	53	117	13	.273
Niehoff, Phl	99	301	25	80	8	.266
Stock, Phl	118	439	59	115	16	.262
Paskert, Phl	113	430	68	110	13	.256

The White Sox wound up their August agenda with a five game set against St. Louis that netted victories six to nine in their streak before falling to the Browns, 6–3, in the last game of the series played on September 1. Ernie Koob, who earlier in the season had no-hit the Sox and Eddie Cicotte, was the culprit once again, this time taking the measure of Dave Danforth, Rowland's choice as a spot starter. The loss left the Chisox with a 3½ game lead over Boston, both teams now even-up in the loss column at 47, as the club geared up for a Labor Day twinbill with Detroit's Tigers, still dangerous, and still hopeful of overtaking Cleveland for third place money at season's end. Doubleheaders on successive days were on tap for September 2 and 3, days that were go down in baseball history as the first glimmer of the team's faustian flirtation with scandal and the ultimate infamy of shame and demise over the 1919–20 scandal that rocked the national pastime.

To put that Detroit series into proper perspective it is necessary to move ahead nearly a decade to 1927. As that year was aborning, a year famous for the exploits of "Lucky Lindy," the record-setting New York Yankees and Babe Ruth with his 60 roundtrippers, headlines in the Detroit and Chicago newspapers announced in pained, stunning alarm that there was more than playful mischief afoot in the September 2 and 3 doubleheaders between the Tigers and White Sox in 1917. There were indeed allegations that the four games were played under a dark cloud of collusion involving the exchange of money "for services rendered." Known then as "sloughing," the unmistakable implication was that members of the White Sox ball club were willing to pay team members of the Tiger ball club to throw one or more of the four games, or at very least, to make it easy for the White Sox to win the four games. The affair, which bubbled to a boiling point during December of 1926, burst with full fury as the New Year's Day issues of 1927 in both cities blared the news abroad. For the next two weeks newspapers, radios and fans across the country kept tabs, day by day and hour to hour, on "the latest" as the hearings made their way from sworn testimony to a final verdict.

It is important *not* to read 1919 into what happened in 1917, as principals, fans and bystanders were able to do in 1927. From the standpoint of the 1917 season, 1919 and its flagrant, scandalous proceedings were, of course, beyond imagining. That was not the case in 1927 when all involved or concerned had the benefit of a 1919 World Series to recall for added perspective.

The 1917 "fix" was summarized in the Sunday, January 2, 1927, edition of the Detroit Free Press in a front page article under the headline: Tigers Sold 1917 Series, Risberg Tells Landis.

> The Detroit series which Swede Risberg referred to in his testimony before Commissioner Landis Saturday, figured in a brilliant sprint down the stretch by the Chicago club, during which the White Sox won 18 out of 19 games.
>
> Their only defeat over that period was at the hands of the St. Louis Browns, to whom they lost the day before taking on Detroit in the series which Risberg charges was crooked. It came after the Chicagoans had won nine in a row.
>
> Then followed seven (ed: the number was actually nine) victories in a row, their string being ended this time when Detroit defeated them 4 to 3 in the first game of a double header on September 11...

The alleged purchase of a four-game series of baseball games by the Chicago White Sox from the Detroit Americans, to help the Sox win the pennant of 1917, was described by Charles A. "Swede" Risberg, the Sox shortstop at that time.

The White Sox contributed $15 apiece to raise a pool of about $1,100, Risberg said, which was given to the Detroit team, principally pitchers, to "slough" the series to the Sox.

The scheme to get the Detroit team to lay down in the series which began Labor Day, 1917, was first broached to him, Risberg said, by Clarence Rowland, then Sox manager and now an American League umpire.

All the members of the Sox team contributed to the $1,100 pool for Detroit, Risberg said, including Eddie Collins and Ray Schalk, the new Sox manager for 1927.

The article continues with allegations against Rowland, who allegedly informed Sox team members in the dugout that everything was set for the fix, indicated by a flagrant error that Tiger shortstop Eddie Dyer would make early in the game. It should be noted without delay that all, especially Pants Rowland, were exonerated at the conclusion of Commissioner Landis' hearings.

The principal White Sox involved in the allegations were Swede Risberg and Chick Gandil. The alleged co-conspirators, headed by Gandil, were members of the White Sox ball club, from manager Clarence Rowland on down, and selected members of the Detroit club. The proceedings that followed were adjudicated by Landis, who served as both judge and jury. It was the baseball czar, Landis himself, who would hand down verdict and punishment.

The unalterable facts and proceedings in 1917 were these: (a) the White Sox won the September 2 doubleheader by scores of 7–2 and 6–5 (in ten innings). The next day they again won twice, 7–5 and 14–8; (b) in the four game series the White Sox stole 21 bases, eight of them in one game; (c) in the four games the White Sox received 21 bases on balls and the Tigers were charged with 11 errors (both of these factors, unusual in their number and in the potential effect they may have had on the games' outcomes, may have lent credence to a "fix theory"); (d) money was indeed collected from White Sox players for payment to Detroit team members and later in September Gandil handed over money ($870 was the amount indicated in sworn testimony) to pitcher Bill James in Philadelphia.

Gandil was accompanied by Risberg; and (e) after summoning 38 players and listening to their testimony, Landis dismissed the allegations of Gandil and Risberg on January 12, 1927, and found all the accused not guilty of the charges brought forward.

Judge Landis followed up his decision with a statement indicating that although the entire affair was reprehensible, there was no criminal intent. He indicated further that he would recommend for approval a number of major legislative measures including a statute of limitations with respect to alleged baseball offenses, ineligibility to play for one year for offenses involving certain betting or reward offenses and permanent ineligibility for "betting any sum whatsoever upon any ball game in connection with which the bettor has any duty to perform."

Some of the White Sox' brightest stars, including Eddie Collins, Red Faber, Ray Schalk and Eddie Cicotte, all of whom were implicated in the alleged fix and contributed money to the pool, asserted that their participation was based on the assumption that the money was intended as a gift to the Detroit club, especially its pitching staff, which had more than average success in beating the Chisox' chief rival for the pennant, the Boston Red Sox. They insisted to a man that there was no previous plan for the two Detroit doubleheaders, nor was it their intention to be part of a fixed series.

What Judge Landis condemned as reprehensible about the case not only had to do with Risberg and Gandil. It also included the practice of collecting monies to be presented to another team as a gift "for services rendered," a condemnation that was understandable and in keeping with the moral foundations of professional athletics.

By 1927, when the news of the 1917 affair broke, the national pastime, American sports and American sports lovers of all kinds had moved far beyond the 1919–20 scandals. The tumultuous days of the Deadball Era, when betting on baseball was a danger of mammoth proportions that threatened to bring down the game even before the Eight Men Out sullied the 1919 World Series, seemed part of a distant past. But the ever present danger of game-fixing and gambling was never more than a heartbeat away from the game, and the bitter aftermath of the 1915–20 era in Chicago White Sox history was the near destruction of one of the American League's premier franchises.

This accounting of the 1917, September 2–3 doubleheaders and

"The Commish," Judge Kenesaw Mountain Landis, brooding and stern, was the judge and jury in the 1927 hearings of the alleged game-fixing between the White Sox and Tigers in September of 1917. He apparently decided that baseball didn't need another Black Sox brouhaha and wound up absolving everybody of all charges made by Swede Risberg and supported by Chick Gandil. There are still questions. (Dennis Colgin)

the subsequent charges, trial and consequences a decade later, is necessarily incomplete though not lacking in essential details. Just enough is included to sketch the outlines of the affair to complete the record of the 1917 season, and for two reasons: (1) it *is* a part of the 1917 season; and (2) involving as it did some of the principal conspirators of the 1919 scandal, which included roomies Swede Risberg and Chick Gandil, as well as Buck Weaver and Fred McMullin, this episode certainly serves as a red light warning signal that there were players on the White Sox roster who apparently would stop at nothing to line their pockets with money. The seeds had been sown with this "little venture" to make these ball players ripe for the plucking when "The Big Fellas," sovereigns of the underworld like Arnold Rothstein, Carl Zork and Abe Attell, would seize on a plum as big as the World Series for their own private use and profit. Little did mere mortals like Swede Risberg, Chick Gandil and Eddie Cicotte realize that they would simply be pawns in the great chess game that would line the pockets of the Big Money in far away places.

The 1917 season also moved on. With 20 games yet to play, the White Sox, after their twinkilling of the Tigers on September 2 and 3, took on the Browns in St. Louis and Cleveland at home, adding another four wins to their latest skein, extending it to eight straight before travelling to the Motor City to take on the Tigers once again. Hap Felsch ignited an eight run, eighth inning rally in the first of the two games in St. Louis with a leadoff double and then doubled again during the inning to spearhead a 13–6 massacre of the Browns. In the two game series Felsch had five hits, leading the Sox to an 11 inning victory the next day with a timely, two-run single after two were out that beat St. Louis 4 to 1. Red Faber and Lefty Williams were the beneficiaries of Felsch's lusty hitting. In the 13–6 rout skipper Rowland rested Eddie Collins during the latter part of the game, giving Bobby Byrne, an 11-year veteran of National League play, picked up by Commander Comiskey as "insurance" for utility infielding after Buck Weaver went down, an opportunity to record his only game and only at bat as an American Leaguer in the record books. Later released after Weaver's return, the at bat in St. Louis proved to be his last major league appearance. The box score of the September 4 game:

Chicago	AB	R	H	PO	A	St. Louis	AB	R	H	PO	A
J. Collins, rf	2	0	0	1	0	Sloan, rf	5	0	1	0	0
Leibold, rf	3	1	1	2	0	Smith, lf	5	0	1	3	1
McMul'n, 3b	6	2	2	0	5	Sisler, 1b	5	1	3	14	1
E. Collins, 2b	4	1	2	2	3	Pratt, 2b	5	0	0	4	4
Byrne, 2b	1	0	0	0	1	Severeid, c	5	2	2	5	3
Jackson, lf	2	3	2	2	0	Jacobs'n, cf	5	2	2	0	0
Felsch, cf	5	3	3	1	0	Johnson, 3b	5	1	3	0	5
Gandil, 1b	4	0	1	14	0	Lavan, ss	5	0	1	1	2
Risberg, ss	3	2	2	3	3	Koob, (LP)	1	0	1	0	1
Schalk, c	5	1	3	1	0	Rumler, ph	1	0	0	0	0
Lynn, c	0	0	0	1	1	Rogers, p	2	0	2	0	3
Faber, (WP)	3	0	0	0	6						
Totals	38	13	16	27	19	Totals	44	6	16	27	20

```
Chicago      031 001 080    13–16–2
St. Louis    000 000 033     6–16–2
```

2B: Leibold, Felsch 2; SB: Severeid, Sisler, E. Collins 2, Jackson, Johnson, Felsch, Risberg, J. Collins; Sac. Hits: Faber, E. Collins, Gandil; LOB: Chicago 8, St. Louis 11; Double Plays: Johnson, Pratt and Sisler, E. Collins, Risberg and Gandil; BB: Koob 3, Rogers 3, Fober 0; K: Faber 1, Koob 2, Rogers 0; Hit by Pitcher: Jackson by Rogers; Umpires: Hildebrand and Dinneen; Time of Game: 1:32.

Oscar Emil Felsch hailed from hardy German stock. He was born and reared in Milwaukee, where the good German burghers worked hard, drank beer by the barrel, ate their bratwurst and potato salad by the plateful and spent their leisure hours either at Borchert Field watching the Brewers play ball, or dancing to polkas. The Felsch family was an enthusiastic part of that entire scenario and young Oscar, whose baseball games were interrupted by bothersome schooltime hours, spent his early years honing his athletic skills. With an easy smile and an upbeat personality, he was one of the more likeable kids in the neighborhood. The name "Happy" was a natural, as was his powerful swing.

By 1914 Hap Felsch had put in the last of his apprentice years in the minors, smacking baseballs around the American Association for his hometown Brewers and leading the league in homers with 19. That caught the eye of Mr. Comiskey in Chicago, and he brought Felsch north with his 1915 Sox club to try out his swing and his speed on American League opponents. That season he won his spurs, helping the team move up to third place under new manager Clarence Rowland, who at the time wasn't much older than the 24 year old Felsch. He didn't tear the league apart, but there were telltale signs that this fellow could run with the swiftest, throw with the stronger arms in the league and hit with authority. Among sluggers in the league, Hap's bat had the kind of pop in it that made him a prime candidate for the middle of Rowland's batting order.

After a .300 season in 1916, during which he nailed down the center field spot and led the league in fielding average, he was ready for heavy duty action with a pennant contender in 1917, installed in the number five spot in the batting order behind Capt. Eddie Collins, who hit third, and Joe Jackson, whose multi-talented hitting skills were used in the cleanup slot. That 3–4–5 lineup in the middle of the order was the best in either league, and the best of the three from a hitting standpoint in 1917 was Hap Felsch, who contributed a strong .308 average and 102 RBI, a total which was unsurpassed in White Sox history to that point.

Strong as a bull, he powered his way through the strongest of the White Sox years of supremacy, the fellow in the lineup who could ruin opponents in one swat. And had it not been for his potent shilelagh, the Chisox would probably not have distanced themselves from the field, especially inasmuch as Eddie Collins and Joe Jack-

The Happy One, Oscar Emil Felsch. Hap led the Sox with a strong .308
in 1917 on his way to a career that might conceivably have merited Hall
of Fame consideration. That was not to be, not after the 1919 World
Series. (Dennis Colgin)

son, while productive in many ways, simply didn't have what for them would have been considered up-to-par years.

The one flaw in all of this, and it proved to be fatal within a very short period of time, was his preference for the bawdy and ribald, which early on led him to consorting with the more adventurous and raucous among the Sox players such as Swede Risberg and Chick Gandil. Although Hap got by 1917 without a scratch, 1919–20 would be another story. These were Hap Felsch's White Sox numbers:

Year	AB	R	H	RBI	3B	HR	BA	SLG	SB	BR	FR	TPR
1915	427	65	106	53	11	3	.248	.363	16	2	-3	-1.4
1916	546	73	164	70	12	7	.300	.427	13	16	7	1.7
1917	575	75	177	102	10	6	.308	.403	26	17	19	3.0
1918	206	16	52	20	5	1	.252	.325	6	-3	5	-0.1
1919	502	68	138	86	11	7	.275	.428	19	7	21	2.1
1920	556	88	188	115	15	14	.338	.540	8	31	18	3.2
Totals	2812	385	825	446	64	38	.293	.427	88	70	67	8.5

As a result of their winning ways, the St. Louis sweep pushed the Sox lead up to six games. Now up 4½ on Boston in the win column, they had also gone ahead in the loss column, 47 losses to Boston's 50. The noose was tightening around The Carmine's neck with every passing inning, their chances to repeat lessening with every passing day.

On September 8 the Rowlandmen checked in at Comiskey Park for a two-game set with Cleveland with 15 games to go in regular season's play. The afternoon bill featured a military celebration, parading some 6,000 soldiers and sailors in front of a sellout gathering—*and* an Eddie Cicotte Special, a polished, 2 to 0 demonstration of the pitching arts that shut down the Indians on four hits and not the faintest glimmering of hope for a run in the nine innings Little Eddie labored on the hill.

The only fire power needed was ignited by Capt. Collins, who led a deadly two-run assault on Cleveland's ace, Jim Bagby, as the Sox picked up another half game on Boston, idled by rain in Philadelphia. And it was Collins who snuffed out the only real shot fired by the Indians all day when he flagged down a missile headed for right center that might have complicated things for Eddie Cicotte and his two run lead.

It was Edward Trowbridge Collins, not Joe Jackson, who was the linchpin Czar Comiskey sought to revitalize his ball club when, in 1914, he vowed to get back into the thick of pennant contention. It cost him dearly to wrap up the deal with Connie Mack, but Commy never wavered, dead certain to the bottom of the soles of his shoes that the first step was the most important and that a player who played the game not only with surpassing skill, but with his head and heart as well, was the very first order of business. Pitchers and sluggers could wait, but a master craftsman who could lead came first. Eddie Collins, made team captain right from the start, filled that bill, paying immediate dividends with a super season in 1915, his first in pale hose, leading the league with a career high 119 walks, stealing 46 bases, hitting right at his lifetime average, .332, and calling the defensive signals for a Chicago club that suddenly began to evidence the ability, smarts and determination to get into the winner's circle. Credit Eddie Collins. He might have been a part of those great Mack championship clubs, adding super numbers to his Hall of Fame credentials, but his glossy play as a consummate professional during his Chicago years, and under the most trying of circumstances, sealed his place among the game's greats at Cooperstown.

Collins' numbers in 1917 were not up to those he usually posted. He found other ways offensively and especially defensively to make the club a winner. He turned in 42 multiple-hit games, seven of them through the torrid winning streak between August 23 and September 14, and he played in every game of the season, igniting or capping rallies when clutch hitting—or bunting, a specialty of his—was called for. He gave the rookie Risberg a comfort zone, easing him into major league play, and, along with Ray Schalk, led the way defensively, spurring infielders and outfielders alike to extra effort and with it, sensational play afield. The Cleveland game (above) was a typical example, a 1 for 2 day with a couple walks, a few assists and that dazzling robbery of what might easily have been an extra base knock.

There's but one thing to add to any discussion about Eddie Collins' role in either Philadelphia or Chicago: he was elected, with the very first class of honorees, to the Hall of Fame in 1936. His Chicago record follows:

Year	GP	AB	R	H	2B	3B	BB	BA	OB%	SB	BR	TPR
1915	155	521	118	173	22	10	119	.332	.460	46	48	6.6
1916	155	545	87	168	14	17	86	.308	.405	40	29	3.0
1917	156	564	91	163	18	12	89	.289	.389	53	22	-0.1
1918	97	330	51	91	8	2	73	.276	.407	22	13	1.6
1919	140	518	87	165	19	7	68	.319	.400	33	20	2.6
1920	153	602	117	224	38	13	69	.372	.438	19	42	5.4
1921	139	526	79	177	20	10	66	.337	.412	12	15	4.1
1922	154	598	92	194	20	12	73	.324	.401	20	12	0.7
1923	145	505	89	182	22	5	84	.360	.455	47	36	3.4
1924*	152	556	108	194	27	7	89	.349	.441	42	34	3.2
1925*	118	425	80	147	26	3	87	.346	.461	19	31	2.5
1926*	106	375	66	129	32	4	62	.344	.441	13	25	2.1
Totals	1670	6065	1065	2007	266	102	965	.331	.426	366	307	35.1

* Served as Playing Manager

The final tilt of the 1917 season between Cleveland and the Sox was a bizarre affair that ended up in a forfeit that went into ten innings. There had been tie games and many rainouts that went into the 1917 record book, but no forfeits involving either team. That all changed on September 9, when umpire "Brick" Owens, in his second year of major league arbitrating, declared Cleveland outfielder Jack Graney out on a play at third base that Owens ruled interference. What preceeded the interference call was as strange as what followed it in the bottom of the ninth. Graney had singled and on the ensuing run and hit play, headed for second with the pitch. Freddie McMullin knocked down Ray Chapman's grounder but got it to Eddie Collins at second too late for a force play, and Collins' relay to Gandil was too late to get the swift Chapman. With runners on first and second, then, Tris Speaker's fly-out was deep enough to permit the runners to advance, putting Graney at third and Chapman at second.

During the course of Bill Wambsganss' at bat Graney took a long lead off third and Ray Schalk, always on the lookout for a quick pickoff, fired one of reliever Dave Danforth's pitches to McMullin, hoping to pick Graney off, but his throw was off the mark and McMullin, just prior to chasing the errant Schalk throw, got all tangled up with Graney on the baseline before he could retrieve the ball near the dugout. As he did Graney and Chapman, who took off from second, both scored. But Owens ruled that Graney had interfered with McMullin, unfairly holding him up to get at the ball. Predictably, a hue and cry was raised and it was twenty minutes before play was resumed with the score still tied at three and the White Sox due up in the bottom half of the inning. Southpaw Danforth was first up for the Sox and reliever Fritz Coumbe made short work of "Dauntless Dave," whiffing him in short order. On the third strike catcher Steve O'Neill fired the ball to third baseman Ivan Howard, as catchers often do after a strikeout, but Howard purposely let the ball go through, as did left fielder Graney, who turned his back on the ball as it sped past him, rolling all the way out to the left field wall. That insolence was too much for umpire Owens, who tore off his mask and declared the game a 9–0 forfeit to Chicago.

Thus ended the game and the season series with the Indians, the Sox victors in 14 of the 22 seasonal matches, the last of which was no doubt grist for Hot Stove League review all winter long. The last Cleveland date also idled the Pale Hose the next four days, with no games scheduled until September 14 at Detroit. Three of those days were promptly filled up with exhibition dates, a common practice among major league franchises.

One of those exhibitions

Even in what for Eddie Collins was an off season, he still was a team leader who found ways and means to win ball games, enabling the Chisox to keep pressure on their opponents both offensively and defensively. (Dennis Colgin)

was played in Fort Wayne, Indiana, where the local Chiefs of the Central League provided the Pale Hose with an afternoon of competition before a sellout crowd. Eager to see the ball club that was on its way to the pennant, the locals cheered enthusiastically with almost every out and every base hit. Long a baseball hotbed, and the site of the first National Association game in 1871, Fort Wayners relished every inning of the 7 to 2 White Sox victory. The game gave Pants Rowland a chance to work out some of his reserves and rest his regulars, though the entire team made each of the Beloit, Fort Wayne and Milwaukee trips. Mellie Wolfgang, still another of the White Sox spitballers, a veteran of several seasons with the Sox who served primarily as batting practice pitcher during the 1917 season, went the route for the winners. The box score of the Fort Wayne game follows:

Chicago White Sox at Fort Wayne Chiefs, September 11, 1917

Chicago	R	H	PO	A	E	Ft. Wayne	R	H	PO	A	E
Leibold, cf	1	1	3	0	0	Rumser, ss	2	3	2	1	2
McMul'n, 3b	0	0	2	4	0	Van'rift, 2b	0	1	2	3	0
Murphy, rf	0	2	0	1	0	Hoffman, 3b	0	1	2	3	1
J. Collins, lf	2	3	4	0	0	Hald'rm'n, lf	0	0	1	1	2
Jourdan, 1b	1	2	9	0	0	Siegfried, cf	0	1	2	1	0
Hasbrook, 2b	1	3	4	2	1	Miller, rf	0	0	1	2	0
Risberg, ss	1	2	1	5	1	Myers, 1b	0	0	8	1	0
Lynn, c	1	1	2	1	0	Kelly, c	0	2	6	0	0
Jenkins, c	0	1	2	0	0	Kowal'i, (LP)	0	0	0	1	0
Wolf. g, (WP)	0	0	0	3	0	Wagner, p	0	0	0	2	0
Totals	7	14	27	16	2	Totals	2	8	24	15	5

Fort Wayne   001 001 001   2–8–5
Chicago   421 110 10x   7–14–2

2B: Hasbrook, Lynn; 3B: Siegfried; HR: Rumser 2, Jourdan; SB: Leibold, Risberg; Sac. Hit: Wolfgang; K: Wolfgang 4, Kowalski 2, Wagner 1; BB: Wolfgang 3, Kowalski 1; Umpires: Slade and Farnan.

Back in Chicago big name sportswriters like Westbrook Pegler and Grantland Rice were already beginning to sharpen their pencils for a Chicago World Series, and in New York, Irvin S. Cobb, one of the *New York Times'* top journalists, and a humorist as well, was given a special assignment to cover the Series.

The *Chicago Tribune* carried an article about tickets for the upcoming Classic, noting that on Ban Johnson's return from some baseball business in St. Louis, the American League's prexy found his desk swamped with ducat requests, many of them from the far reaches of the country. I. E. Sanborn, in the *Trib*'s September 13 issue quoted Johnson on ticket sales:

> Judging by the flood of requests that has already started, Comiskey Park would not be large enough to hold half the people from other western cities who want to come here for the games...Chicago's patrons should come first, however, for they make possible the playing of the world's series.

So the cat was out of the bag and betting money was already on the Pale Hose to close out the season in another three weeks at the head of the pack. Although talk about World Series ball games was the rage downtown, it wasn't part of the ball club's banter around the clubhouse. A seven game lead, garnished by Boston losses in Washington and New York, was all well and good, but there was still a Red Sox series to get through in Boston among another 14 games to play. But the underlying feeling up and down the roster from Commisar Comiskey on down to the bucket boy was that this Chicago ball club was going to be a champion, and the quiet confidence they manifested from day to day underscored their considerable talents, versatility and determination, suggesting that they would get the job done, and in style.

On then, to Detroit, where the team had been involved in those controversial back-to-back double-headers on September 2 and 3 for a single game on Saturday, the 14th, and another twinbill on Sunday, the 15th. The three-game series would complete the Chicago-Detroit competition for the season.

With everyone rested and none of his players except Buck Weaver suffering from undue physical stress, White Sox manager Pants Rowland, by this time more respected around the league than he had been in previous years (winning *does* solve so many problems!), named Eddie Cicotte to pitch the opener in his home town. Detroit manager Hughie Jennings, the famed Eeeeyah!-man of baseball, countered with southpaw Willie Mitchell.

Eddie Cicotte beat Willie Mitchell, the Sox added their ninth straight to their latest victory run and maintained their eight game lead over Boston's Red Sox, who beat the Yankees behind Carl Mays, successful for the 20th time during the course of the season.

On the Bosox' victory, the *New York Times* had this interesting note:

> September 15, 1917. The Yankees, who have been helping the Chicago White Sox win the American League pennant by persistently nagging Boston, withdrew their support yesterday, and the Red Sox won a game at the Polo Grounds by a score of 6 to 5. The White Sox do not seem to be gravely in need of this assistance, but the oftener Boston is beaten, the sooner the inevitable will happen. Harry Frazee, who owns the Bostons, had offered his players $1,000 each if they beat the White Sox. His pocketbook would be just as safe if he offered them $10,000 each.

In the National League the McGrawmen, moving along on cruise control, backed up a Pol Perritt shutout with a five-run, nine-hit attack that distanced the New Yorkers from second place Philadelphia by 11 games. John McGraw's patented winning formula, which depended on strong defense (three double plays in their Philadelphia conquest and a pair of spectacular fielding gems helped deny the A's a single run although they got to Perritt for 12 hits), timely hitting and stingy pitching that emphasized, as always, pinpoint control, had New Yorkers raving as they expected not only a pennant but a World Series triumph. McGraw, as always, expected the victory, going so far as indicating already in mid-September that it wouldn't matter who the Giants played; they would beat either of the Sox teams, though he preferred to play against the Red Sox. That latter bit of pomposity did not escape the notice of Rowland, his number one side-kick Bill Gleason, a crusty old veteran of baseball wars both with and against McGraw, and the White Sox players.

The White Sox victory over the Tigers on September 14 featured a 3 for 4 day by Chick Gandil, who tripled, singled twice, drove in a run and handled 13 chances flawlessly. The '17 season for Gandil, not the best of his three years with the Pale Hose, was nonetheless a steady, strong-fielding campaign for the veteran. He had done for Comiskey what the big boss expected back in March when he came to terms with the sure-handed first-sacker. On this particular day he shared offensive fireworks with Eddie Collins, both of them registering three safeties in the 7 to 3 victory.

Arnold Gandil was born in St. Paul, Minnesota, and in 1917,

at 30, was into his eighth major league campaign. Although 1917 was not a career year for the Sox' first baseman, it was a productive season of solid fielding (Gandil's .995 fielding average in 149 games led American League first sackers) along with a number of games in which his timely hitting paved the way to important White Sox victories. One of those came on September 14 in the 7 to 3 triumph over the Tigers at Detroit, a day on which the Sox maintained their eight-game edge on the Red Sox, and moved them to within eight victories of the coveted 100-win mark.

The box score follows:

Chicago	AB	R	H	PO	A	Detroit	AB	R	H	PO	A
J. Collins, rf	5	0	0	3	0	Bush, ss	4	1	1	6	3
McMul'n, 3b	5	0	2	1	3	Vitt, 3b	3	0	0	1	2
E. Collins, 2b	5	2	3	0	6	Cobb, cf	2	1	0	3	0
Jackson, lf	3	2	0	1	0	Veach, lf	4	1	2	1	1
Felsch, cf	3	2	1	5	0	Heilman, rf	4	0	2	1	0
Gandil, 1b	4	1	3	13	0	Burns, 1b	3	0	0	12	1
Risberg, ss	3	0	1	2	3	Young, 2b	3	0	2	1	2
Schalk, c	3	0	1	2	1	Stanage, c	3	0	0	2	4
Cicotte, (WP)	4	0	1	0	2	Mitchell, (LP)	2	0	0	0	2
						Ehmke, p	0	0	0	0	0
						Harper, ph	1	0	0	0	0
Totals	35	7	12	27	15	Totals	29	3	7	27	15

Chicago	020 002 030	7–12–0
Detroit	100 100 001	3–7–3

2B: Bush, E. Collins; 3B: Gandil; SB: Cobb, E. Collins 2; Sac. Hits: Vitt, Jackson, Schalk, Burns; Sac. Fly: Cobb; LOB: Chicago 5, Detroit 4; DP: Mitchell, Stanage, and Vitt; BB: Mitchell 1, Cicotte 2; K: Mitchell 3, Cicotte 2; Hit by Pitcher: Felsch (by Mitchell); Wild Pitch: Mitchell; Passed Ball: Stanage; Umpires: Owens and Evans; Time of Game: 1:33.

Chick Gandil, who had left home at 17 to do things on his own and in his own way, wandered a long way from his early years in Minnesota, winding up, finally, in the rough and tumble Southwest where he played ball, did some boxing, and acquired the tough hombre characteristics that were to mark his personal and ball playing persona. He didn't smile much, was quick to draw a line in the dirt over what he perceived to be assaults on his manhood, and was in the forefront of every battle, *mano a mano*, in which the Sox were involved.

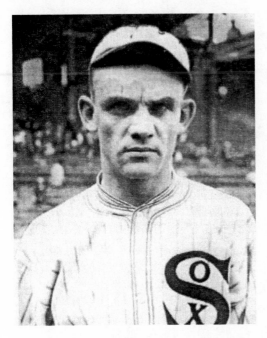

Charles "Chick" Gandil's major league career started at Comiskey Park in 1910, but from 1911 to 1915 he was with the Washington Senators and then moved to Cleveland for the 1916 season. Comiskey brought him back to Chicago for the 1917 season. He led American League first basemen in fielding average four times, including his .995 mark in 1917. (Dennis Colgin)

One such encounter had come up earlier in the season when the Red Sox, at Comiskey Park in August, sailed into bases with spikes flying. On a play that doubled Del Gainer at first, Shano Collins relayed a strike to Gandil for a double play after snaring Red Sox Harry Hooper's line drive. Gainer slid back into first, spikes high, attempting to beat the throw. That brought on an exchange of threats and support for Gainer from the Red Sox dugout. Chief among the Red Sox was relief pitcher Lore "King" Bader, who was singled out by Gandil for futher "consultation." According to Irv Sanborn of the *Chicago Tribune*, this is the way it ended:

After the game Gandil tarried on the way to the dressing rooms until the Red Sox bunch overtook him, then had it out with Bader before a small group of spectators. All accounts agree that one punch settled the argument for the rest of the season and Bader was the recipient of the punch. (*Chicago Tribune*, August 22, 1917.)

Gandil's Chicago years were to receive much closer scrutiny during 1919 and 1920, of course, when his leadership in the World Series fix made headlines nationwide. Although he sat out the 1920 season because he refused to sign the contract President Comiskey offered him, there was no denying his steep involvement in baseball's most celebrated scandal. And that, after Commissioner Landis' decree, marked the end of his major league career.

Chick Gandil's four-season White Sox record follows:

Year	GP	AB	R	H	3B	OB%	BB/K	SB	FA	FR	BA	TPR
1910	77	275	21	53	3	.262	24/-	12	.989	7	.193	-0.5
1917	149	553	53	151	7	.316	30/36	16	.995	-6	.273	-1.8
1918	114	439	49	119	4	.330	27/19	9	.992	-3	.271	-1.0
1919	115	441	54	128	7	.383	20/20	10	.997	-4	.290	-1.0
Totals	455	1708	177	451	21	.323	101/75	47	.993	-6	.264	-4.3

By September 19 the Pale Hose were in Philadelphia, just having concluded a three out of four set in three different cities, which ran their current streak of winning baseball to 20 wins in the last 22 games. That included two wins in Detroit after Eddie Cicotte's 2 to 1 loss to the Bengals, a 4 to 3 victory over the St. Louis Browns that rang down the curtain on their 1917 home schedule, and finally, a 6–1, Red Faber triumph that opened their last series of the season with the Mackmen. The victory, the Sox' 95th, enabled them to move on up the coast to Boston with an eight game bulge. The pennant race was over and everybody knew it. The only race that was left was the one to the box offices in Chicago and New York where World Series tickets would soon be available to White Sox and Giants fans, and to the countless numbers of other interested bystanders, media and officials of one kind or another.

CHAPTER 10

The Champs

Charley Comiskey, the Old Roman, finally had his championship ball club. Red Faber and his pale hosed teammates saw to that on September 21 when they beat the Red Sox at Fenway Park in a ten inning thriller 2 to 1. The winning tally was produced by Ray Schalk's double and a single by Shano Collins. The big redhead breezed through the first five stanzas as though he were about to hurl a perfect game, but the Carmine got to him for three hits and a game-tying run during the remaining four innings, and a pair of singles that put Charles Shorten on third and Larry Gardner on first raised Red Sox hopes in the bottom of the tenth. Then Babe Ruth came off the bench to hit for Ev Scott and rifled a shot toward right that Eddie Collins converted into a lightning double play, Collins to Weaver to Gandil, ending the game, sealing the victory and putting the American League flag beyond the reach of Boston—or anybody else—for 1917.

There were several things that were characteristic, as well as significant, about the flag-clinching triumph that day. For one, though they were tied, the White Sox refused to lose, winning when they had to, manufacturing the winning run with timely hitting. In this instance, it came from the little battler behind the plate, Ray

163

Schalk, and the unheralded John "Shano" Collins. The lineup from top to bottom seemed to be just as dangerous as it had to be, with everyone contributing, as it won game after game in clutch situations. For another, Red Faber, crowning the final third of the campaign with stellar pitching, battled Hub Leonard down to the last out to annex his 16th triumph. His performance spoke volumes about his readiness for the impending Fall Classic. Another factor that was indispensable to the Chicagoans during the 1917 campaign was their team speed in every phase of the game, whether shutting down enemy rallies with double plays, catching up with fly balls and line drives to make breath-taking catches in the outfield, or staging hit and run and run and hit plays, or stealing bases when needed. The team possessed awesome speed afoot and used it to equally awesome advantage. Yet another factor, among more to be mentioned later, was Fred McMullin's fine play as a stand-in for Buck Weaver during his convalescence, followed by his move to third base when "The Ginger Kid" returned to the lineup in Philadelphia on September 18 that underscored the ball club's depth and versatility.

The box score of the pennant-clinching game follows.

Chicago White Sox at Fenway Park, September 21, 1917

Chicago	AB	R	H	PO	A	Boston	AB	R	H	PO	A
J. Collins, rf	5	0	2	3	1	Hooper, rf	4	1	1	0	0
McMullin, 3b	4	0	1	0	3	Barry, 2b	4	0	2	2	2
E. Collins, 2b	4	0	1	2	7	Hoblitzel, 1b	4	0	0	9	1
Jackson, lf	3	0	0	1	0	Lewis, lf	4	0	0	3	0
Felsch, cf	4	1	1	1	0	Shorten, cf	4	0	1	4	0
Gandil, 1b	4	0	0	10	0	Gardner, 3b	3	0	1	0	2
Weaver, ss	2	0	1	3	4	Scott, ss	2	0	0	6	2
Schalk, c	4	1	2	1	0	Thomas, c	3	0	0	5	4
Faber, (WP)	3	0	0	0	6	Leonard, (LP)	3	0	0	1	2
						Ruth, ph	1	0	0	0	0
Totals	35	2	8	30	21	Totals	32	1	5	30	13

Chicago	000 100 000 1	2–8–0
Boston	000 000 100 0	1–5–1

2B: Schalk; 3B: Hooper; Sac. Hits: McMullin, Scott; LOB: Chicago 8, Boston 3; DP: J. Collins and Gandil, E. Collins, Weaver and Gandil; Scott and Hoblitzel; BB: Leonard 3; K: Faber 1, Leonard 4; Hit by Pitcher: Gardner by Faber, Weaver by Leonard; Umpires: Hildebrand and Dinneen; Time of Game: 1:48.

The following excerpts from the pages of the *Chicago Tribune*'s September 22 edition tell us about the Chicago Baseball Czar's emotional reaction to the Chisox victory in Boston. The Trib carried a copy of the wire Commy sent to manager Rowland:

To: C. H. Rowland, Mgr., Champion White Sox
Brunswick Hotel, Boston, Mass.

The fondest hopes of all Chicago and the wonderful legion of White Sox fans as well as myself have come true—after eleven long years of patient waiting. Our heartiest congratulations are due your team and self for winning the American League pennant, and we are all wishing you Godspeed and good luck in the coming world's series. Give the club and party as fine a dinner as you can with my compliments.

Charles. A. Comiskey

John Alcock wrote one of several articles in the *Tribune* heralding the victory, and had this to say about Comiskey's personal reaction in Chicago:

September 22, 1917.
"After eleven years."

Ticker service was too slow. Comiskey had opened a telephone wire to an afternoon sporting editor as early as the third inning. He had followed the White Sox battle at Boston almost play by play. Then the tenth inning ended with the White Sox winners of the one game needed to assure them the American League championship...

It was too much for the Old Roman. His hand shook so that safety required he hang up the telephone receiver. But he turned to his son, Commy Lou, and said: "Better tell your mother." Big Lou had Mrs. Comiskey on the phone in a minute or so, and the whole family was rejoicing long before Chicago fandom knew the glad news.

There was no chance for a coherent statement from Comiskey after his Sox had clinched the pennant. When the finish came he was just so happy to talk...

After the first excitement subsided, Comiskey was almost as cool as the Comiskey most folks know. He went back as far as 1908 recalling other championships that were within his grasp. "Twice I had the pennant all ready to nail to the pole, and both times they snatched it from my hands," he said. "This one is mine, though. And after eleven years!

The Pale Hose clinched the 1917 pennant on September 21, 1917. Red Faber's 16th win of the season turned the trick.

Eight games remained yet to be played before the relentless grind of the 154-game schedule would be completed. During that time the club's physical welfare would be just as important as winning ball games. This was no time for big guns to go down, so there would be time off for some of the brighter stars while the reserves got a chance to strut their stuff. Given those considerations it was inevitable that the two pennant winners would lose as many as they won in ringing down the final act of the 1917 season.

On September 24, three days after Chicago's victory celebration, crossfiring Slim Sallee and the Men of McGraw clinched the National League pennant with a 2 to 1 victory over the Cardinals in St. Louis. The win maintained the Giants' ten-game lead over the Phillies despite another heroic, season-long effort by Pete Alexander, who would add a third straight, 30-win season to his growing list of Hall of Fame credentials. And so the World Series opponents were officially set. That battle would begin in Chicago on October 6.

There are two games among the remaining eight that merit more than a passing comment or two. These two games involved moundsmen Joey Benz and Eddie Cicotte. In the first of these Benz, a.k.a. Blitzen among his Sox teammates, beat the Senators in Washington, going the route in a 6–1 victory.

Beating the Senators was one thing Joey Benz knew how to do, and in 1917 he really took Washington's Nationals to the cleaners. Including his 6–1 conquest on September 27, he won four times without a loss, hurling in still another Sox triumph over the Senators without gaining the victory. In a 7–3 year, he also beat the Athletics 11–0, the Brownies 11–1 and Cleveland 2–1. Not bad at all for a spot pitcher.

The White Sox ball club behind the Hoosier righthander in 1914 wasn't nearly as good as his 1917 teammates and his record suffered accordingly (14 and 19), but during one over-the-edge stretch he was almost untouchable, no-hitting the Indians on May 31, 1914, despite three Chisox errors, and following that with another no-hit stretch of eight innings against Walter Johnson. In the ninth frame an Eddie Ainsmith rope was deflected off third sacker Scotty Alcock's glove, making its way into left field for the only Wahington safety of the day. Blitzen won that one, too, beating the one and only Johnson—as he had said he would!

By 1917 Joey Benz, whose Me Worry? visage (from the *Mad* magazine era) and go-along-get-along personality made him a big hit with players, fans, and even umps, had been throwing his spitters and knucklers for the Sox some six seasons. He made one last appearance during the 1919 season, a two inning stint, then called it a career, having enjoyed the best of White Sox times, but not having suffered through the worst, though he was as dejected about the Scandal Years as everyone else in Chicagoland. His career record showed 77 wins against 75 losses, all achieved in White Sox flannels. His record follows:

Year	Won	Lost	Pct.	IP	BB/K	OBA	RAT	PR	PD*	ERA	TPI
1911	3	2	.500	55.2	13/28	.251	10.8	7	1	2.26	0.4
1912	13	17	.433	237.2	70/96	.259	11.7	11	1	2.90	0.5
1913	7	10	.412	151.0	59/79	.254	12.3	3	4	2.74	0.7
1914	14	19	.424	283.1	66/142	.236	9.9	15	6	2.26	2.1
1915	15	11	.577	238.1	43/81	.238	9.6	22	3	2.11	2.2
1916	9	5	.643	142.0	32/57	.214	9.1	13	1	2.03	0.8
1917	7	3	.700	94.2	23/25	.220	9.6	2	0	2.47	0.1
1918	8	8	.500	154.0	28/30	.269	10.9	3	3	2.51	0.5
1919	0	0	.000	2.0	0/0	.250	9.0	1	0	0.00	0.0
Totals	76	75	.503	1358.2	334/538	.243	10.5	76	19	2.42	7.3

*PD (Pitcher's Defense) is a sabermetric measure that calculates how many runs a pitcher saves beyond what a league-average pitcher saves his team. An excellent season rating would be 2; superior, 4; and 6 and above outstanding.

The White Sox closed out the 1917 season with a three game

series at the Polo Grounds, a place they would be visiting soon
again to see what they could do about winning the World Series.
This time, however, the three game engagement would involve
them with manager "Wild Bill" Donovan's New York Yankees.
The Sox entered the series with 99 wins behind them and skipper
Rowland slated Lefty Williams and Eddie Cicotte to pitch the series
opening doubleheader on September 29.

In the twinbill's first game of the day, the Yanks landed on
Lefty Williams like a long lost brother and chased him in the opening frame. Williams escaped the loss only because the Sox managed a four-run uprising in the second inning that moved them
ahead of the Yankees 5 to 4. By that time Dave Danforth was on
the mound in relief of Williams. As the game wore on both teams
pounded the pitchers around, the Yanks finally bombing the Sox
into submission by a 12–8 margin. Rowland left Danforth in the
game the rest of the way and, though it wasn't one of the tall southpaw's better days, he did survive in one piece, albeit having been
tagged with the loss. As a result the Sox' win column was stalled
at number 99, a number that exceeded by six any previous total in
the 17 seasons of major league baseball on the South Side.

For the second game Rowland used his regular starting lineup
and entrusted the outcome to his ace, the 27-game winner, Eddie
Cicotte, and after giving up a run in the first inning, little Eddie
put on a pitching clinic for some 15,000 plus New Yorkers, shutting out the Yanks the rest of the way. The winning runs were engineered by Hap Felsch, who grounded into a fielders' choice, stole
second, moved on to third on catcher Roxy Walter's erring throw,
and scored on a Chick Gandil single, and a screaming line drive off
the bat of Buck Weaver that scored Gandil. Another seventh inning
tally made the final score 3 to 1, enabling Eddie "C" to notch his
28th conquest of the season. Equally important, it raised the Sox'
victory number to the century mark, a record that still stands.

Jim Crusinberry, the *Chicago Tribune* sports scribe covering
the game, took note, also, of three very interested spectators, Giant
players Heinie Zimmerman, Benny Kauff and George Burns.

September 30, 1917. New York's baseball fans, who are greatly
excited over the coming world's series between the White Sox
and the Giants, experienced both joy and despair today while
giving the Sox the once over, or rather the twice over, in a double header against the Yankees. They were joyful in the first

game when the Yanks ran away with it by a count of 12 to 8, but they were left in doubt regarding the chances of their Giants when they saw the Sox take the second, 3 to 1.

There were more than 15,000 fans present, not because the games amounted to anything, but because it had been announced in advance that Cicotte would hurl. All New York was interested in what this clever little shine ball, knuckle ball, and spitball flinger of the Chicago team would do and the crowd was a Giants' crowd, who came out just to speculate on what Cicotte would do with Heinie Zim, Benny Kauff, George Burns, and the other sluggers of the local champions.

Bennie and Heinie and George were in the grand stand themselves, probably as interested in the actions of Cicotte as anyone in the throng and indications are that in Gotham tonight the fans have less confidence in victory than

They called this fellow Blitzen. The popular Joe Benz spent his 9-year career in Chicago, winning 77 ball games for the Pale Hose. He specialized in beating Washington. (Brace photograph)

they had this morning or even after the first game was played today. There will be less of that six to five stuff in the gambling halls tonight.

The Sox' 100th victory left them 8½ games ahead of Boston's Carmine and 13 ahead of Cleveland, in third place. Detroit rounded out the first division at 79 and 55, followed by Washington, New York, St. Louis and Philadelphia. The box score of that epochal White Sox victory follows:

White Sox–Yankees Game at the Polo Grounds, September 29, 1917

Chicago	AB	R	H	PO	A	New York	AB	R	H	PO	A
J. Collins, lf	4	0	0	2	0	Miller, cf	4	1	2	2	0
E. Murphy, ph	1	0	0	0	0	Ward, ss	4	0	1	2	2
McMullin, 3b	4	1	0	1	1	Baker, 3b	3	0	0	0	2
E. Collins, 2b	4	0	1	0	3	Pipp, 1b	4	0	0	10	0
Jackson, rf	4	0	1	0	0	Lamar, lf	4	0	1	2	0
Felsch, cf	4	1	1	3	0	Vick, cf	4	0	1	2	0
Gandil, 1b	3	1	2	9	1	Fewster, 2b	4	0	2	2	4
Weaver, ss	4	0	2	3	3	Walters, c	3	0	1	6	1
Schalk, c	3	0	0	7	1	Thorm'len, (LP)	2	0	0	0	0
Lynn, c	1	0	1	2	0	Brady, p	0	0	0	0	0
Cicotte, (WP)	3	0	1	0	0	Hendryx, ph	1	0	0	0	0
Totals	35	3	9	27	9	Totals	33	1	8	26*	9

*Felsch out, hit by batted ball.

Chicago	000	002	100	3–9–2
New York	100	000	000	1–8–4

2B: Vick; 3B: Miller; SB: Felsch, Vick; LOB: Chicago 9; New York 6; DP: Gandil and Schalk, E. Collins, Weaver and Gandil; BB: Thormahlen 4, Cicotte 1; K: Thormahlen 5, Cicotte 7; Umpires: Hildebrand and Dinneen; Time of Game: 1:45.

Eddie Cicotte's 28th victory, two less than Pete Alexander's in the National League, led the American league. His nearest competitors were Babe Ruth with 24 and two 23-game winners, Walter Johnson and Cleveland's Jim Bagby. But Cicotte's 28-game total, outstanding though it is, might just be a lesser accomplishment than some of the other numbers he posted as his league's best hurler that season. He led the league in innings pitched with a whopping 346.2, dazzled opposing teams with a miniscule 1.53 ERA, led in opposing teams' BA with .248, paced the circuit with an 8.28 ratio (ratio, it will be recalled, is the sum of hits and walks allowed per nine innings pitched), and registered the best pitcher runs total (44) and Total Pitcher Index (5.4) in the American League. He was, arguably, the best pitcher in baseball *the summer of 1917*, even ahead of Pete Alexander and his 30 wins. He was, for a fact, the American League's MVP, relegating Ty Cobb's greatest individual season, which did not help to produce a league champion, to a runnerup spot because without little Eddie there is absolutely no way that the Comiskeymen could have won the pennant. That marks him as indispensable and irreplaceable in the Chicago scheme of things. And this, mind you, over the singular and invaluable contributions of team captain Eddie Collins, or Hap Felsch with his banner year, or Joe Jackson, or any of the others on a stellar ball club. And it goes with, or without saying, that had there been a Cy Young Award in 1917, it would have been garnered by Mr. Cicotte.

Eddie Cicotte had been around the American League since his September, 1905, debut with Detroit's Tigers. Ty Cobb had debuted just a week earlier as both players were brought into Detroit for a look-see. The Tigers kept Cobb but passed on Cicotte, who surfaced three seasons later with the Red Sox for whom he pitched the next four-plus seasons. Then he was purchased by the White Sox during mid-season of 1912. During the next four seasons he became one of the league's best hurlers, and by 1917, at 33, was at an apex point in a career that might well have merited Hall of Fame consideration, winning 80 games between 1917 and 1920 while losing but 48. An off year (12 and 19) during the height of the Great War's demands and anxieties in 1918, put a serious dent into what might have been close to 100 victories as against 35–40 losses.

Conjecture about his Hall of Fame candidacy came to a shuddering halt, of course, because he was one of the key operatives in the 1919 World Series fix. Had Eddie Cicotte been able to continue his career after 1920 it is reasonable to assume that he would have been effective for a few seasons more, possibly extending his win total up to the 250 mark or more. There might conceivably have been enough strength in his career record to gain admission to The Hall. Though this was not to be, it was a measure of his greatness, especially during the two White Sox pennant years, that he might well have been named the Cy Young pitcher of the year during those two championship seasons. Pitchers have made it to The Hall on less, after all.

White Sox fans are left with the gnawing emptiness of what might have been. So also was Eddie Cicotte. There are realities, and then there are grim realities, and the little shine-baller had to live with them the rest of his days. The Cicotte record with the White Sox follows:

Year	Won	Lost	Pct.	IP	CG	SH	BB/K	OBA	OB%	PR	ERA	TPI
1912	9	7	.563	152.0	13	1	37/70	.277	.320	8	2.84	1.0
1913	18	11	.621	268.0	18	3	73/121	.226	.281	40	1.58	5.0
1914	11	16	.407	269.1	15	4	72/122	.232	.288	21	2.04	2.7
1915	13	12	.520	223.1	15	1	48/106	.261	.306	-2	3.02	0.0
1916	15	7	.682	187.0	11	2	70/91	.218	.296	22	1.78	2.9
1917	28	12	.700	346.2	29	7	70/150	.203	.248	44	1.53	5.4
1918	12	19	.387	266.0	24	1	40/104	.271	.300	0	2.64	0.0
1919	29	7	.806	306.2	35	5	49/110	.228	.261	48	1.82	5.3
1920	21	10	.677	303.1	28	4	74/87	.275	.320	18	3.26	1.4
Totals	156	101	.607	2323.1	188	28	533/961	.252	.291	199	2.29	23.7

On October 1 the White Sox played their final game of the season, a losing effort to the Yankees, 4–2. Urban Shocker was the winner in a game that Lefty Williams started and Red Faber, the loser, finished. No game is a meaningless exercise, but this one was less meaningful than others and it was a day the Sox used to get in some playing time for Ted Jourdan at first base and Swede Risberg at short to brush up on his shortstopping skills (Buck Weaver had the day off and Freddie McMullin played third, as he had been doing). It presented still another opportunity for Joe Jackson to play some right field, with Shano Collins switching over to left field from his accustomed spot in right.

Though other teams had not yet finished their 1917 schedule, the Sox wound up theirs with a 100 and 54 mark, outdistancing the Bosox by nine games. The final standings, including the Sox' record against each team:

Team	Won	Lost	Pct.	GB	R*	OR*	W/L vs.
Chicago	100	54	.649		656	463	
Boston	90	62	.592	9	555	454	12–10
Cleveland	88	66	.571	12	584	543	14–8
Detroit	78	75	.510	21.5	639	577	16–6
Wash'ton	74	79	.484	25.5	543	566	15–7
New York	71	82	.464	28.5	524	558	12–10
St. Louis	57	97	.370	43	510	687	16–6
Philadelphia	55	98	.359	44.5	529	691	15–7

*R designates Runs Scored and OR, Opponents' Runs Scored.

Over in the Senior Circuit the 1917 race wound up this way:

Team	Won	Lost	Pct.	GB	R	OR	NYG W/L vs.
New York	98	56	.636		635	457	
Philadelphia	87	65	.572	10	578	500	14–8
St. Louis	82	70	.539	15	531	567	14–8
Cincinnati	78	76	.506	20	601	611	11–11
Chicago	74	80	.481	24	552	567	15–7
Boston	72	81	.471	25.5	536	552	15–7
Brooklyn	70	81	.464	26.5	511	559	13–9
Pittsburgh	51	103	.331	47	464	595	16–6

White Sox and Giant players finished among league leaders in these departments:

The Hitters

Runs Scored:	George Burns	NYG	1st	103
	Joe Jackson	CWS	4th	91
Hits:	Burns		2nd	180 Triples
	Jackson	CWS	2nd	17
Home Runs:	Dave Robertson	NYG	tied 1st	12
Total Bases:	Burns	NYG	3rd	246
RBI:	Heinie Zimmerman	NYG	1st	102
	Hap Felsch	CWS	tied 2nd	102
	Jackson	CWS	5th	75
Runs Produced:	Zimmerman	NYG	1st	158
	Bennie Kauff	NYG	3rd	152
	Felsch	CWS	3rd	171
Bases on Balls:	Burns	NYG	1st	75
	Eddie Collins	CWS	2nd	89
	Nemo Leibold	CWS	5th	74
BA:	Kauff	NYG	4th	.308
	Felsch	CWS	5th	.308
On-Base Percentage:	Burns	NYG	3rd	.380
	E. Collins	CWS	5th	.389
	Kauff	NYG	4th	.379
Slugging Average:	Jackson	CWS	5th	.429
Adjusted Batter Runs:	Burns	NYG	4th	35.4
	Jackson	CWS	5th	26.9
Clutch Hitting Index:	Ray Schalk	CWS	1st	135
	Zimmerman	NYG	1st	146
	Felsch	CWS	3rd	133
	E. Collins	CWS	5th	128
Runs Created:	Burns	NYG	1st	102

Eddie Cicotte beat the Yankees at the Polo Grounds on September 19, 1917, for his league-leading 28th triumph and the White Sox' 100th, an all time franchise high. Who better to win it than little Eddie? (Brace photograph)

Stolen Bases:	E. Collins	CWS	2nd	53
	Burns	NYG	2nd	40
	Kauff	NYG	3rd	30
Fielding Runs:	Artie Fletcher	NYG	2nd	27.4
	Felsch	CWS	2nd	18.9
Total Player Rating:	Fletcher	NYG	3rd	4.4

The Pitchers

Wins:	Eddie Cicotte	CWS	1st	28
	Ferdie Schupp	NYG	4th	21
Win Percentage:	Reb Russell	CWS	1st	.750
	Schupp	NYG	1st	.750
	Harry "Slim" Sallee	NYG	2nd	.750
	William "Pol" Perritt	NYG	3rd	.708
	Cicotte	CWS	3rd	.700
	Claude "Lefty" Williams	CWS	4th	.680
GP:	Dave Danforth	CWS	1st	50
	Cicotte	CWS	2nd	49
Complete Games:	Cicotte	CWS	3rd	29
	Schupp	NYG	5th	25
Shutouts:	Cicotte	CWS	4th	7
	Schupp	NYG	4th	6
Saves:	Danforth	CWS	1st	9
	Sallee	NYG	1st	4
Innings Pitched:	Cicotte	CWS	1st	346.2
Fewest Hits per game:	Schupp	NYG	1st	6.68
	Fred Anderson	NYG	2nd	6.78
	Cicotte	CWS	2nd	6.39
Fewest Walks per game:	Russell	CWS	1st	1.52
	Sallee	NYG	2nd	1.42
	Cicotte	CWS	3rd	1.82
Strikeouts:	Cicotte	CWS	2nd	150
	Schupp	NYG	4th	147
K/Gm:	Schupp	NYG	2nd	4.86
	Danforth	CWS	5th	4.11
Ratio:	Cicotte	CWS	1st	8.28
	Schupp	NYG	2nd	9.13
	Russell	CWS	4th	9.65
ERA:	Cicotte	CWS	1st	1.53
	Anderson	NYG	2nd	1.44
	Perritt	NYG	3rd	1.88
	Faber	CWS	4th	1.92
	Schupp	NYG	4th	1.95
Opp. BA:	Cicotte	CWS	1st	.194

	Schupp	NYG	tied 1st	.209
	Anderson	NYG	tied 1st	.209
Opp. On-Base Percentage:	Cicotte	CWS	1st	.248
	Anderson	NYG	1st	.255
	Schupp	NYG	2nd	.265
	Russell	CWS	4th	.279
Starter Runs:	Cicotte	CWS	1st	43.5
	Schupp	NYG	tied 3rd	22.7
	Anderson	NYG	tied 3rd	22.7
Clutch Pitching Index:	Faber	CWS	1st	136
	Perritt	NYG	3rd	118
Total Pitcher Index:	Cicotte	CWS	1st	5.4
	Anderson	NYG	tied 4th	1.9

Between their final game of the season at the Polo Grounds against the Yankees on October 1 and the World Series opener, which was set for Saturday, October 6, the White Sox spent a few days and the nervous energy that goes with the anticipation of playing in The Big Show maintaining their playing edge with an exhibition game in Cleveland on Tuesday the 2nd, and working out on the days following. The Giants, meanwhile, due in Chicago to play the first Series game, arrived during the week, first, to take on the Cubs in a practice game at Weeghman Park, and then to go through batting and fielding drills at Comiskey Park.

Both teams were at full strength as they awaited the Classic's first pitch. Now, if only Friday's rain and dank, Windy City weather would break, there would be nothing left to interfere with the impending Armageddon. The nation's two top metropolises, wrapped up in their own private baseball warfare for national bragging rights, would have at it in the best four out of seven.

Charley Comiskey had his winner, John McGraw was back in the World Series limelight, and both would soon find out whether the Comiskeymen could repeat their 1906 world's championship, or if McGraw's Giants, on the other hand, would finally break through the championship drought that had gone through a dozen years since their electrifying victory over Connie Mack's Athletics way back there in 1905. Adding zest and salsa to the extravaganza (both would see to it that it would indeed be an extravaganza) was that "inside matchup" featuring those old adversaries and globe-trotting baseball emmisaries, The Old Roman and Little Napoleon.

A final touch during the hoopla and hype of the week pre-

Double Trouble, all dressed up in new World Series garb, The Shoeless One, Joe Jackson (left) and Hap Felsch ready to take their licks at Giant pitching. In the Series Jackson hit a creditable .304 and Felsch poled the only Sox homer, a game-winner in game two at Comiskey Park. (Dennis Colgin)

ceeding this extraordinary World Series pairing worth noting was added by the White Sox' redoubtable fan club, The Woodland Bards, who planned a gala affair in celebration of the Chisox' championship season at the Marine Cafe of the Edgewater Beach Hotel. The Wednesday night affair would be replete with the usual banquet-style meal, the ball club on hand and seated in the place of honor in the center of the banquet hall, and more than a thousand of the Sox faithful, all bent on letting one and all know that their boys would most certainly humble the mighty men of McGraw. At ten smackers a ticket, a pretty steep investment those days, they were no doubt entitled to their optimism. It remained to be seen, however, whether or not their supreme confidence in skipper Rowland's boys was justified.

CHAPTER 11

The World Champs

The third time was the charm. After failing twice in a coin toss that landed on the floor rather than its designated spot, President Navin of the Detroit club, assigned the task of flipping a coin as a means to decide which team would be the home team for the first two games of the Series, tried once more, and this time, while it was in the air, the New York Giants' President, Harry Hempstead, called "heads" only to have the coin land "tails" up, thus giving President Comiskey the opportunity to host the first two games of the 1917 World Series. It seems Commy won the opening round of the World Series competition, and with it, both hometown and home field advantage. One ought not to make more of that little incident than it was actually worth. Nonetheless, The Old Roman seemed to have the baseball gods smiling his way right from the start of The Classic's proceedings. The Series would begin on October 6, then, in Charley Comiskey's own Chicago.

The Series, rated as a toss-up, was analyzed in excruciating detail, especially in the New York and Chicago press. The *Chicago Tribune* quartet of sports writers, Jim Crusinberry, Irving Sanborn, Jack Lait and the renowned Ring Lardner, as might have been expected, favored the men of Comiskey. Citing previous World

Series experience in the persons of Buck Herzog and Heinie Zimmerman, the vast array of New York writers favored the Giants, led by the game's number one field boss, at least in their estimation, John McGraw, who was appearing as a manager in his fifth Fall Classic. Walter Trumbull was just a bit more cautious in analyzing the Giants, writing in a September 29 special to the *New York World*:

> New York will be represented in the coming series with the White Sox by the best team the National League has known since the days of the great Cub machine driven by Frank Chance.
>
> This team has not the wonderful asset of a Christopher Mathewson, but in other respects it is a far better club than the Giants beaten twice by the Athletics and once by the Red Sox for the highest honors in baseball...
>
> In studying the chances of a team in a world's series the general records of the season's play are of minor importance. A league season is a distance event. A world's series is a dash.

He went on to point out, after analyzing the teams position by position, that the Series looked pretty much like an even draw despite the heady, consistent play of Chicago on the one hand, and the fiery determination of the Giants on the other, which, all other things considered, countered one another.

Amid all the conjecture and imponderables, one thing had been set in stone after the coin toss had established the winner of the first series games, and that was the Series schedule: October 6 and 7, at Chicago; October 9 and 10, at New York; October 12, at Chicago if needed; October 15, at New York if needed; and October 17 for the final game if needed, the site to be determined by the toss of a silver dollar coin. With a schedule like that it was predictable that the pitching aces of both staffs would be well rested between starts, and further, that they would be available for relief work if needed. Although the Series schedule was impartial to both teams in that respect, that very factor made all the difference in the world to Sox manager Rowland whose plan was to extract every last inning he could out of Eddie Cicotte and Red Faber during the seven game series.

It also meant that baseball's Fall Classic would be in the headlines for nearly two weeks. The grand old game was about to give its national audience an extended look at America's premium ball clubs in the sporting world's autumnal showcase *par excellence.* It's worth noting that Charley Comiskey had done his part in elevating the event to epic proportions. His Baseball Palace had been enlarged to accommodate upwards of 33,000 spectators, and it was awash in red, white and blue bunting. Every effort had been made to scrub up every last square inch of the property, to extend guest and celebrity amenities and to shoehorn as many of the thousands on the wire and ticket lines into the ball park as possible. Beyond that, he had decked out his ball club in specially designed red, white and blue uniforms, deserting the old, all-white hose for white socks with two broad stripes, one red and the other blue. To top off the patriotic, wartime theme, the uniform jerseys would bear a flag patch. And in New York the stately Polo Grounds would also be ready with equally colorful "dressing" that would put the finishing touches to the most carefully staged World Series event in the game's history up to that point.

Two future Hall of Fame umpires, the National League's inimitable Bill Klem, baseball's most demanding arbiter, ever, and the highly respected Billy Evans of the American League, a sports writer who took up umpiring and brought to his profession a refined and diplomatic demeanor behind the plate, headed up the specially selected umpiring team for the Series. They were complemented by two veterans, the National League's Charles "Cy" Rigler, into the 11th season of his 30 year career, and colorful Francis "Silk" O'Loughlin of the American League, of whom it was said: "The Pope for religion, O'Loughlin for baseball. Both infallible." Their outstanding credentials wouldn't intimidate John McGraw, of course, nor would there be any hesitancy on the part of the ball players to fight and scream for every advantage, but the Series would nonetheless be called by the best the game had to offer.

Over 32,000 fans, including a galaxy of stars from the world of entertainment and baseball, dignitaries and 1,500 servicemen from nearby Fort Sheridan were crammed into Comiskey Park for the World Series opener on October 6, and after both teams' managers and captains, John McGraw with Buck Herzog for the Giants and Pants Rowland with Eddie Collins for the White Sox, met with the umpires for the pre-game discussion about ground rules, the military's color guard presented the flag, followed by the National

Anthem. With all formalities completed, "Silk" O'Loughlin, plate umpire for the Series inaugural, yelled: "Play ball!"

The "Mutt and Jeff" of the two pitching staffs opposed each other, lean and lanky Slim Sallee for the Giants and the little White Sox wizard, Eddie Cicotte. McGraw's selection of Sallee came as a bit of a surprise, though choosing him over staff ace Ferdie Schupp was easily justified on the basis of his late season record, eight wins against but a pair of losses in his last twelve starts, resulting in a strong 18 and 7 season. There was no hesitation on the part of Clarence Rowland in handing the ball to Eddie C. The diminutive trick-pitch meister was ready, willing, and the ablest American Leaguer hurler of them all. The challenge lay directly ahead.

Game 1

After a pair of scoreless innings the White Sox drew first blood in Game One on a Fred McMullin single that scored John Collins, who, moments before, had registered his second straight hit. He scored easily on the McMullin blow when centerfielder Benny Kauff misplayed McMullin's line drive into a double. That was followed by the Series' first big blow, a Hap Felsch shot in the bottom of the fourth that was fielded by a Mr. Maurice De Vry in the left field stands. The gentleman, according to Ring Lardner, "paid a dollar and a half to get in and wouldn't take half that sum for the ball." (*Chicago Tribune*, October 7, 1917.) Hap Felsch, not at all shy about taking in a greenback, accepted a $50 Liberty Bond as a reward for his game-breaking blow.

The very next inning the Giants responded with a mild uprising against Cicotte with a Lew McCarty howitzer shot that drove Hap Felsch all the way to the wall in right center. The heavy-legged Giants receiver made it to third but was held up there for fear that he would be thrown out at the plate trying to stretch his triple into a homer. The next man up, Cicotte's counterpart Slim Sallee, arched a Texas Leaguer between the two Collins men, scoring McCarty. George Burns followed that with a grounder to Buck Weaver that was promptly converted into a 6-4-3 doubleplay, ending the threat and the inning.

The play of the game occurred two innings later after Giant first baseman Walter Holke singled in the seventh. That brought up Lew McCarty, whose triple previously indicated that he had found little Eddie's pitches much to his liking. He found another that he liked and ripped it to left. This one, however, got Joe Jackson's attention, and Jackson made a sensational tumbling catch to snuff what would surely have been another three-bagger had it gotten past him.

As for the rest of Game One, it was a matter of Cicotte's knucklers and moistened deliveries and his razor-edged control that kept the Giants at bay, thus assuring the Sox of an opening game victory, 2 to 1. The story

Pregame One Greetings. John McGraw (left) and Pants Rowland exchange a few words at Comiskey Park before the World Series inaugural begins. (Dennis Colgin)

line on the game's pitching was that Slim Sallee pitched a great game for the Giants, but Cicotte was better. That was pretty much the story of Eddie Cicotte's summer. The summary:

New York	000 010 000	1-7-1
Chicago	001 100 00x	2-7-1

2B: McMullin, J. Collins, Robertson; 3B: McCarty; HR: Felsch; SB: Gandil, Burns; LOB: New York 5; Chicago 2; DP: Weaver, E. Collins, Gandil; K: Cicotte 2, Sallee 2; BB: Sallee 0, Cicotte 1; Umpires: O'Loughlin, AL (plate); Klem, NL (1st); Rigler, NL (2nd); Evans, AL (3rd). WP: Cicotte, 1-0; LP: Sallee, 0-1; Time of Game: 1:48; Attendance: 32,000 plus.

Heroes: Jackson—catch of McCarty's liner; Cicotte—complete game opening game victory; J. Collins—three hits; McMullin—great play afield and timely RBI; Felsch—game winning homer.

Goats: Kauff—misplayed the McMullin line drive; Kauff—picked off first in the eighth; Holke—picked off first in the second; McGraw—didn't use the sacrifice to put men in scoring position.

Game 2

On a sun-drenched, 60 degree autumn day at Comiskey Park another sellout crowd in excess of 32,000 was on hand to watch 21-game winner Ferdie Schupp duel the White Sox' Red Faber. That particular matchup didn't provide much of a duel, however. By the time the second inning was over John McGraw's top southpaw was gone, having yielded four hits and a pair of runs in 1⅓ innings before being lifted in favor of Giants relief pitcher Freddy Anderson.

The White Sox found Anderson's offerings even better than Schupp's, pounding him for another four runs and five hits. The key hits that paved the way for a five-run Sox outburst in the bottom of the fourth inning were registered in succession by Nemo Leibold, who scored Buck Weaver on a hit and run play, a line drive single by Fred McMullin scoring Ray Schalk, and another single by Eddie Collins, who greeted Anderson's replacement, Pol Perritt, with an RBI that plated Leibold.

Joe Jackson and his Black Betsy then smashed one of those hissing liners that Sox fans came to hear as well as to see. That one scored two more and the count suddenly stood at 7 and 2. Happy Felsch then hit a screamer that got to Buck Herzog so fast that Jackson, leading off second at the time, simply didn't have time to get back to the base to avoid the inning-ending twinkilling. But for all practical purposes the game—and scoring—was over at that point.

And so the big redhead, Urban Faber, had fashioned a strong 7 to 2 victory, disposing of the Giants with 99 pitches and eight goose egg innings. Although the McGrawmen momentarily forged ahead in this game on the strength of a two-run second, the big spitballer got through that thicket, settled down and both pitched and fielded his way to the Sox' second triumph in as many days.

One of the better plays of the day was made by Faber himself on a Benny Kauff dribbler down the first base line that the sturdy righthander shoveled into his glove, then registering the putout himself with a lunging dive to first base, putting his glove to the base a split second before the Giant speedster arrived.

Leaving Chicago with an 0 and 2 deficit was the last thing John McGraw might have imagined before the Series began, but there it was, and it had to be dealt with. What better place than the Polo Grounds?! The Giants' little generalisimo's confidence was unshaken. The boys from the backwaters of Lake Michigan had taken him for two straight, but that would change in a hurry once his troops were back at their familiar Coogan's Bluff battlelines. What's more, Ferdie Schupp would be asked to go right at the upstart Rowlandmen. Was that a wise move? What timorous soul would question Little Napoleon! Schupp it would be and Schupp would win—period.

The Hap Felsch swing that put the Giants away 2 to 1 with a towering smash into the left field stands of Comiskey Park, putting the first World Series game on ice for Chicago. (Dennis Colgin)

The Game Two summary:

New York	020 000 000	2-8-1
Chicago	020 500 00x	7-14-1

There were no extra base hits in this game. SB: E. Collins 2, Jackson; LOB: New York 7, Chicago 3; DP: Herzog unassisted, Faber, Weaver and Gandil, Felsch, E. Collins and Weaver, Weaver and Gandil; K: Schupp 2, Anderson 3, Tesreau 1, Faber 1; BB: Schupp 1, Perritt 1, Tesreau 1, Faber 1; Passed Ball: McCarty; WP: Faber (1-0); LP: Anderson (0-1); Umpires: Evans (plate), Rigler (1st base), Klem (2nd base), O'Loughlin (3rd base); Time of Game: 2:13; Attendance: 32,000 plus.

Heroes: Faber—Scattered eight hits while providing 2-0 Series lead; Sox defense—Three DP's and some eye-popping throws to blunt the Giants' attack; Jackson—A perfect 3 for 3 day; Weaver—three hits and steady shortstopping (13 chances).

Goats: Faber—Baserunning *faux pas* at third with Weaver already on the bag.

Bungling Embarassment: Pants Rowland—Sox skipper, who combined with Bill Gleason in coaching duties on the baselines, would have to use his left hand in New York to direct traffic because he burned his right hand when he turned scalding water on it in his after-game shower.

Great Play: Felsch—Shoestring catch in the seventh robbed Holke of a hit that Felsch turned into a DP with his off-balance throw to Eddie Collins, who, in turn, relayed it to Buck Weaver to retire Artie Fletcher.

Game 3

The big news in Gotham on October 9 was neither the Sox nor the Giants. It was Old Man Weather who frowned on Game Three of the World Series by dousing New York with a deluge that postponed it to Wednesday, the 10th. The inclement weather, however, changed no plans in either camp. Pants Rowland would send Eddie Cicotte to the mound and John McGraw would counter with his big lefty, Rube Benton, giving Ferdie Schupp an additional day of rest before starting game four. Benton, thus, became the third straight southpaw to start in the Series, and, as a matter of fact, those three lefthanders would be John McGraw's starters in each of the Series clashes, a still-standing record.

On the rainy day of October 9 the *Chicago Tribune*'s Jim Crusinberry filed this interesting report:

Red Faber warms up before Game Two in the specially designed 1917 World Series uniform worn by the White Sox. Big Red subdued the Giants with a 2.33 ERA in 27 innings of championship pitching. (Brace photograph)

Covering a World Series in New York on a rainy day is just like reporting a battle in France from an Atlantic port in the United States. One can make one hotel and one taxi to another and then to another and perhaps the result will be an interview with Capt. Joe Jenkins of the White Sox bull pen. However, we were far more fortunate than any of the other three hundred war scribes here. We actually saw Charley Comiskey. He was seated in a cafe in mid-afternoon eating breakfast or lunch or supper or something with Mrs. Comiskey and Ted Sullivan and John T. Connery and John Burns and a lot of other people.

The next day, October 10, however, was a different matter. New York's disposition matched the sunshine that bathed the Polo Grounds, as the Giants got back into the Series with big Rube Benton's five-hit mastering of the White Sox, defeating them in a 2-0 game the Giants dominated. The *New York Times* favored the Giants' victory with a front page story:

Joe Jackson's big bat, Black Betsy, was
busy with a perfect day in the Chisox'
big 7 to 2 humiliation of the Giants in
Game Two. (Dennis Colgin)

John Calhoun Benton of North Carolina, with his left-handed curves performing tricky capers, hauled the Giants out of the cavern of adversity at the Polo Grounds yesterday, halting the triumphant march of the White Sox in the third game of the world's series, and planted McGraw's tottering club on the joyous end of a 2 to 0 victory. Warmed by a thundering reception from 33,777 loyal fans, the New York players shook off the lethargy which weighed them down in the first two games in Chicago, and in one swift, pungent batting rally hammered Rowland's mysterious pitching sensation, Eddie Cicotte, down to defeat.

One "pungent batting rally" was all it took, lighting up Coogan's Bluff with the only two tallies of the game, and narrowing the White Sox' Series margin to a discomfiting 2-1 lead. Three of the Giants' eight hits off Eddie C came in the fourth inning. In that stanza the Giants parlayed a Dave Robertson triple followed by Walter Holke's double to the Polo Grounds' sun field in left on a ball that Shano Collins misplayed, into the game's first tally, sending the Giants' hitting star of the Series home with the first run. The second run of the inning came home when Holke scored on a scratch infield hit by George Burns with just enough sting in it to enable Holke to score while the unsuccessful play was being made on Burns at first base.

The Sox came closest to doing something about Benton's slants in the top of the fourth when, after two out, Hap Felsch singled through the hole for one of the five hits Benton gave up in his shutout victory. That was followed by a vicious shot off the bat of Buck Weaver to the right field wall that Robertson snatched for the third out.

Manager Rowland observed after the game that Eddie Cicotte actually pitched a better game in the 2-0 loss than he did in the Series opener he won 2-1. Both he and Commisar Comiskey acknowledged Benton's superior effort, noting that there just isn't much offense with five hits. Accordingly, the story line of the game, much as it was in The Classic's opener, was that Eddie Cicotte pitched a great game, but big Rube Benton was just that much better.

The Game Three summary:

Buck Weaver, one of the Sox' hitting heroes in game two won by Chicago. He had three hits in the 7–2 triumph. (Dennis Colgin)

Chicago	000 000 000	0-5-3
New York	000 200 00x	2-8-2

2B: Holke, Weaver; 3B: Robertson; SB: Robertson; Sac. Hit: Rariden; SB: Robertson; LOB: Chicago 4, New York 8; DP: Rariden and Herzog; K: Cicotte 8, Benton 5; BB: none; Umpires: Klem (plate), O'Loughlin (1st base), Evans (2nd base), Rigler (3rd base); WP: Benton (1-0); LP: Cicotte (1-1); Time of Game: 1:55; Attendance: 33,777.

Heroes: Benton—Superbly pitched shutout; Robertson—Three more hits to raise his Series average to .545 (6 for 11); McGraw—Surprise selection of Benton to pitch put Schupp in a position to tie up the Series with a win in game four.

Goats: J. Collins—Shano's two errors in left field were instrumental in defeat.

Great Play: Gandil—The Sox first baseman climbed the roll of canvas behind first base for covering the field to make an outstanding, one-handed grab of Buck Herzog's pop fly, ending the Giants' two-run fourth.

Boner: Weaver—Sox shortfielder was trapped between second

and third by Benton who tagged Weaver himself, ending any possibility of getting a rally going.

Game 4

Irvin S. Cobb, *New York Times* humorist assigned to cover the World Series, summed up the stern 5 to 0 beating administered by the Giants, evening the Series count at 2-2, and restoring New York's faith in their team, this way in the October 12 *New York Times*:

> ...naught that the Rowlandites could do was of avail, for the Giants played like ball players inspired and were not to be denied. Sustained by the impeccable work of Ferdie Schupp in the box, cheered by the conduct of Mr. Benny Kauff and Mr. Heinie Zimmerman, both of whom suddenly decided, after a long period of total eclipse, to win for themselves a place in the sun, with the result that Benny knocked two Liberty Bond home runs and Heinie graduated out of the class of the confirmed anti-batters by responding to the popular demand for a hit on his part with a three bagger—as I say, buoyed and uplifted by these things and by other contributing factors, the Giants made merry and five runs at the expense of the erstwhile haughty children of the killing pens. The members of the Stock Yards' younger set, who now have gone scoreless for twenty-two consecutive innings, were a gloom-ridden lot when the finish came, and for some time *before* the finish came.

John McGraw was right after all. Saving Ferdie Schupp for game four proved to be the finishing touch following Rube Benton's 2-0 masterpiece. This one, however, was even tastier for New Yorkers. With three games left it meant that the Series had been reduced to a best two out of three set and not a person along the Great White Way the evening of October 11 could be found who would believe the Giants couldn't keep right on winning.

Schupp, at his 1917 best, had maneuvered the Sox, despite seven hits, six of which were singles, into the loss column for a second scoreless day in a row. Whiffing seven, including Hap Felsch twice, he was in command all the way, taking the Sox and Red Faber to the cleaners in a convincing triumph. Though it took four games, 34 innings to be exact, to finally see a Chicago pitcher other than Eddie Cicotte or Red Faber, the Giants, with their characteristic persistence and fury, finally crashed through to set matters even in the 1917 Series for all the marbles.

Fleet little Benny Kauff, the "Ty Cobb of the Federal League," had what was probably the best day of his baseball career considering the circumstances. A noisy, wildly supportive cast of 27,000 plus Gothamites cheered ecstatically when Benny hit the first of his two roundtrippers. The way Schupp was out-finessing Chisox hitters, that one was enough, but just for good measure, Kauff popped another into the seats near the foul line of the Polo Grounds' short right field porch scoring Buck Herzog ahead of himself. That upped the count to five, and when Chick Gandil flied out to Mr. Benjamin Michael

Chick Gandil, whose fine fielding and clutch hitting helped the Sox win the world's championship. The alleged ringleader of the "Eight Men Out" though he was, he was also one of the most sure-handed first basemen of his era. (Dennis Colgin)

Kauff for the third out in the ninth, Ferdie Schupp, with Kauff's help, had evened everything up including his own Series record and the Series standings, as well.

The Game Four summary:

Chicago	000 000 000	0-7-0
New York	000 110 12x	5-10-1

2B: E. Collins; 3B: Zimmerman; HR: Kauff 2; Sac. Hit: Herzog; SB: E. Collins; LOB: Chicago 6, New York 3; DP: Herzog, Fletcher and Holke; Faber, Schalk and Gandil; BB: Schupp 1; K: Faber 3, Danforth 2, Schupp 7; Hit by Pitcher: Holke by Faber; Wild Pitch: Faber; WP: Schupp (1-0); LP: Faber (1-1); Umpires: Rigler (plate), Evans (1st base), O'Loughlin (2nd base), Klem (3rd base); Time of Game: 2:09; Attendance: 27,746.

Heroes: Kauff—Supplied the offensive punch with two four-baggers; Schupp—Applied the whitewash brush with a 7-hit shutout.

Unsung Hero: Rariden—Called two heady games behind the plate for the Giants in their two successive shutout victories in New York.

Goat: E. Collins—Picked off second after doubling in the fourth inning with one out and Hap Felsch up.

Great Play: The Giants stole the hit and run sign with Hap Felsch up in the fourth, then put Eddie Collins away with a snap throw from Schupp to Herzog, who relayed to third where Zimmerman nailed Collins.

Game 5

From his San Francisco vantage point Duffy Lewis, the Red Sox' slugging outfielder and World Series veteran, predicted that the White Sox would win game five and "put the Giants on the toboggan." John McGraw thought otherwise. Pants Rowland naturally agreed with Lewis. Chicago fandom, stunned and sobered by the New York shutouts at the Polo Grounds, weren't quite so sure, but reasoned that Eddie Collins, Joe Jackson and Hap Felsch couldn't be throttled forever. They were hoping that on October 13 Pale Hose hits would be rattling all over Comiskey Park.

They did. Fourteen of them. But Sox fans had to wait on edge until late in the game before any celebrating could be done. Going into the bottom of the seventh the Giants held a reasonably safe lead, 5 to 2. Then lightning struck in the form of a Jackson single, followed by another shot through the infield by Felsch and a Chick Gandil two bagger that scored two. That blow hit the Giants like a sledgehammer. After Ray Schalk walked, the Rowlandmen still had two runners on base, Gandil, by this time at third, and Schalk at first. Rowland then sent Schalk on his way to pull off the front end of a double steal. When Giants' catcher Bill Rariden saw that Gandil had decided not to break immediately for the plate from third, he fired Slim Sallee's pitch to Buck Herzog at second base, hoping to nail Schalk. But Herzog bobbled the throw, and Gandil, by that time in a full sprint, was on his way to the plate to complete the delayed double steal. He beat Herzog's throw back to Rariden, scoring the game's tying run. It was the pivotal play of the day.

Another three spot in the home eighth salted the game away,

Ferdie Schupp, the Giants' little lefty, was a 9 and 3 pitcher with the game's all time low ERA for a single season (0.90 in 1916). He came back in 1917 to win 21 for New York and shut out the Sox in Game Four of the World Series. (Transcendental Graphics)

the Sox winning it 8 to 5. The bitterness of that loss, a loss that the Giants themselves snatched from the iron jaws of victory, was reported by Walter Trumbull in a wired story to the *New York Herald* on October 13:

> It was a bitter contest played upon a bitter autumn afternoon, but bitterest of all to the Giants was the fact that defeat came only after victory seemed sure. Up to the last half of the seventh inning the White Sox were reeling and broken from the power of the New York attack. The Giants had scored five runs to their opponents' two. They had driven Lefty Russell from the hill after only three batters faced him and they had pounded Cicotte hard.
>
> The White Sox appeared to be fighting desperately but hopelessly. The crowd of over 27,000 rooters sat in sullen silence and dismay. The warriors whom they had come to cheer appar-

ently were outclassed by a superior foe. Then came the sudden, sweeping onslaught which turned the Giants' offensive
into a rout and hurled them from the very heights of victory
to the valley of defeat.

Ahead of those big seventh and eighth innings, however, it was
all New York, and that was due as much to the blundering Pale
Hose as it was to the Giants' attack. Fielding miscues, no less than
six of them, and bad judgment kept a steady parade of McGraw's
hitters moving into the batter's box. Nor was the pitching any better in the game's early stages.

For game five Pants Rowland, somewhat against his own better judgment, gave in to Reb Russell's pleas for a shot at the Giants
and started him against Slim Sallee. That backfired in a hurry under
the barrage of George Burns' leadoff walk, Buck Herzog's single
and a two base laser to the right field fence by Benny Kauff. No
one was out and Heinie Zimmerman, the Giants' leading run producer, was the next hitter. That brought on Eddie Cicotte, who
struggled through six innings as the McGrawmen ran up a 4 to 2
lead. He was followed by Lefty Williams, who lasted through three
outs and another run. Finally, after the Sox tied it at 5 and 5, Rowland threw tomorrow to the winds and brought on Red Faber, who
tore through the heart of the Giants' order in the eighth and then
disposed of Artie Fletcher, Dave Robertson and Walter Holke in
the ninth to salt away the victory that put the Sox up 3 to 2 as the
teams headed back to The Big Apple for game number six.

The Game Five summary:

New York	200 200 100	5-12-3
Chicago	001 001 33x	8-14-6

2B: Kauff, Felsch, Fletcher, Gandil; Sac. Hits: Sallee, McMullin; SB: Kauff,
Robertson, Schalk; LOB: New York 11, Chicago 10; DP: McMullin and Gandil,
McMullin, E. Collins and Gandil; K: Cicotte 3, Williams 3, Faber 1, Sallee 2;
BB: Russell 1, Cicotte 1, Sallee 1; WP: Faber (2-1); LP: Sallee (0-2); Umpires:
O'Loughlin (plate), Klem (1st base), Rigler (2nd base), Evans (3rd base);
Time of Game: 2:37; Attendance: 27,323

Heroes: Faber—Held down the Giants with shutout ball in brilliant relief stint; McMullin—Made a spectacular play on Art
Fletcher's line drive and then completed a fast twinkilling to choke
off further Giant scoring in the third

Goats: Herzog—Dropped Rariden's throw permitting successful double steal that tied the game; McGraw—Left Sallee in

the game during the seventh inning Sox rally deciding not to go to the bullpen for help.

Bum Choice: Rowland—He brought Cicotte in after three hitters convinced him Reb Russell wasn't up to the task, but should have started Cicotte if his intent was to use him anyway.

Interesting Quotes: Comiskey—"I was afraid they (the Sox players) weren't going to get into it until next season, but they finally awoke and went through in great shape." Eddie Collins—"I have been in many a world's series game but never in one like this one today!"

Game 6

Back to New York, to Broadway, to the Big Apple—and to Coogan's Bluff. Knowing that a seventh game, if necessary, would also be played in New York, Pants Rowland and Co. were bent on getting the final win in the very next game, scheduled for October 15. No point in exposing themselves to any more New York tomfoolery than necessary.

For that one Rowland, against the advice of some in Chicago, decided to go with the most effective pitcher he had in the Series so far, and that would be the big lad from Cascade, Iowa, Red Faber. In weighing Faber's effectiveness against Giant hitting opposed to using him directly after his impressive finish in the previous game, Rowland also took into consideration that Eddie Cicotte had gone six innings in game six and that Lefty Williams, another possible starter, didn't exactly overwhelm the men of McGraw. So the decision came down to Red Faber, and he didn't mind that a bit.

John McGraw, on the other hand, cast his lot with Rube Benton, ordering Fred Anderson and Pol Perritt to stand by for relief pitching duty. No one challenged that decision and the Giants were pretty upbeat about their chances now that they had started to hit and were back in front of their New York fans.

Though there were little snorts and stabs at getting something started, neither the White Sox nor the Giants were able to do anything about scoring during the first three rounds. Then came the fourth inning, that most tumultuous of stanzas in each of the Series games. That inning in Game Six would be no exception.

Nothing will be remembered about the Sox' three run outburst in the fourth frame that paved the way to victory more than the play that featured the foot race to home plate between Heinie Zimmerman and Eddie Collins which the fleet Collins won, boosting the Chisox' advantage to 3–0. It was the run that proved to be the winner in a 4 to 2 ball game that meant Chicago's Comiskeymen had won the ultimate prize, the world's championship. And it was the signature play of the 1917 World Series, chronicled and analyzed *ad infinitum*, a play that grouped another of McGraw's fine players with the two Freds, Snodgrass and Merkle. But it happened nonetheless, and though the Giants still had another 18 outs with which to overcome a five-star boner on the part of no less than five Giant players collaborating to make Collins' run possible, that play, like the lighthouse searchlight, stands out as the unpardonable error that gave the Chisox the winner's share of the World Series money.

The most woebegone comment of the 1917 Series was made by the same Heinie Zim after the game in answer to questions about "the play": "Who was I supposed to throw the ball to—Bill Klem?" His answer exposed the the shoddy back-up defensive play that saw neither first baseman Walter Holke, nor the pitcher Rube Benton make a move to cover an unguarded home plate, left that way by catcher Bill Rariden. The fifth culprit involved in this mother of all unfortunate World Series plays was right fielder Davy Robertson, who let Joe Jackson's fly ball dribble through his hands, enabling Collins to move from second to third and into a position to make his run to gold and glory. Hap Felsch's come-backer to Rube Benton then set the stage for "the play."

It was a mess, all right. But, as pointed out above, there was still plenty of time to right the wrongs of the fourth inning. The problem for the Giants, however, was the real hero of the Series, Red Faber, who simply turned the lights out on the McGrawmen with another gritty triumph, his third of the championship set, thus tying him with ten other pitchers in the Series' history who have won three of the four possible victories it takes to win it all in a seven-game series. There was one other record: in the 1917 Series two pitchers, Red Faber and Eddie Cicotte, pitched 50 of the 52 innings it took to complete the six-game set, Cicotte with 23 and Faber with 27. The remaining two innings belonged to relievers Lefty Williams and Dave Danforth with an inning each. It appears that when Pants Rowland determined before the Series to get as many innings as possible out of his two stars, he was bound and determined to do just that. The numbers underscore his determination. The final game summary follows:

Chicago	000 300 001	4-7-1
New York	000 020 000	2-6-3

2B: Holke; 3B: Herzog; Sac. Hit: Faber; LOB: Chicago 7, New York 7; BB: Faber 2, Benton 1, Perritt 2; K: Benton 3, Perritt 3, Faber 4; Hit by Pitcher: Robertson by Faber; WP: Faber (3-1); LP: Benton (1-1); Umpires: Klem (plate), O'Loughlin (1st base), Evans (2nd base), Rigler (3rd base); Time of Game: 2:18; Attendance: 33,969

Heroes: Faber—Pitched a complete game winner; Gandil— More hitting in the clutch, this time the fourth inning single that scored two, enough to beat the Giants; Collins—Finished off a great Series with the fourth inning dash to home plate and the winning tally.

Goats: Rariden—All five contributed to one of the World Series' classic boners: Benton, Holke, Robertson, Zimmerman.

Absolutely the worst post-game comment: McGraw—In replying to Pants Rowland's comments after the game McGraw parted ways with the White Sox pilot by delivering himself of the most peevish, ill-chosen World Series comment of all time: "Get away from me, you god-damned busher."

Series Recap

The *Reach Official American League Guide,* published by former major leaguer Al Reach, a prominent Philadelphia sports equipment supplier in his later years, summed up the Series in his 1918 Guide, which reviewed the 1917 season, in the following words (page 79):

> There were upsets of the dope in every department of the game all along the line, and the close followers of the series hardly knew what to expect from one game to another. Pitching, batting, fielding, generalship, gameness, crowds, everything, ran at variance with the early predictions, but in the final autopsy of the series it must be frankly admitted that by all odds the gamer and the better team won. Chicago so far outclassed the National League champions that in the final analysis the wonder is that the White Sox did not clean up the series sooner.

When Pants Rowland's eyes fell on that paragraph of terse, well
chosen words, he must have murmured, "At last!" He had risen
from the depths of minor league baseball to the top of the baseball
world within a span of just over five years despite all the deroga-
tory and demeaning things that had been said about his capabilities, managing and baseball savvy, not least of which was the
stinging, bitter McGraw insult at the Polo Grounds. Despite the
fact that he would be unceremoniously dumped in favor of Bill
Gleason after the 1918 season, the man did have the last laugh.
Pants Rowland had his day, and many years after, as a matter of
fact, in a baseball career that encompassed managing, scouting,
umpiring, club ownership and executive responsibilities plus the
respect of the baseball world—on into his 90th year. It was that 1917
World Series, in which he out-managed the mighty McGraw, that
he came into his own, however, and it was his management of a
volatile, at-the-edge ball club, however talented, that brought the
1917 Comiskeymen to the Series.

There was one other statement in the *Reach Guide* (p. 86) that
reads like an incongruous testimonial, totally unbelievable to readers who lived after the disastrous World Series scandal of 1919.
Here is what the Guide had to say about the Commisar, Charles
A. Comiskey:

> In conclusion we desire to say that the victory of the White Sox
> was not only deserved but most popular, principally on account
> of President Comiskey, the beloved owner of the Chicago club.
> Charles Comiskey, through the liberal methods in running his
> club, endeared himself to the fans of his own city and earned
> prestige abroad. The man outside of Chicago gauges
> "Commy" as the ideal type of the man to conduct a ball club.
> First of all, "Commy" loves base ball; he started as a player
> and graduated into the ownership class through his vision and
> perseverance. Surely nobody begrudges this jovial, white-
> haired man his success. A big part of his profits this year he
> gave to the Red Cross; his gifts to charities are unending; he
> always has a kind word and meal for the down-and-out. No
> wonder Comiskey is the most popular man in base ball today.

Is this the Comiskey today's readers know? Yet, whether he
knew it or not, the Czar of Chicago Baseball stood at the very apex
of his career, his profession, if you please, during those deliriously
exhilarating days following his White Sox' World Series victory

over the Giants. In October of 1917 there were still no catastrophic events, like the gruesome last several months of World War I, the war's effect on the baseball industry, and no scandals that would ruin his career—indeed his life. As Comiskey, his Bards, the ball players and Chicago fandom celebrated their good fortune, all of that was an unknown quantity that, if forecast, would have been written off as a macabre, incredulous, indeed unthinkable prediction, a very, very bad joke. Almost a century later, of course, we know better.

As for the Series' ball players and the games themselves, there are, indeed, several stick-out games, plays and performers:

The Series MVP—Red Faber, whose three wins and 2.33 ERA spearheaded the Sox.

Best All-around Performance—Eddie Collins, basestealing (3), hard-hitting (9/22, .409 BA) hero who directed the Chisox fielding; the brains of the ball club on the field of play.

Most Pleasant Surprise—Fred McMullin, whose fielding helped steady the Sox' defense at the corners.

Pivotal Game—Game 5, featuring the Sox' come-from-behind, late inning victory that gave them the opportunity to win the Series with but one more victory.

Single Most Important Blow: Happy Felsch's Game 1 moonshot that downed Slim Sallee and the Giants.

Most Important Blow(s), II: Benny Kauff's two Game 4 homers that paced Schupp's shutout win, 5–0.

Most Respected Giants Hitter: Davy Robertson (11/22, .500 BA), who led the Giants' attack.

The Series' Most Unfortunate Baseball Boner: Giants' defense, "led" by Heinie Zimmerman; they completely messed up the fourth inning play on Eddie Collins that handed the White Sox the game's (and Series) winning run.

CHAPTER 12

How Good Were the
1917 White Sox?

There are many things that cannot be said of the 1917 White Sox, but one thing certainly *can* be said: they were the best ball club in professional baseball in 1917. Further, a strong claim could be made that they had crossed the threshold of a dynastic reign in the American League. Though they could not be listed among the 25, or 50, or even 75 of the best teams in the game's history, given what happened in 1919 and after, they were good enough to win it all in 1917 and on their way at that point to a greatness of an even more enduring nature.

The nucleus of this championship aggregation, with Joe Jackson, 27, Hap Felsch, 25, Eddie Collins, 30, Buck Weaver, 26, Ray Schalk, 24, and pitchers Red Faber, 28, Lefty Williams, 24 and Eddie Cicotte, at 33 the elder statesman among them, could be expected to roll along at top speed another several seasons, and did. They were well equipped for the "Big Crunch" era of the 1920s, the livelier ball and the stepped-up tempo of the game they themselves featured. Their 1919 and 1920 record showed that they could win and win big when they put their minds and skills to it, and given Charley Comiskey's oversized pocketbook along with his thumb on the pulsebeat of player development and acquisition, it is reasonable to assume that the Willie Kamms, Dickie Kerrs and Ted Lyonses of the '20's would have checked in to patch up or fill in the missing pieces. That was all in the more-than-likely future from the vantage point of 1917.

This ball club had the pop in the middle of the order to break ball games wide open, and conversely, it excelled at the hit and run game that depended on speed, smarts and hitting behind runners to move men around the bases and into scoring position. Bunting and stealing bases were additional parts of a lethal arsenal of tricks that kept the enemy guessing, wreaking havoc with speed to burn up and down the lineup.

It is well to remember that the White Sox didn't appear overnight to challenge the upper crust in the American League. With the advent of Eddie Collins, a foundation piece dating to 1915, and Joe Jackson, Happy Felsch and Lefty Williams in 1916, the Comiskeymen gave the Red Sox and other contenders fits in the race for the 1916 pennant. During three out of the next four seasons (the wartime year of 1918 when the bottom fell out and they dropped to 6th in the standings was the exception) they were *the* team to beat.

And what might be said of Chicago's pitching and defense? First, with respect to the defense, the very speed that was such an important factor in the offense was put to good use defensively. Felsch, quick and strong-armed, anchored an outfield that boasted another fine outfielder in his own right, Jackson. Comiskey Park's spacious outer gardens were as well patrolled as any outfield in either league, including John McGraw's unit of George Burns, Benny Kauff and Davy Robertson in an equally spacious outfield with a deep, deep centerfield.

Around the infield Collins provided the savvy not only to keep the pitchers on course, but to place infielders according to pitches and the hitting strengths and weaknesses of opposing hitters, as well as burning up the right side of the infield with often sensational play. Buck Weaver, Freddie McMullin and the youngster of the lot, Swede Risberg, ever improving and ever a thorn in the side of enemy offenses, held down the left side of the diamond. Chick Gandil, no slouch around first base, could be counted on to dig throws out of the dirt as well as to thwart opposing bunters. A fine first baseman, his only weakness, an admittedly big one, was his own disposition, something that all too often affected his play.

Behind the plate future Hall of Famer Ray Schalk took charge of the defense, a brainy, aggressive catcher who hustled with the best of them and constantly brought new twists to the catching arts. That made it easy for the pitching staff to rear back, concentrating on pitches and spots, rather than having to worry about the whole infield, setups and which pitch to throw. They all trusted Schalk implicitly.

A pitching corps led by Eddie Cicotte, who enjoyed a career year, and Red Faber, both in their prime, is bound to have its effect on any pennant race and that was certainly the case in 1917, especially after Faber overcame early season injuries and layoffs to finish up the season on an upswing that carried him through an outstanding World Series performance. Ewell "Reb" Russell, at 15 and 5, who had his greatest outings against the Red Sox in clutch pitching assignments, had remarkable success for a sore-armed pitcher. Spotted strategically by Pants Rowland as demand or circumstance dictated, he backed up the Sox' "Big 2" with pinpoint pitching, and wound up leading the league in winning percentage. Young Claude Williams, who admittedly pitched in good luck during the summer of '17, nonetheless was a 17-game winner who earned a starting berth. The Sox depended on him all the way through the final days of "The Eight Men Out" when he, along with Chick Gandil, pitching partner Cicotte, et al., were bounced out of the game forever. And in Dave Danforth the Chisox possessed one of the most versatile pitchers in either league, heading up AL hurlers with 50 appearances (Cicotte's 49 finished up a close second), and specializing in relief stints that went anywhere from one or two on up to seven and more frames.

A look at some of the more telling numbers gives an even better clue as to this ball club's achievements in 1917. The list, with more than the usual number of firsts and seconds for a pennant winner, is imposing:

The Offense

Run Differential   192; led ML. This category is viewed by many baseball analysts as one of the most significant in measuring the team's dominance factor. In 1917 the Chisox finished better by 92 than the team that finished second in this category (Boston).

On Base Percentage .329; led ML. Not spectacular but better than the rest.

Clutch Hitting Index 108; led ML. This index (CPI) is a sabermetric measurement that calculates how many runs were driven in above the number of Batting Runs (a linear measurement of runs the team accounts for beyond league-average teams), and it gives an indication as to the team's ability to drive in runs with men on base.

Stolen Bases 219; led ML. The Giants led the NL with 162, 57 less than Chicago.

Runs Scored 656; led ML. Speed and consistently solid hitting with men on bases accounted for more runs than any other team.

Triples 80; led AL. Spacious Comiskey is partly responsible for this league-leading total, just four more than Detroit's 76.

Team BA .253; 2nd AL. Detroit led Team BA with .259.

Team SA .326; 2nd AL. Detroit led Team SA with .344.

Bases on Balls 522; 2nd AL. Cleveland led with 549.

Pitching and the Defense

ERA 2.16; led ML. Shaded Boston (2.20) for AL leadership, but 11 percentage points better than the Giants (2.27), who led the NL.

Fewest Home Runs 10; led ML. Four better than Pittsburgh's 14.

Team Pitching Runs 79; led ML. Cicotte's individual 49 PR was also an ML best.

Shutouts 22; tied 1st, ML. The Phillies also registered 22 Shutouts.

Clutch Pitching Index 102; tied 1st, AL. New York's CPI was also 102.

Fewest Walks 413; tied 1st, AL. The Phils' and New York Giants' 327 led both leagues.

Saves 21; 2nd, ML and AL. Cleveland led both leagues with 22.

Fewest Errors 204, 2nd, ML and AL. Boston led both leagues with 183.

Fielding Wins 2.3; 2nd, ML and AL. Boston led both leagues with 4.0.

Fielding Average .967; 2nd AL. Boston led with .972.

Opponents' On-Base Percentage   2nd, AL; .298. The Giants were ML leaders at .283.

Opponents' BA   .238; 2nd, AL. The Giants' .234 led both leagues.

Respected baseball analysts and historians Marshall Wright and Bill James* are both agreed that the 1917 White Sox were clearly the best team in the major leagues that year and probably the best team at the end of the Deadball Era (1915–1920). But as to their ranking among teams like the 1975 Cincinnati Reds, the 1998 Yankees or the 1930 Philadelphia Athletics there is a far road for the '17 world's champions to travel to catch up with the brilliance of those aggregations. That necessarily puts them out of reach of any top-50 listing, and a fair assessment might put them in the 90 to 110 range of the top teams in baseball history. Finally, it is well to remember that many fine ball clubs didn't win the pennant or playoffs. Many of them were actually better than some ball clubs that were World Series winners, and that also affects any ranking of baseball's top teams.

In answer to the question, was this the best White Sox team in the franchise's history, an accompanying table lists the fifteen best Pale Hose ball clubs in a priority order (with added statistics to flesh out each team's accomplishments a bit) according to Run Differential (RD). RD would be a major factor in deciding which team is best, but not the only one. Thus, the listing is intended as a thought-provoker and a conversation-starter, leaving up to the reader a final arrangement of the pecking order. From the author's corner, the suggestion would be that in the final analysis the 1917, 1920, 1959, 1983 and 1994 White Sox teams would be the top five clubs (Author's preference: 1917, 1994 [despite the strike-shortened season that year], 1920, 1959 and 1983.) The complete listing of the 15 teams follows the explanatory Legend:

Y/F—Team's Finish in the league or division in a given year (Y).
RD—Run Differential (Runs Scored minus Opponents' Runs).
W/L%—Team's Win-Loss record and Winning Percentage.
OB%—Team On Base Percentage.
OBA—Opponents' Batting Average.
H/G—Hits per 9 innings pitched by pitching staff.
Note: Numbers in parentheses indicate finishing position in the league.

*Correspondence with Marshall Wright (October 15, 2002) and Bill James (August 9, 2002).

Y/F	RD	W/L%	Tm BA	OB%	SB	ERA	H/G	SV	OBA	Ratio
1915 3rd AL	208	93–61, .604	.258 (3)	.345 (2)	233 (2)	2.43 (3)	8.0 (3)	9 (5)	.241 (3)	10.5 (1)
1917 1st WS Winner	192	100–54, .649	.253 (3)	.329 (1)	219 (1)	2.16 (1)	7.9 (4)	21 (2)	.238 (2)	10.7 (2)
1901 1st AL No WS	188	83–53, .610	.276 (5)	.350 (2)	280 (1)	2.98 (1)	9.3 (2)	2 (4t)	.263 (2)	12.0 (2)
1983 1st AL West	150	99–63, .611	.262 (2t)	.332 (1)	165 (3)	3.67 (2)	8.5 (1)	48 (2)	.248 (1)	11.5 (1)
1920 2nd, AL	129	96–58, .623	.295 (3)	.357 (3)	108 (3)	3.59 (3)	9.6 (4)	10/4t	.280 (4)	12.4 (3)
2000 1st, AL Cent	137	95–67, .586	.286 (3)	.359 (2)	119 (2)	4.67 (1)	9.4 (1)	43 (2)	.270 (1t)	13.6 (2)
1994 1st AL Cent Strike year	135	67–46, .593	.287 (2)	.370 (1)	77 (4)	3.96 (1)	8.6 (1)	20 (5)	.250 (1)	12.1 (1)
1919 1st AL	133	88–52, .629	.287 (1)	.351 (2)	150 (1)	3.04 (3)	8.9 (3)	3 (7t)	.262 (2)	11.6 (2)
1993 1st AL West	112	94–68, .580	.265 (2)	.342 (1t)	106 (4)	3.70 (1)	8.7 (2)	48 (1t)	.255 (2)	12.5 (1t)
1906 1st AL WS Winner	110	93–58, .616	.230 (8)	.301 (5)	214 (3)	2.13 (2)	8.0 (5)	5 (2t)	.239 (4)	9.9 (1)
1916 2nd AL	104	89–65, .578	.251 (3)	.251 (2)	197 (2)	2.36 (1)	7.6 (1)	15 (4)	.236 (1)	10.4 (1)
1959 1st AL	81	94–60, .610	.250 (6)	.330 (3)	113 (1)	3.29 (1)	8.2 (2)	36 (1)	.242 (2)	11.8 (2)
1991 2nd AL West	77	87–75, .537	.262 (4)	.338 (3)	134 (2)	3.79 (4t)	8.8 (4)	40 (7)	.239 (1)	11.8 (1)
193 3rd, AL7	50	86–68, .558	.280 (4t)	.350 (6)	70 (5)	4.17 (2)	9.6 (3)	21 (1t)	.273 (2)	13.3 (2)
1967 4th AL	40	89–73, .549	.225 (9t)	.293 (9)	124 (2)	2.45 (1)	7.3 (1)	39 (4t)	.219 (1)	10.4 (1)

The final summary has been ably stated by baseball historian David Nemec.*

> The popular belief is that the 1919 team was the best in the history of the Chicago White Sox franchise even apart from the fact that it threw the World Series. But the evidence leans heavily toward the 1917 crew. In the process of winning a club-record 100 games, Pants Rowland's bunch also proved to be the only White Sox team to date to capture a pennant with ease. The comfortable nine-game margin over a powerful Red Sox club that was coming off two straight pennant romps, and would win again in 1918, ostensibly can be traced to a particularly strong season from pitcher Eddie Cicotte and stout offensive backing from Eddie Collins, Joe Jackson and Happy Felsch.
>
> However, there was a less obvious factor. In 1917 Dave Danforth blossomed into arguably the first outstanding southpaw relief pitcher, posting 11 wins, a .647 winning percentage, and a league-leading total of nine saves. Danforth's scarcely recognized contribution more than any other, at least to my mind, is what puts the 1917 team a notch at the head of the pack in White Sox history.

There you have it, White Sox fans. It remains up to you to dig around in the White Sox past to come up with your own list of great teams and the franchise's all-timers.

---

*Correspondence with David Nemec, October 17–18, 2002.

They Were the Champs—
And Their Sox Were White

The Old Roman, Pants, Kid Gleason, the players, The Bards—
and Chicagoland—had their world's championship and they rev-
eled in it. What's more, the White Sox had beaten John McGraw's
Giants fairly and squarely.

Note: fairly and squarely. This ball club, featuring the eight
frontliners who, just two seasons later, turned the mighty Chicago
franchise inside-out with its involvement in the worst scandal to hit
the national pastime in its storied history, had dethroned Boston's
Red Sox, whipped the New York Giants, and ruled the baseball uni-
verse by dint of its artistry, power, smart baseball and superb pitching—and had done it on the up and up.

The unfounded and peevish charges leveled against their
teammates ten years later by Swede Risberg and Chick Gandil with
respect to the Labor Day doubleheader "fix" in games with the
Detroit Tigers on September 2 and 3, 1917, were all dismissed by
Judge Landis in exhaustive hearings and detracted not one iota
from the team's achievement, or from its integrity. As they stood
atop baseball's unique world, they had every right to the rewards

they received for their accomplishments both individually and as a team, during a season that has been unjustly overlooked in the rush to get not only at the infamous Black Sox Scandal, but to hasten on to the roaring '20's, Babe Ruth, and the era of the Big Sticks.

Chicago's heroes of the day, Eddie Cicotte, Red Faber, Reb Russell, Eddie Collins, Buck Weaver, Joe Jackson, Hap Felsch, Ray Schalk, and all the others who played supportive, yet strategic roles in the drive to World Series glory, had bent their backs and collective will to the task at hand, putting their names and that of the 1917 White Sox alongside the names of baseball's greats, past and present, who grace the game with their skill and artistry. They were the champs—and their socks were white.

Appendix A: The 1917 Chicago White Sox Game Log

Date	Site/Opponent/Result	CWS Starter	Opp. Starter	CWSP/Rec.
4/11	At St. Louis W 7–2	Lefty Williams	Earl Hamilton	Scott, 1–0
4/13	At St. Louis L 3–4	Red Faber	Ernie Koob	Faber, 0–1
4/14	At St. Louis W 11–0	Eddie Cicotte	Earl Hamilton	Cicotte, 1–0
4/15	At Detroit W 6–2	Jim Scott	Harry Coveleski	Scott, 2–0
4/16	At Detroit W 4–0	Red Faber	Deacon Jones	Faber, 1–1
4/17	At Detroit W 4–2	Dave Danforth	Howard Ehmke	Danforth, 1–0
4/19	St. Louis L 2–6	Jim Scott	Eddie Plank	Scott, 2–1
4/20	St. Louis W 5–2	Eddie Cicotte	Allen Sothoron	Cicotte, 2–0
4/21	St. Louis W 2–0	Red Faber	Ernie Koob	Faber, 2–1
4/22	St. Louis W 3–2	Dave Danforth	Earl Hamilton	Williams 1–0
4/24	Cleveland W 1–0	Jim Scott	Stan Coveleski	Scott, 3–1
4/25	Cleveland L 1–4	Eddie Cicotte	Fritz Coumbe	Cicotte, 2–1
4/26	Cleveland L 0–3	Red Faber	Jim Bagby	Faber, 2–2
4/27	Cleveland L 1–2	Lefty Williams	Ed Klepfer	Scott, 3–2
4/28	Detroit W 2–1	Jim Scott	Harry Coveleski	Faber, 3–2
4/29	Detroit L 0–3	Red Faber	Willie Mitchell	Faber, 3–3
5/2	At Clevel'd W 8–3	Lefty Williams	Fritz Coumbe	Williams, 2–0
5/3	At Clevel'd L 1–2	Jim Scott	Ed Klepfer	Scott, 3–3
5/5	At St. Louis L 0–1	Eddie Cicotte	Ernie Koob	Cicotte, 2–2
5/6	At St. Louis L 4–8	Reb Russell	Allen Sothoron	Russell, 0–1
5/6	At St. Louis L 0–3	Joey Benz	Bob Groom	Benz, 0–1
5/8	At St. Louis W 4–3	Jim Scott	Dave Davenport	Cicotte, 3–2
5/8	At St. Louis W 9–7	Lefty Williams	Allen Sothoron	Russell, 1–1

Date	Site/Opponent/Result	CWS Starter	Opp. Starter	CWSP/Rec.
5/9	At St. Louis W 4–2	Lefty Williams	Bob Groom	Cicotte, 4–2
5/10	New York L 0–1	Reb Russell	Bob Shawkey	Russell, 1–2
5/11	New York L 1–6	Dave Danforth	Ray Caldwell	Danforth, 1–1
5/12	New York W 2–1	Jim Scott	George Mogridge	Scott, 4–3
5/13	New York W 1–0	Eddie Cicotte	Nick Cullop	Cicotte, 5–2
5/14	Philadel'ia W 6–2	Reb Russell	Walter Anderson	Russell, 2–2
5/15	Philadel'ia W 11–0	Joey Benz	Walt Johnson	Benz, 1–1
5/16	Philadel'ia W 3–2	Lefty Williams	Bullet Joe Bush	Williams, 3–0
5/17	Philadel'ia W 7–0	Eddie Cicotte	Cy Falkenberg	Cicotte, 6–2
5/18	Boston W 8–2	Reb Russell	Babe Ruth	Russell, 3–2
5/19	Boston W 8–2	Lefty Williams	Dutch Leonard	Williams, 4–0
5/20	Boston L 1–2	Jim Scott	Carl Mays	Scott, 4–4
5/23	Washingt'n W 2–1	Eddie Cicotte	Jim Shaw	Cicotte, 7–2
5/24	Washingt'n W 1–0	Reb Russell	George Dumont	Russell, 4–2
5/25	Washingt'n W 5–1	Joey Benz	Harry Hopper	Benz, 2–1
5/26	Washingt'n T 1–1	Jim Scott	Bert Gallia	Tie
5/27	Washingt'n W 4–1	Eddie Cicotte	Walter Johnson	Cicotte, 8–2
5/29	St. Louis W 4–2	Reb Russell	Bob Groom	Russell, 5–2
6/2	At Phil'a W 4–0	Eddie Cicotte	Bullet Joe Bush	Cicotte, 9–2
6/4	At Phil'a W 4–2	Reb Russell	Wynn Noyes	Russell, 6–2
6/5	At Phil'a W 6–3	Joey Benz	Rube Schauer	Benz, 3–1
6/6	At Wash'n L 0–3	Eddie Cicotte	George Dumont	Cicotte, 9–3
6/7	At Wash'n L 0–1	Reb Russell	Walter Johnson	Russell, 6–3
6/8	At Wash'n W 11–4	Joey Benz	Jim Shaw	Benz, 4–1
6/9	At Wash'n W 5–4	Jim Scott	Harry Harper	Danforth, 2–1
6/10	At Clevel'd W 10–4	Lefty Williams	Fritz Coumbe	Williams, 5–0
6/12	At New York L 3–4	Eddie Cicotte	George Mogridge	Cicotte, 9–4
6/13	At New York L 6–7	Reb Russell	Nick Cullop	Benz, 4–2
6/15	At Boston W 8–0	Lefty Williams	Ernie Shore	Williams, 6–0
6/16	At Boston W 7–2	Eddie Cicotte	Babe Rurh	Cicotte, 10–4
6/18	At Boston L 4–6	Reb Russell	Carl Mays	Danforth, 2–2
6/18	At Boston L 7–8	Jim Scott	Rube Foster	Faber, 3–4
6/20	Cleveland W 3–2	Lefty Williams	Stan Covelieski	Williams, 7–0
6/21	Cleveland L 0–1	Eddie Cicotte	Jim Bagby	Cicotte, 10–5
6/22	Cleveland W 4–1	Red Faber	Otis Lambeth	Faber, 4–4
6/23	Cleveland W 2–1	Joey Benz	Guy Norton	Williams, 8–0
6/24	Cleveland W 1–0	Dave Danforth	Joe Boehling	Danforth, 3–2
6/26	Detroit L 2–9	Red Faber	Willie Mitchell	Faber, 4–5
6/26	Detroit W 4–3	Lefty Williams	Bill James	Williams, 9–0
6/27	Detroit W 5–2	Eddie Cicotte	Hooks Dauss	Cicotte, 11–5
6/27	Detroit W 3–2	Dave Danforth	Howard Ehmke	Danforth, 4–2
6/28	Detroit L 5–6	Reb Russell	Bernie Rowland	Williams, 9–1
6/29	At Clevel'd W 3–1	Red Faber	Stan Coveleski	Faber, 5–5
6/30	At Clevel'd L 1–11	Lefty Williams	Jim Bagby	Williams, 9–2
7/1	At Clevel'd L 4–5	Eddie Cicotte	Guy Morton	Cicotte, 11–6
7/2	At Clevel'd W 4–3	Dave Danforth	Joe Boehling	Danforth, 5–2
7/3	At Detroit W 5–1	Red Faber	Harry Coveleski	Faber, 6–5
7/4	At Detroit W 4–3	Eddie Cicotte	Bill James	Cicotte, 12–6
7/4	At Detroit W 4–3	Lefty Williams	Willie Mitchell	Williams, 12–2

Date	Site/Opponent/Result	CWS Starter	Opp. Starter	CWSP/Rec.
7/5	At Detroit L 6–11	Dave Danforth	Howard Ehmke	Danforth, 5–3
7/6	At Detroit L 1–4	Red Faber	Hooks Dauss	Faber, 6–6
7/7	Philadel'ia L 2–4	Jim Scott	Elmer Meyers	Scott, 4–5
7/8	Philadelp'a W 8–4	Eddie Cicotte	Rube Schauer	Cicotte, 13–6
7/9	Philadelp'a L 2–5	Lefty Williams	Bullet Joe Bush	Williams, 10–3
7/10	Philadelp'a L 3–7	Red Faber	Wynn Noyes	Russell, 6–4
7/12	New York W 2–1	Eddie Cicotte	George Mogridge	Cicotte, 14–6
7/12	New York W 5–3	Jim Scott	Bob Shawkey	Russell, 7–4
7/13	New York L 5–6	Lefty Williams	Ray Caldwell	Faber, 6–7
7/14	New York W 4–1	Reb Russell	Slim Love	Russell, 8–4
7/15	Washingt'n L 5–6	Lefty Williams	Jim Shaw	Williams, 10–4
7/17	Washingt'n W 5–0	Eddie Cicotte	George Dumont	Cicotte, 15–6
7/17	Washingt'n W 3–2	Red Faber	Walter Johnson	Faber, 7–7
7/18	Washingt'n W 4–0	Joey Benz	Harry Harper	Benz, 5–2
7/18	Washingt'n W 7–4	Dave Danforth	Bert Gallia	Danforth, 6–3
7/19	Boston L 2–3	Lefty Williams	Babe Ruth	Williams, 10–5
7/20	Boston W 5–2	Eddie Cicotte	Rube Foster	Cicotte, 16–6
7/21	Boston T 5–5	Red Faber	Dutch Leonard	Tie
7/22	Boston W 2–0	Reb Russell	Carl Mays	Russell, 9–4
7/23	Boston W 5–3	Lefty Williams	Ernie Shore	Williams, 11–5
7/25	At New York W 4–1	Eddie Cicotte	George Mogridge	Cicotte, 17–6
7/25	At New York W 5–1	Red Faber	Ray Fisher	Faber, 8–7
7/26	At New York L 5–6	Joey Benz	Nick Cullop	Williams, 11–6
7/27	At New York W 9–5	Reb Russell	Ray Caldwell	Russell, 10–4
7/28	At New York L 4–5	Red Faber	Allan Russell	Faber, 8–8
7/28	At New York L 3–4	Jim Scott	Bob Shawkey	Scott, 4–6
7/30	At Boston L 1–3	Lefty Williams	Babe Ruth	Williams, 11–7
7/31	At Boston L 2–5	Eddie Cicotte	Dutch Leonard	Cicotte, 17–7
8/1	At Boston W 4–0	Reb Russell	Carl Mays	Russell, 11–4
8/2	At Boston W 7–1	Red Faber	Ernie Shore	Faber, 9–8
8/3	At Phil'a W 4–0	Jim Scott	Socks Siebold	Scott, 5–6
8/4	At Phil'a W 7–3	Joey Benz	Elmer Meyers	Faber, 18–7
8/4	At Phil'a W 4–3	Lefty Williams	Jing Johnson	Williams, 12–7
8/6	At Phil'a L 4–5	Reb Russell	Wynn Noyes	Scott, 5–7
8/7	At Phil'a L 1–8	Red Faber	Rube Schauer	Faber, 9–9
8/8	At Wash'n L 0–2	Eddie Cicotte	Harry Harper	Cicotte, 18–8
8/9	At Wash'n W 3–2	Joey Benz	Bert Gallie	Benz, 6–2
8/10	At Wash'n L 0–4	Red Faber	Walter Johnson	Faber, 9–10
8/11	At Wash'n L 2–3	Eddie Cicotte	Jim Shaw	Cicotte, 18–9
8/12	At Clevel'd W 4–3	Jim Scott	Jim Bagby	Danforth, 7–3
8/14	At Clevel'd W 3–2	Lefty Williams	Stan Coveleski	Williams, 13–7
8/14	At Clevel'd L 3–4	Red Faber	Guy Morton	Faber, 9–11
8/15	At Clevel'd W 5–4	Eddie Cicotte	Ed Klepfer	Scott, 6–7
8/17	Philadel'ia L 7–9	Jim Scott	Rube Schauer	Cicotte, 18–10
8/18	Philadel'ia W 5–4	Lefty Williams	Walter Anderson	Faber, 10–11
8/19	Philadel'ia W 14–6	Reb Russell	Elmer Meyers	Russell, 12–4
8/20	Boston W 7–0	Red Faber	Rube Foster	Faber, 11–11
8/20	Boston L 1–3	Eddie Cicotte	Carl Mays	Cicotte, 18–11
8/21	Boston W 2–0	Reb Russell	Babe Ruth	Russell, 13–4

Appendix A

Date	Site/Opponent/Result	CWS Starter	Opp. Starter	CWSP/Rec.
8/22	Boston L 1–5	Lefty Williams	Dutch Leonard	Williams, 13–8
8/23	Wash'n W 6–0	Eddie Cicotte	Jim Shaw	Cicotte, 19–11
8/25	Wash'n W 4–1	Red Faber	Walter Johnson	Faber, 12–11
8/26	New York W 8–3	Reb Russell	George Mogridge	Russell, 14–4
8/27	New York W 3–0	Eddie Cicotte	Bob Shawkey	Cicotte, 20–11
8/28	New York W 4–3	Lefty Williams	Ray Caldwell	Williams, 14–8
8/29	St. Louis W 6–0	Reb Russell	Ernie Koob	Russell, 15–4
8/29	St. Louis W 11–1	Joey Benz	Tom Rogers	Danforth, 8–3
8/30	St. Louis W 8–4	Eddie Cicotte	Bob Groom	Cicotte, 21–11
8/31	St. Louis W 8–2	Red Faber	Dave Davenport	Williams, 15–8
9/1	St. Louis L 3–6	Dave Danforth	Ernie Koob	Danforth, 8–4
9/2	Detroit W 7–2	Eddie Cicotte	Willie Mitchell	Cicotte, 22–11
9/2	Detroit W 6–5	Reb Russell	Geo. Cunningham	Williams, 16–8
9/3	Detroit W 7–5	Red Faber	Howard Ehmke	Danforth, 9–4
9/3	Detroit W 14–8	Red Faber	Bernie Boland	Cicotte, 23–11
9/4	At St. Louis W 13–6	Red Faber	Ernie Koob	Faber, 13–11
9/5	At St. Louis W 4–1	Lefty Williams	Allen Sothoron	Williams, 17–8
9/8	Cleveland W 2–0	Eddie Cicotte	Jim Bagby	Cicotte, 24–11
9/9	Cleveland W★ 3–3	Reb Russell	Stan Coveleski	Danforth, 10–4
9/14	At Detroit W 7–3	Eddie Cicotte	Willie Mitchell	Cicotte, 25–11
9/15	At Detroit L 3–4	Reb Russell	Hooks Dauss	Danforth, 10–5
9/15	At Detroit W 2–1	Red Faber	Geo. Cunningham	Faber, 14–11
9/16	St. Louis W 4–3	Lefty Williams	Dave Davenport	Cicotte, 26–11
9/18	At Phil'a W 6–1	Red Faber	Bullet Joe Bush	Faber, 15–11
9/19	At Phil'a L 1–2	Eddie Cicotte	Jing Johnson	Cicotte, 26–12
9/20	At Phil'a W 5–3	Lefty Williams	Elmer Meyers	Danforth, 11–5
9/21	At Boston W★★ 2–1	Red Faber	Dutch Leonard	Faber, 16–11
9/22	At Boston L 1–4	Joey Benz	Carl Mays	Benz, 6–3
9/24	At Boston L 0–3	Reb Russell	Babe Ruth	Russell, 15–5
9/25	At Wash'n W 7–5	Eddie Cicotte	Harry Harper	Cicotte, 27–12
9/26	At Wash'n L 4–5	Red Faber	George Dumont	Faber, 16–12
9/27	At Wash'n W 6–1	Joey Benz	Jim Shaw	Benz, 7–3
9/29	At New York L 8–12	Lefty Williams	Bob Shawkey	Danforth, 11–6
9/29	At New York W# 3–1	Eddie Cicotte	Hank Thormahlen	Cicotte, 28–12
10/1	At New York L 2–4	Lefty Williams	Urban Shocker	Faber, 16–13

★　　Chicago declared winner by forfeit in the ninth inning of this game.

★★　　This victory in Boston clinched the pennant

\#　　This victory, Chicago's 100th, set a still-existing franchise record for victories in one season.

The 1917 White Sox won 30 and lost 25 one-run games.

4 games were won by 1–0 scores.
4 games were lost by 1–0 scores.

7 games were won by 2–1 scores.
4 games were lost by 2–1 scores.

Appendix B: The 1917
Chicago White Sox Statistics

I) Offensive Statistics

Name	GP	AB	H	3BH	HR	RBI	BB/K	SH	SB	BA
Joe Benz	19	30	5	0	0	0	0/11	3	0	.167
Bobby Byrne	1	1	0	0	0	0	0/0	0	0	.000
Eddie Cicotte	49	112	20	2	0	8	12/23	8	1	.179
Eddie Collins	156	564	163	12	0	67	89/16	33	53	.289
Shano Collins	82	252	59	3	1	14	10/27	6	14	.234
Dave Danforth	50	46	6	1	0	5	6/19	5	1	.130
Red Faber	41	69	4	0	0	2	10/38	8	0	.057
Hap Felsch	152	575	177	10	6	102	33/52	18	26	.308
Jack Fournier	1	1	0	0	0	0	0/1	0	0	.000
Chick Gandil	149	553	151	7	0	57	30/36	13	16	.273
Ziggy Hasbrook	2	1	0	0	0	0	0/0	0	0	.000
Joe Jackson	146	538	162	17	5	75	57/25	19	13	.301
Joe Jenkins	10	9	1	0	0	2	0/5	1	0	.111
Ted Jourdan	17	34	5	1	0	2	1/3	0	0	.147
Nemo Leibold	125	428	101	6	0	29	74/34	6	27	.236
Byrd Lynn	35	72	16	0	0	5	7/11	4	1	.222
Fred McMullin	59	194	46	1	0	12	27/17	21	5	.237
Eddie Murphy	53	51	16	1	0	16	5/1	3	4	.314
Swede Risberg	149	474	96	8	1	45	59/65	25	16	.203

Reb Russell	39	68	19	3	0	9	2/10	4	0	.279
Ray Schalk	140	424	96	5	3	51	59/27	17	19	.226
Jim Scott	24	42	5	0	0	0	4/9	9	0	.119
Zeb Terry	2	1	0	0	0	0	2/0	0	0	.000
Buck Weaver	118	447	127	5	3	32	27/29	35	19	.284
Lefty Williams	45	67	6	1	0	2	8/19	6	0	.090
Mellie Wolfgang	5	4	0	0	0	0	0/10	0	0	.000
Team totals	156	5057	1281	83	19	535	522/479	235	219	.253

(II) Pitching Statistics

Name	GP	IP	W/L%	ERA	OB%	SV	SH	CG	BB/K
Joe Benz	19	94.2	7-3,.700	2.47	.272	0	2	7	23/25
Eddie Cicotte	49	346.2	28-12,.700	1.53	.248	4	7	29	70/150
Dave Danforth	50	173.0	11-6,.647	2.65	.325	9	1	1	74/79
Red Faber	41	248.0	16-13,.552	1.92	.319	3	3	16	85/84
Reb Russell	35	189.1	15-5,.750	1.95	.279	3	5	11	32/54
Jim Scott	24	125.0	6-7,.462	1.87	,341	1	2	6	42/37
Lefty Williams	45	230.0	17-8,.680	2.97	.321	1	1	8	81/85
Mellie Wolfgang	5	17.2	0-0,.000	5.09	.379	0	0	0	6/3
Staff	156	1421	100-54, .648	2.16	,298	21	21*	78	413/517

Total does not include one combined shutout.

(III) Defensive Statistics

Name	Pos	G	PO	A	E	DP	Ave.
Joe Benz	P	19	3	42	5	0	.875
Eddie Cicotte	P	49	14	94	5	2	.956
Dave Danforth	P	50	0	42	4	0	.913
Red Faber	P	41	13	84	8	0	.924
Reb Russell	P	35	11	51	1	2	.984
Jim Scott	P	24	7	37	2	1	.957
Lefty Williams	P	45	8	46	4	2	.931
Mellie Wolfgang	P	5	0	5	1	0	.833
Joe Jenkins	C	1	0	0	0	0	.000
Byrd Lynn	C	29	104	13	5	4	.959
Ray Schalk	C	139	624	148	15	18	.981
Chick Gandil	1B	149	1405	77	8	84	.995
Ted Jourdan	1B	14	68	5	2	2	.973
Bobby Byrne	2B	1	0	1	0	0	1.000
Eddie Collins	2B	156	353	388	24	68	.969
Ziggy Hasbrook	2B	1	0	2	0	1	1.000
Fred McMullin	3B	52	61	90	11	4	.932
Buck Weaver	3B	107	154	218	20	18	.949
Fred McMullin	SS	2	2	2	4	0	.500

Swede Risberg	SS	146	291	352	61	57	.913
Zeb Terry	SS	1	0	1	0	0	1.000
Buck Weaver	SS	10	20	39	1	9	.983
Shano Collins	OF	73	125	6	1	4	.984
Happy Felsch	OF	152	440	24	7	5	.985
Joe Jackson	OF	145	341	18	6	4	.984
Nemo Leibold	OF	122	204	18	9	3	.961
Eddie Murphy	OF	9	2	0	0	0	1.000
Reb Russell	OF	1	3	0	0	0	1.000
Team		156	4290	1793	204	288*	.967

*Team total really is 117. The 288 figure is combined total.

Bibliography

Alexander, Charles C. *John McGraw*. New York: Viking-Penguin, 1988.

Asinof, Eliot. *Eight Men Out: The Black Sox and the 1919 World Series*. New York: Holt, Rinehart and Winston, 1963.

Axelson, Gustav. *"Commy": The Life Story of Charles A. Comiskey*. Chicago: Riley and Lee, 1919; reprint, Jefferson, NC: McFarland, 2003.

Aylesworth, Thomas, Benton Minks, and John S. Bowman, eds. *The Encyclopedia of Baseball Managers*. New York: Brompton Books, 1990.

Benson, Michael. *Ballparks of America*. Jefferson NC: McFarland, 1989.

Berke, Art, and Paul Schmitt. *This Date in Chicago White Sox History*. New York: Stein and Day, 1982.

Cohen, Richard M., David Neft, and Roland Johnson. *The World Series*. New York: Dial, 1976.

Costello, James, and Michael Santa Maria. *In the Shadows of the Diamond*. Dubuque IA: Elysian Fields, 1992.

Dewey, Donald, and Nicholas Acocella. *The Biographical History of Baseball*. New York: Carroll and Graf, 1995.

Dickey, Glenn. *The History of the American League Since 1901*. New York: Stein and Day, 1980.

Durso, Joseph. *Baseball and the American Dream*. St. Louis: The Sporting News, 1986.

Frommer, Harry. *Shoeless Joe and Ragtime Baseball*. Dallas TX: Taylor, 1992.

Gropman, Donald. *Say It Ain't So, Joe!* Boston: Little, Brown, 1979.

Holtzman, Jerome, and George Vass. *Baseball Chicago Style.* Chicago: Bonus Books, 2001.

Hynd, Noel. *The Giants of the Polo Grounds.* Dallas TX: Taylor, 1995.

James, Bill. *The New Bill James Historical Baseball Abstract.* New York: Free Press, 2001.

Johnson, Lloyd, and Brenda Ward. *Who's Who in Baseball History.* New York: Barnes and Noble, 1994.

Leventhal, Josh. *The World Series.* New York: Black Dog and Leventhal Publishers, 2001.

Lieb, Fred. *Baseball As I Have Known It.* New York: Tempo Star, 1977.

Pietrusza, David, M. Silverman and M. Gershman, eds. *Baseball: The Biographical Encyclopedia.* Kingston NY: Total/Sports Illustrated, 2000.

Ritter, Lawrence. *Lost Ballparks.* New York: Penguin, 1994.

Robinson, Ray. *Greatest World Series Thrillers.* New York: Random House, 1965.

Seymour, Harold. *Baseball: The Early Years.* New York: Oxford University, 1960.

Thorn, John, with Pete Palmer and M. Gershman, eds. *Total Baseball,* 7th Edition. Kingston NY: Total Sports Publishing, 2001.

White, G. Edward. *Creating the National Pastime: Baseball Transforms Itself, 1903–1953.* Princeton NJ: Princeton University Press, 1996.

Wilbert, Warren N. *A Cunning Kind of Play: The Cubs-Giants Rivalry, 1876–1932.* Jefferson NC: McFarland, 2002.

Newspapers

Boston Globe
Chicago Sun-Times
Chicago Tribune
Cleveland Plain Dealer
Detroit Free Press
Detroit News
Fort Wayne Press Gazette
Milwaukee Journal
New York American
New York Herald
New York Times
St. Louis Post Dispatch
Sporting Life
Sporting News

Guides and Magazines

The Baseball Research Journal (SABR).
The Chicago White Sox Media Guide 2000.
The National Baseball Hall of Fame and Museum Guide, 1984 and 1997.
The National Pastime (SABR).
The Reach Baseball Guide, 1918.
The San Francisco Giants Yearbook, 1985.
The Sporting News Official World Series Records, 1982.

Index